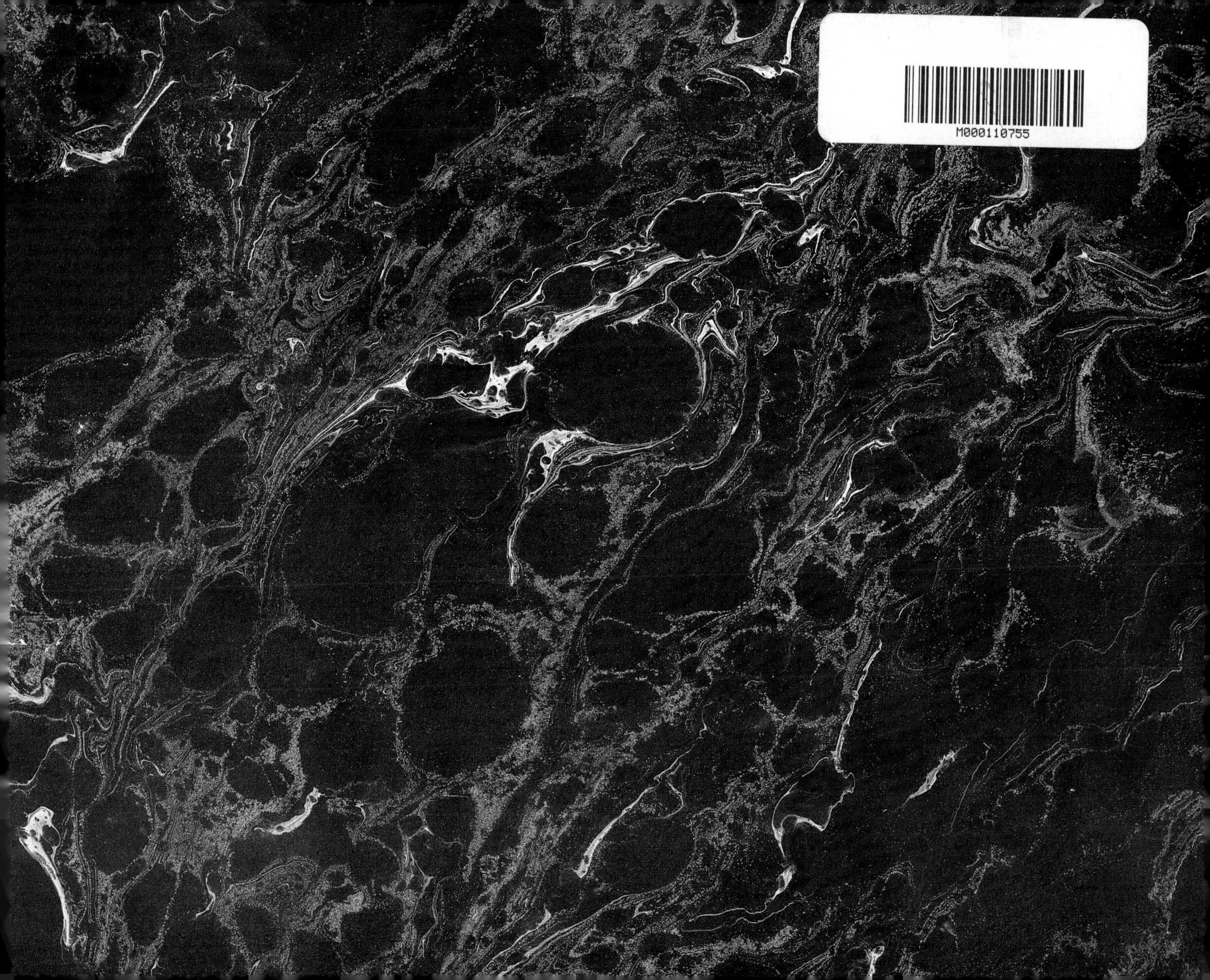

A EUROPEAN JOURNAL

A EUROPEAN JOURNAL

TWO SISTERS ABROAD IN 1847

MARY WILSON WITH ILLUSTRATIONS BY ANNE WILSON

EDITED AND INTRODUCED BY JENNIFER SIMPSON

BLOOMSBURY

TO THE MEMORY OF MY FATHER, J H SIMPSON – A GRANDSON OF HENRY AND CHARLOTTE WILSON

I WOULD LIKE TO ACKNOWLEDGE THE HELP OF MANY LIBRARIANS AND ARCHIVISTS IN LONDON, IN THE COUNTIES OF NOTTINGHAMSHIRE, SURREY AND HAMPSHIRE, AND IN MELBOURNE, AUSTRALIA. I AM ESPECIALLY GRATEFUL FOR HELP GIVEN BY MEMBERS OF THE STAFF AT THE BIRMINGHAM CENTRAL REFERENCE LIBRARY.

I THANK MY FAMILY FOR THEIR PATIENCE AND HELP; MY SON MARK WATERSON FOR UNDERTAKING RESEARCH FOR ME IN AUSTRALIA; AND MY SISTER MARY DRAKE, WHO DUG DEEPLY INTO BOXES IN HER ATTIC AND FOUND PAPERS WHICH ENABLED ME TO START FAMILY HISTORY RESEARCH. ALSO TO GILLIAN WINTER AND BETTY WALKER, TWO WILSON DESCENDANTS, OWNERS OF MANUSCRIPTS AND PAINTINGS BY ANNE S. WILSON.

MY THANKS GO TO XANDRA HARDIE, MY LITERARY AGENT, TO JANE CARR, MY EDITOR, AND TO ALL THOSE CONCERNED WITH THE PRODUCTION OF THE BOOK. ALSO TO LIZ CHERRY WHO TYPED THE MANUSCRIPT, TO JOHN STANBURY WHO HELPED WITH PHOTOGRAPHY, AND TO KATHLEEN BETTERTON, MYFANWY SINCLAIR, BETTY BARKER, IRENE WIENER, ILENE SIDWELL, AUDREY NOHRA, AND MANY OTHER FRIENDS WHO HAVE GIVEN ENCOURAGEMENT.

I AM ALSO GRATEFUL TO THE LA TROBE LIBRARY IN MELBOURNE, AUSTRALIA AND TO BETTY WALKER FOR ALLOWING ME TO REPRODUCE THEIR WATERCOLOUR PAINTINGS.

FIRST PUBLISHED IN GREAT BRITAIN 1987

BLOOMSBURY PUBLISHING LTD, 4 BLOOMSBURY PLACE, LONDON WC1A 2QA

ISBN 0 7475 0022 3

DESIGNED BY FIELDING ROWINSKI
PHOTOTYPESET BY SX COMPOSING LTD, RAYLEIGH, ESSEX
PRINTED AND BOUND IN PORTUGAL BY PRINTER PORTUGESA INDUSTRIA GRAFICA
MAP COURTESY OF THE BRITISH LIBRARY

Contents

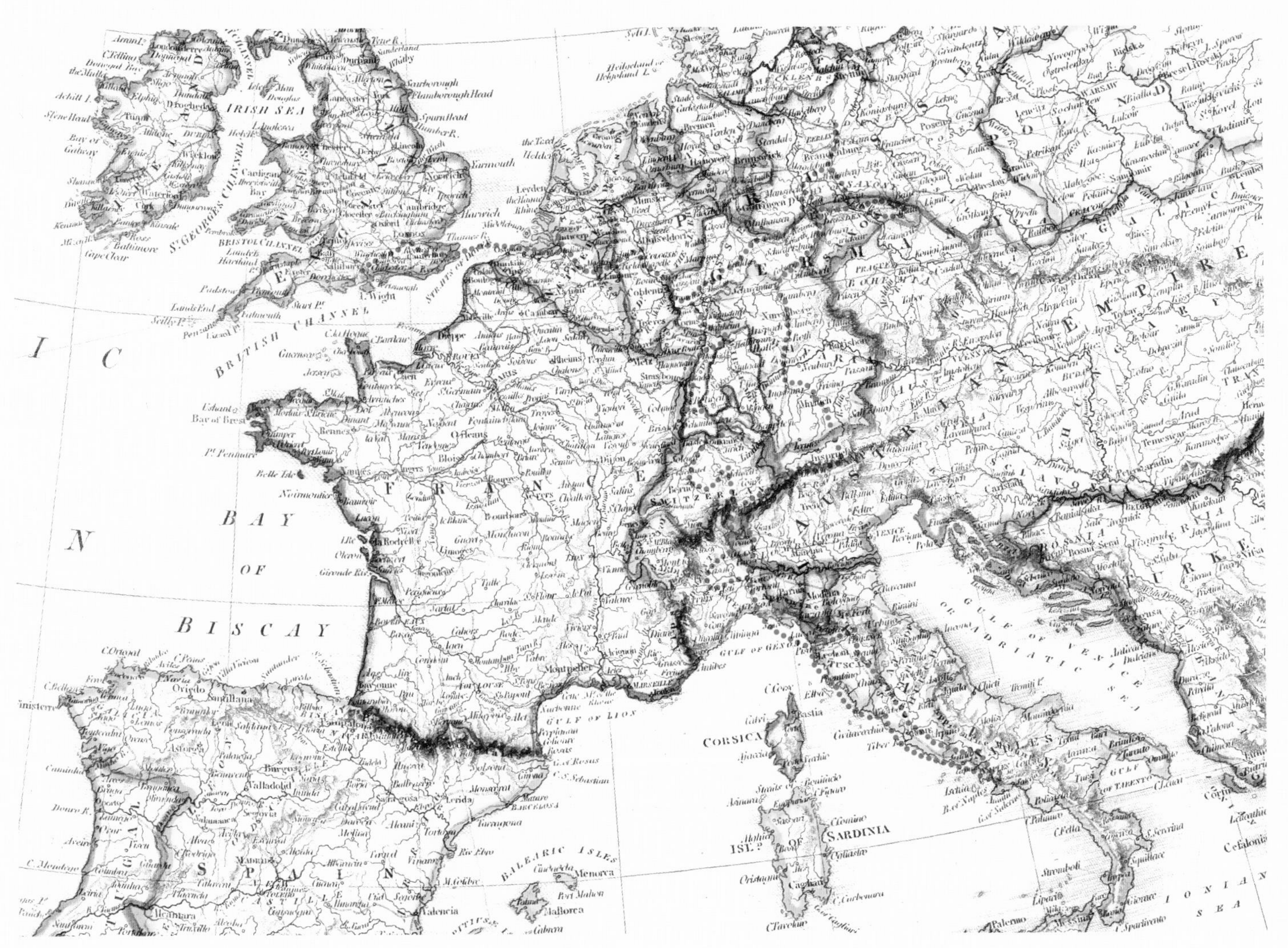

THE ROUTE FOLLOWED BY ANNE, MARY AND JOHN WILSON

Introduction

When Pope Pius IX took a ride among his people in Rome in the summer of 1847, there were two English women standing in the crowd at the bottom of the Palace steps waiting to see the ceremony. (According to family legend, they refused to curtsy.) One of them was Mary Wilson and, when His Holiness appeared, her first interest was in the kind of cloth he was wearing – Mary and her sister Anne were the daughters of a London linen-draper. They were born over the shop in Tavistock Street and were baptized at St Paul's Church, Covent Garden. When they went on their journey in 1847, Mary the journal writer was 36, Anne the illustrator was 41 and their brother John who accompanied them was 39 years old. Their brothers William, Gilbert and Henry were left behind shop-keeping in London and their brother Edward was working in Australia. Their parents had died in the 1830s and, with a successful shop, had left them very comfortably off. This was not their first expedition abroad; they had been to the Rhine and beyond in 1834, and there had been three visits to France.

In mid-winter they crossed the channel from Dover, went by train across Belgium and then travelled through large parts of Germany. They mounted the Alps by carriage and went into Italy for two exceedingly hot and unforgettable months, during which they ventured as far south as Naples. Then to Switzerland where the mountains and the Swiss people delighted them. After staying at Heidelberg, where Anne made her last sketches, they hurried back home before the winter started and to see a dying friend. Altogether they stayed at more than 50 hotels and inns. They used the new railways where they existed, otherwise they travelled by boat (even though Mary was a bad sailor), by diligence – the Continental stagecoach – or by hired carriage and driver. During the nine-month journey, they spent ten weeks in Dresden, the capital of the kingdom of Saxony, where John had stayed before and had friends. They had memorable visits to the Court Theatre and Royal Opera where Wagner was conducting, they took German lessons and became part of the Anglican congregation.

Their activities were disturbed by the bad wintry weather but they were perfectly resigned to that: the weather and conditions underfoot always dominated their lives. But unless something special was happening, they liked to take some exercise out of doors every day if possible in addition to their daily 'work' – reading, writing, drawing or needlework.

Their eldest brother William visited them briefly, a treat marred by illness and bad weather, and many long letters were written between the sisters and brothers during the tour. They were a very close and devoted family – so much so that their youngest brother Henry joined them at Zurich with his bride for their honeymoon.

The Wilsons' journey took very much the same route as a Grand Tour of the seventeenth and eighteenth centuries, but by the nineteenth century the era of the Grand Tours was over. Aristocrats still toured – they turn up every now and again in the journal – but many other, more ordinary people were travelling, to carry on with their work and business, to learn languages and to see the sights – the 'lions', as Mary called them.

Europe at that time was a relatively safe place; there were no longer bandits or bands of demobilized soldiers roaming menacingly about and there were better arrangements for crossing frontiers. (They missed the revolutions in Germany and Italy during the following year.) Public health and sanitation were improving, although Mary's disgust in places like Bormio in Northern Italy was caused, probably, by the very low standard of hygiene.

On the Continent the English on their Grand Tours had been notorious for their arrogance, insensitivity and extravagance, and *Murray's Handbooks For Travellers*, which began to be published in 1836, suggested to contemporary travellers that it would be commendable if tourists could behave in a more sensitive and understanding manner. The Wilsons did their best, but they did not like many of the 'foreigners' they saw and mixed with, and they were often irritated by their fellow English travellers as well. They did make some friends of various nationalities. They liked the small number of Americans they met, including one of the sons of John James Audubon, the naturalist. However, Mary had a deep dislike for Roman Catholic priests and their religion.

For John, the journey was partly a business trip; with his brother William he had inherited the linen shop and they imported fine merchandise from the Continent to sell in the shop. For all three, the journey was also an opportunity to educate themselves. With their newly acquired wealth and their inquisitive minds, travelling was an interesting and instructive way of spending the time – even if there were some discomforts. They took only a moderate amount of luggage, were careful with their money and generally kept themselves to themselves – quite unlike the travellers on the Grand Tour.

To understand the Wilsons' attitudes and character, some details of their background and family life may be helpful. When the Industrial Revolution was at its peak in England, very many people had moved into the towns and cities looking for work, following the enclosure of land and the development of the new manufacturing industries. A new social class was forming of wealthy urban tradesmen, and Anne and Mary's father, John

The Rhine from the bridge of boats at Coblenz, 1834

Wilson, was a member of this new social order. His father had been a farm labourer who had fortunately, and very unusually for the period, married his yeoman master's[1] daughter. The young couple started farming, in a very small way and before the enclosure of the land, at Knapthorpe near Caunton in Nottinghamshire in 1768. With very many children to feed and clothe, they sent their eldest son at the age of twelve to be apprenticed to a linen-draper in Newark for seven years.

In 1793, when the apprenticeship had ended – it was the year of the fateful enclosure of farmland at Knapthorpe – he went to London to find work and soon found a job with a fashionable linen-draper[2] in the City of London. By the end of the century, the young man from Nottinghamshire had been offered a partnership and a business arrangement was made in 1802 for the establishment of his own shop at Covent Garden. Two years later he married one of the daughters of the widow[3] of a Lambeth potter who was a customer and the next year William Wilson was born, named after his farming grandfather. The following year, Anne Sanders Wilson was born, and then followed John, Mary and three more sons.

By this time Covent Garden was a centre of great activity. The original seventeenth-century terraced square, built as a quiet dwelling-place for gentlemen and with the splendid Inigo Jones Church of St Paul standing on the west side, had been transformed into a large market place surrounded by coffee houses, shops and lodging houses. The linen shop in Tavistock Street lay just to the south-east and was two minutes' walk from the Strand, the main highway between the City of London and Westminster. Close by stood the Covent Garden Theatre (now the Royal Opera House) and the Drury Lane Theatre. These two great centres of music and drama in London were destroyed by fire and rebuilt when William and Anne were small children. Many artists, writers and engravers lived and worked in the area and there were numerous shops selling paintings and prints, as well as publishers producing books and journals. Mr and Mrs Wilson began to buy pictures and books for a library.

So the Wilson children started life in this interesting part of London in a busy and well organized home. Their mother took care of each child's education until the age of eight, and then the boys went to a private boarding school in Lambeth, whilst the girls continued with lessons at home and visited a French teacher. Their father worked hard in his flourishing shop and was a devout member of the Church of England. He was involved in attempts to stop corruption in parish affairs and gave generously to charitable causes. He helped relatives and friends in need by giving them lodgings or financial assistance. He was a devoted husband and father and taught his young children to be truthful and dutiful, believing that industry, integrity and temperance were of great importance.

In 1821 the family moved to Greenhill[4], a 15-acre farm in the village of Hampstead on the hills north of London. Here they lived for eight years in the old house in Hampstead High Street where the painter Clarkson Stanfield lived later in the century. William joined his father at the shop and in 1823 the business moved to 159 New Bond Street, where the same building still stands today. John and Edward went to a private school in Hampstead and Anne and Mary and the youngest boys had a part-time governess. By this time their father's health was failing

Entrance to the garden, Green Hill, Hampstead, 1829

and their mother had to spend time at the shop. Anne was busy at home; now a young woman of 16 she helped to entertain the many visitors who came to the house as well as looking after the younger children and their friends. Even with a good big income, the family did not have the usual number of servants. Anne cooked and sewed, made small articles of clothing and artificial flowers, called on friends, went often to church and exercised the children and dogs on the heath.

In her spare time Anne drew and painted. A flower painting was exhibited at the Society of British Artists in Suffolk Street in 1825, when Anne was 19, and, according to records, this was the only time her work was seen in public. In 1970, a volume containing some of Anne's early work was given to the La Trobe Library in Melbourne, Australia, by one of Gilbert's descendants. There are paintings of Hampstead and of flowers, but also finely painted copies of professional artists' work which give us some clues as to how she first learned to draw and paint. At the beginning of the nineteenth century, Rudolph Ackermann had started a scheme whereby, for an annual subscription, prints and drawings were circulated with instructions for copying. This was cheaper than individual tuition. (This method of teaching was later criticised and sketching from nature took its place.)

After painting a large picture of her father's favourite roses, Anne was allowed lessons with Sydenham Edwards[5], an illustrator of botanical and sporting publications and an exhibitor at the Royal Academy. He died in 1819 so the tuition did not last long.

By 1829 the three oldest Wilson boys were working at the shop and their father's health was rapidly deteriorating. With little notice, the landlord at Greenhill asked them to leave and there was a quick search for a new home. After looking in Hammersmith and Wandsworth, they found Wandle Grove, a larger house and farm at Mitcham in Surrey where Anne painted their lovely river walks, the house and their pet animals. The house stands today as a company's offices and the walks beside the River Wandle and its water-meadows are preserved – one of the little green 'islands' in Greater London. Soon her father asked Anne to live as housekeeper with her brothers at the shop in New Bond Street which she did 'though at some sacrifice of my own taste and pleasure' as she wrote many years later – she had less time for painting. In 1834 her father died. The family stayed at the farm, except for William who married Emily and lived over the shop, and Edward who went to work in Manchester. Suddenly – once again – the landlord wanted the property back[6] and in 1838 they were obliged to move, this time to fashionable Chester Terrace in

Brookfield Cottage, Mitcham, May 1840

One of the Wilsons homes, probably the house at Shirley

Regents Park, one of John Nash's handsome London terraces. In the same year, Anne, Mary and John took their mother to Paris. Two weeks after returning home she died of apoplexy.

After losing three infants, not unusual for wealthy as well as poor families in the nineteenth century, William and Emily moved to Mitcham with their surviving child, Arthur, and lived in Brookfield Cottage on land belonging to the farm where the family had once lived. Anne and Mary stayed there on the last night of their 1847 journey.

In 1841 there was a family crisis. Edward, the brother living in Manchester, who had already perturbed the family with his interest in radical politics, appalled them by losing his inheritance after a business failure. They supported him and encouraged him to return to London and work in the family business, but he could not be persuaded and sailed off to Australia to be a farmer. The family was heartbroken and Edward's name is not mentioned once in the journal, so painful had his departure been. With Edward abroad, William married and Gilbert running his own hosiery shop in Oxford Street – where he lived – the family was scattering, so in 1843 Anne, Mary and John decided to leave London and live in the countryside. They chose Shirley Common, close to the New Forest, and near Southampton, where they had friends. It was convenient for John's work: close to the docks for his importing business and also served by the recently constructed London and South Western Railway line for visits to London and the linen shop.

In 1846 Gilbert married a Miss Perfect and a year later Henry married a Miss Good (what an excellent pair) and by the 1860s Anne and Mary had many nephews and nieces. Early letters and diaries suggest that they had little desire to be married themselves. Having helped their mother run the home and bring up five brothers, they realized marriage could mean drudgery. Being single had its advantages, but only, of course, because they had financial independence. In Anne's case she wanted to draw and paint and if she had been born later in the century she might well have attended art school and become a professional artist. As it was, she painted, privately, hundreds of watercolours and produced beautiful needlework. Many of her watercolours were mounted and bound into leather volumes which she gave to her nephews and nieces. Before she died she wrote a little book reminding them of their humble origins and about their good and hardworking grandfather and uncle Edward Wilson.

William and Henry looked after the shop until they died in the 1850s. Gilbert took it over until his death and then it was managed by his eldest son[7]. John travelled a lot on business and died unexpectedly at the age of 45, just six years after the tour with his sisters. Edward, in Australia, became the only member of the family to make his mark in the public sphere. Whilst still a farmer, he found he disliked what was going on in the state of Victoria, and he therefore bought the *Melbourne Argus* newspaper. For a number of years, including the time of the Goldrush, he was the paper's editor. He promoted reforms and upset the Governor and many in the Establishment with his radical ideas, but the newspaper flourished and he made a fortune. Starting to go blind, he returned to England in 1863 and had a farm and a small zoo at Hayes Place in Kent, the eighteenth-century house built by William Pitt where the second William Pitt was born. The house became a centre for colonial visitors, for large numbers of family and friends, for people who were interested in reform and for many others in the world of science and the arts. Edward was a founder of the Royal Colonial Institute and the only member of the Council who was neither titled nor a privy councillor. When Edward died in 1878, most of his fortune was put into a charitable trust which is still helping people in the state of Victoria[8].

Anne and Mary left Shirley in 1859 and went to live near friends and relatives at Harpenden in Hertfordshire. The Church of St Nicholas at Harpenden was rebuilt in 1862 and, according to a late nineteenth-century *Kelly's Directory*, the east window, of stained Munich glass, was the gift of the late Misses Wilson. Could this have been the glass which was seen and bought in Munich in 1847?

The sisters' last move was to Bray in Berkshire where they lived at Chauntry House – now a hotel – which stands next to the churchyard, and where Mary died in 1873 and Anne in 1883.

Mary's journal, about 86,000 words in length, is written in ink in small, neat handwriting with very few errors and no wasted paper. It describes a broad range of the Wilsons' activities and interests and gives some outspoken opinion as well as a little worldly wisdom. Scholars may discover some errors of fact. For instance, the Bernini statue in the Piazza Navona in Rome is not of bronze although in 1847 the marble was blackened by smoke, according to a contemporary painting.

In the dim light of the evenings, Mary wrote about the day's events in her journal and, as there were language problems, it is not surprising if she made one or two mistakes. In addition, it should be remembered that cities and towns, as well as some of the customs and traditions prevalent at the time, have changed during the last one and a half centuries.

The little red leather journal book travelled round Europe with its author in all sorts of conditions and the quality of ink varied from place to place. Small parts of the text are now indistinct, making transcription difficult and in one or two places impossible. The text has been given a minimum of editing so that dull days with bad weather are left out and a little modern punctuation has been introduced. Inconsistencies and errors in spelling have been preserved as in the original.

Anne started making pencil and wash sketches, with notes, after reaching Germany. When time and weather allowed, she recorded in her sketchbooks, one of which has survived. She painted the 97 watercolour pictures which make up the full collection once she had returned home, using her sketchbooks as source material, which was the practice of many professional artists of the period. During the last part of the 18th Century watercolour painting had become very popular, mainly because people wanted to record their travel experiences and firms such as Reeves and Ackermann had started making and selling watercolour paints. Both the journal and the illustrations were undertaken by the sisters to describe and illustrate their journey for the benefit of family and close friends left behind in England, and they have been passed down the generations to the delight of all who have seen them.

From England to Saxony

January 11th to February 22nd

BY TRAIN FROM SHIRLEY TO DOVER VIA LONDON · BY STEAMER TO OSTEND · BY TRAIN TO BRUSSELS · EIGHT NIGHTS AT THE HOTEL BELLEVUE · BY TRAIN TO AIX LA CHAPELLE, CROSSING FRONTIER INTO GERMANY · SEVEN NIGHTS AT LA COURONNE IMPERIALE · BY TRAIN TO COLOGNE · FIVE NIGHTS AT THE HOTEL DE HOLLANDE · STEAMER TRIP ON THE RHINE, ONE NIGHT AT COBLENZ, THEN TO MAYENCE · BY TRAIN TO FRANKFURT · FIFTEEN NIGHTS AT THE HOTEL RUSSIE · BY CARRIAGE TO FULDA · ONE NIGHT AT THE HOTEL DE POSTE · BY CARRIAGE TO GOTHA, WITH ONE NIGHT AT THE HOTEL DU MOHR · TO WEIMAR VIA ERFURT · ONE NIGHT AT THE ERBPRINZ · BY TRAIN TO LEIPZIG VIA HALLE · TWO NIGHTS AT THE HOTEL DE BAVIÈRE · BY TRAIN TO DRESDEN

From England to Saxony

January 11th to February 22nd

Monday January 11, 1847 We left Shirley and went up to London by the 9 o'clock train accompanied by Henry who was to be our guide to Dover. We lunched at the Bridge Hotel[1] where William and Gilbert came to say good-bye, and proceeded to Dover by the ½ past three o'clock train, and at a little after 7 found John waiting to receive us, and went to the Ship Hotel, where we dined and went for a few hours to bed, as we found the boat was to depart at 4 in the morning. Accordingly at 4 we took leave of Henry and made ourselves snug in the cabin which Anne and I had all to ourselves, and there we stayed until 9 when we found ourselves at Ostend. We landed and went to the Hotel des Bains, a large wandering dirty place, to have breakfast and await the administration of our luggage. The morning was bright and beautiful but bitterly cold, after breakfast we had a walk to see what we could of Ostend and found it much cleaner and pleasanter than we expected, at 12 we went to the railway station and started at ½ past 12 for Brussels, passing through Bruges and Ghent. Our fellow passengers, who had crossed with us from Dover, were a young German returning from a tour in America, and an old Englishman, whom we set down as a Jew and as he kept up a constant conversation with the young German partly in bad French and the rest in bad English on the German's side, and was a shrewd clever old fellow, he served to amuse us during our 5 hours ride which might have been otherwise somewhat tedious as the country had no particular beauty to recommend it. We had three other passengers a part of the way, an old Belgian and his lady & an elderly man, country unknown, who came to the train with a great tall soldier and kissed him all over his face at parting. We arrived very comfortably at the Hotel Bellevue and got a very nice sitting room with paintings of the Zoological Gardens on the walls, and bedrooms looking on to the huge square opposite to the Hotel. We dined and had tea and then were not sorry to take possession of our beds. In the course of the evening we were very much delighted with a beautiful piece of music played by a military band at the barracks close to the hotel, before the drums went round to parade the streets.

Wednesday January 13 After breakfast Anne and John wrote home and I worked and looked out at windows and wondered what they would ever do with the huge quantity of ice that they were taking in at a house opposite, and then we all went out, and walked up one street and down another admiring all the beautiful things in the very nice handsome shops. We went round the exterior of the Cathedral and into the park to see the Palace, and were exceedingly amused to see all the statues in the Park thatched like hay stacks to preserve them from frost. We returned along one of the Boulevards and saw a very fine collection of tropical plants in the Botanical gardens, certainly the largest plants of some kinds that I ever saw, but what very much surprised us was to see the common laurustinus and cypress kept as tender plants in the greenhouse, and certainly they did look more tender than those that grow in England in the open air, but the climate of Germany[2] is evidently too severe for evergreens, for no such thing is to be seen, not even a common laurel. The people are generally speaking very nice respectable looking folk, very like ourselves, we agreed. The poorer classes of course have a different look to English poor, the favourite dress with the poor women here seems a sort of loose cloak made of coloured cotton print, which looks a very light covering for such severe weather. We often see them carrying the bright brass vessels that the old dutch painters are so fond of introducing in their pictures. We dined at the Table d'Hote where there were six English ladies besides ourselves, and a large party of foreigners, a very handsome dinner and everything very well managed, after dinner which was at ½ past 4 we returned to our own rooms for the evening, and amused ourselves with work on translations according to our several tastes.

Thursday January 14 We worked a little and were just preparing to sally forth in quest of adventures, when we heard the drums beating and presently several regiments of soldiers both horse and foot, and two pieces of artillery came into the square in front of our windows, and after the band had played for some time, they went through a variety of evolutions and then marched away again. We were rather afraid we were going to have a flogging or an execution for while the soldiers were arranging themselves around the square a deserter handcuffed was marched in, between two Gens d'armes and we were most thankful to see he was marched out at the other side of the square without being shot, it was a beautiful sight though. The troops are not by any means equal to our own in appearance, though they must have sacrificed an immense quantity of comfort to the wasp like figures that they pride themselves on, they seemed nearly cut in two, some of them. When they were all gone we put on our bonnets and went to see if we could get into the Cathedral but again found it closed, so made our way through the city in a different direction to that we had taken the day before and walked on. We got quite into the outskirts, and making a little detour, we found ourselves again on the Boulevards and returned home. The shops in Brussels are beautifully clean and well kept, and full of beautiful things of all sorts, the outside of the town seems very much devoted to vegetable gardens, and beautifully cultivated. We dined at the Table d'Hote and met a much larger party than the day before, and spent the evening as usual. The walls of our sitting room are marked in several places by the bullets that were fired into the hotel at the last revolution, when there was an Englishman shot in the hotel by the mob, the holes were left for some time, to gratify the curiosity of visitors but they are now stopped and painted over. The military band play one piece of music every evening, and then the trumpets sound and the drums set forth to parade the city to call the soldiers.

Friday January 15 We went by the ½ past ten o'clock train to Antwerp, and got there tolerably comfortably in an hour and ¼ in spite of the intense cold which made the rails so slippery that we were delayed more than once in starting. We engaged a young peasant as a guide, who took us first to see the house where the idol of Antwerp, Rubens, lived and the statue erected to his memory in the square in front of the Cathedral, then to the Exchange, a very curious old building from which our old Exchange[3] was copied, then to the Cathedral, the spire of which is most beautiful. The interior is nothing out of the way, the painted glass was all destroyed, and only partially restored, there are some beautiful wood carvings to the stalls, which though quite modern are to my thinking the most beautiful things there. We saw the master piece of Rubens, the descent from the cross and several other very fine paintings, of course all scriptural subjects. After the Cathedral we went to see the two churches Les Jesuites and St Jacques, the latter designed by Rubens, and where he and his family are buried in a small chapel which he built and decorated for the purpose, and where there is one of his finest paintings, portraits of himself and family, including his cousin, the original of the famous Chapeau de paille, but formed into an allegory quite beyond our comprehension even with the kind explanation of the Sacristan who went round with us. They are still preserving the Rubens designs for ornamenting the church, and have recently added two beautiful marble figures of Saints executed by a native of Antwerp. We made acquaintance with two new styles of headdress at Antwerp, one, a black shining leather bonnet, worn by the little girls, & I should say more useful than ornamental, but withal very neat looking, and the other a very singularly shaped straw bonnet, worn by the market women over nice white caps with large flaps hanging down to their shoulders, the rest of their dress was nothing peculiar except the sabots. We went round the church of St Jacques and then to the picture gallery, where there are some very beautiful and some not at all so, and as they are almost all confined to two or three subjects, and those the most fanciful in scripture history, it is not altogether a pleasing collection. We had a very pleasant walk round the immense quais & docks and saw shipping from all countries hemmed in by the ice, which is just now very thick and when broken floats down the river in huge masses. We had several good views of the cathedral from different parts of the city during our promenade, and were on the whole very much pleased with Antwerp. We returned to Brussels by the 4 o'clock train, the country between the two is very flat & uninteresting, so was the less regretted the windows being so hard frozen that we could not see through them. We were too late for the Table d'hote and dined by ourselves and spent the evening in our usual avocations.

Saturday January 16 We went directly after breakfast to see the Cathedral, and just walked round it. There is nothing in the interior much worth notice except the painted windows and the pulpit, which is one of the finest specimens of wood carving in the world, it is a representation of the exclusion of Adam and Eve from Paradise. The figures the size of life, and most gracefully designed, form the support of the Pulpit, and the stairs and Pulpit itself are covered with foliage, the apple tree, the Guelder rose, ivy and several other trees like nature, and the serpent, a huge creature, is creeping away and coiling itself round the sounding board of the pulpit, where a figure of religion is crushing his head with a cross. The figures, and trees, and numerous birds and animals that are introduced are all most admirably represented. We went from the Cathedral to have another look at the gay shops and examined the beautiful lace and other vanities exposed therein. And then as John wanted a new outfit and had to hunt a tailor we parted company and Anne and I went on with the shops and explored streets leading out of the square where the hotel was situated, & tried to find out the way to the Protestant chapel & then having, as usual, called in to get our avant diner collation at one of the numberless beautiful confiseurs for which Brussels is celebrated, we returned to the hotel, and amused ourselves with books and work and dinner for the rest of the day. The party at dinner generally consisted of seven or eight foreigners, relations or friends of Madame Proft the hostess, who sat altogether at the top of the table, then came on either side an English lady and her two daughters, then ourselves and another Englishman or two and generally two or three Frenchmen at the bottom. The people who had been accustomed to meet each other seemed to talk away very pleasantly, but we did not make acquaintance with any one except the lady who sat next to Anne, and whom she questioned on various points of interest. The six English ladies had been boarding at the hotel for two months and we fancied meant to stay over the winter as living is very reasonable in hotels during the leisure season abroad especially if you do not mind making a bargain.

Sunday January 17 Finding the services at the chapel were at nine and ½ past two, we could not summon sufficient courage to go to early service in such pinching cold weather, so after breakfast we went to the post, and then walked some considerable distance through the city into the suburbs and were nearly bitten to death by the cold, which I certainly think I never felt so intensely before, and after a brisk trot that thawed our feet, and just peeping into one of the churches, which was quite crowded, and where the congregation seemed to do their business and leave the Priest to do his, we took our brioche lunch and returned home. At ½ past two Anne and I went to the Chapel royal, near the museum, where we heard the afternoon service and a sermon for the relief of the poor, there was a very good congregation, we returned to dinner and sat down 24 in number.

Monday January 18 We walked in the morning to the Boulevards and a very cold walk it was, the trees covered

Apartment in the Hotel de Hollande at Cologne, January 1847

with frost and a cutting wind, we went to the post office and got our letters, and then went to see the Picture gallery. There are some very large nasty martyrdoms of Rubens' and some more modern paintings that are very beautiful, especially we noticed a herd of sheep that positively looked quite woolly. When we returned home John and Anne finished writing letters, and the evening passed as usual. We had two or three strangers at dinner, but one curious little man that amused us very much has gone, John fancied he was the celebrated cricket player Felix[4].

Wednesday January 20 We left pleasant Brussels at 11 o'clock to go by railway to Aix la Chapelle, we were very sorry to go as Brussels is a very agreable place to stay in and especially if at the Hotel Bellevue, which is most comfortable and well managed. The shops are beautiful and the only disagreable we met with in walking about the city was the dirty condition of our dress when we got home, owing I suppose to their custom of strewing their ashes along the streets which makes them very dirty in dry weather. We had a very comfortable journey to Aix & from Liège to Aix a very beautiful one, with scenery like Derbyshire appearing like a picture between the numerous tunnels that we passed through. We had our luggage examined when we reached Aix, but they behaved very well and only just opened them and closed them again and we drove to 'Le Couronne Imperiale' where we dined, and made our first acquaintance with German stoves and eiderdown quilts.

Sunday January 24 We could not go out for the snow and thaw have made it too dirty for petticoats, so John went to the Cathedral by himself and heard a very fine mass performed, but found the streets perfect torrents of mud. When we went down to dinner we found a party of about 24 mostly young men, who made such a noise all dinnertime as I never heard, all in high good humour, one of them whom we heard afterwards was a public performer, was exhibiting 'leger de main' tricks for the amusement of his companions, one of whom was in such ecstasies, that he gave him a hug when he did anything very clever. We had a band too, who played three or four pieces of music very nicely. The German dinners, so far, we had liked very much, and the stoves and eiderquilts I thought charming, though in my constant attention to the stove I sometimes contrived to make my two mates rather warmer than they liked. We were sorry that we could not see more of the neighbourhood of Aix, but the melted snow had made every place so dirty as to be quite impossible.

Monday January 25 We sat at home all the morning, watching for the sun to make his appearance, which he did at last, and as it looked bright and fine overhead we determined after dinner to wade through the mud as far as the Cathedral, we accomplished it better than we expected. We walked round the interior, watched for a short time the service that was performing and listened to the fine organ and beautiful chanting which is always a treat to me. Assuredly if anything would make me a Catholic the music would be that thing, and only that, for all else that one sees of their ways and doings is contemptible and revolting. We walked along one or two of the best streets in Aix, saw the bathrooms and theatre, and then as there is nothing much worth doing in the city we returned to our nice quiet room, here we breakfasted at 9 – dined at one, drank tea at seven and to bed between ten and eleven as regularly as if we were at home.

Tuesday January 26 We gave up the idea of stirring out as it had poured with rain during the night, and we had no object in braving the consequences, so John went to the post office and we worked & read, and watched a pigeon fancier that lived in a loft near the hotel, and who is strongly suspected of spending a good part of his time in decoying pigeons that did not belong to him into his house.

Wednesday January 27 We took an affectionate leave of our worthy host and his establishment and left Aix by the 12 o'clock train for Cologne. We had the good fortune to travel with the most agreable Scotchman that ever came out of Scotland, he had been a Russian merchant living for many years at St Petersburg, and was on his way thither when we met him, to wind up his affairs intending to retire and live in Derbyshire, where he was building a house. He seemed to have every place we could mention at his fingers' ends, knew all the principal Towns & Cities in Europe, the people, manners, the best way of travelling, and in fact there seemed to be nothing that he did not know, and we were really sorry to part with him when we came to the end of our journey in three hours and a quarter. We got to the Hotel de Hollande a little before 4 and after dinner made ourselves at home in our new residence. Our windows look out upon the Rhine with a very good view up the river to the Seven mountains. The host Monsr Illig came and talked with us during dinner and amused us very much by telling us that his three sons had excused themselves from serving as soldiers, by declaring that they had 'foul interiors', a curious anatomical description.

Thursday January 28 John had a very bad cold and preferred staying at home, so he ordered a carriage and valet for us to see the 'Lions' of Cologne and of course the first was the Cathedral, the height of which exceeds anything one could have imagined, and if it is ever completed it will certainly be one of the wonders of the world, but that seems more than doubtful as one part decays and falls into ruins while they build another. We saw the shrine of the three Kings, but did not think it worth while to pay the large sums charged for seeing the tombs, the most beautiful part I thought was the painted glass in the windows, which is very rich. We went from the Cathedral to the Church of Les Jesuites, which is exceedingly richly ornamented with carved work and gildings and very much in want of soap and water. The magnificent inlaid marble pavement was in such a filthy condition that we could scarcely see it, and we wondered our conductress was not ashamed to point out its beauties through such a veil of dirt, more especially as from our entering the Church through her dwelling we suspected it was her business to do the cleaning, if any is ever done. They have twelve different Altar pieces here which they change during the year, and in one of the small chapels, a painting of Ignatius Loyola said to be by Michael Angelo. We went next to the Church of St Gerion built by the Empress Helena[5] after the model of the Church of the Holy Sepulchre at Jerusalem, and a most curious

Cologne, 29th January 1847

and interesting old building it is, the most ancient part is circular with a dome, and in consequence the altar is placed on the middle of a very steep flight of steps leading to another chapel. Our guide took us down under the chapel to show us some very curious mosaic in the crypt, but when we got there it was too dark to see anything except a large quantity of oleanders & other shrubs that had been placed there as a protection from frost and the candles for the use of the church hanging in every direction making it look more like a chandler's shop than any part of a church. We went next to the Church of St Jacques to see a celebrated picture by Rubens, the crucifixion of St Peter. There is a copy of the painting at the back of the original, and we were obliged to pay to have the real one turned round, which is only done on Sundays and holidays, it is a horrible picture as most of the martyrdoms are, but Rubens is said to have considered it his finest work. He was christened at St Jacques and they point out the large brazen font where the ceremony was performed, but excepting the font and picture it is a wretched poverty-struck looking place. We now went to the church of St Ursula and the 11,000 virgin martyrs[6], where they profess to have all the bones that once belonged to the said ladies except three or four of the sculls, which we had previously seen at Les Jesuites, bound up with gay embroidery and tinsel crowns. At St Ursula the bones are placed all round the church exposed to view except those of the Saint herself, which are in a marble sarcophagus near the Altar. There was a ceremony going on while we were there, as far as we could understand, the admission of a new curé into the service of the church, at any rate there were quantities of candles lighted, and the church hung round with crimson calico and evergreens, and the choristers were singing something very like a dirge and the marble figure of St Ursula was crowned with flowers and garnished with evergreens. I was very glad to get out again, for I always feel like an intruder on the devotion of others, though they do not seem to think anything of it and I suppose would not allow it, if it was offensive to them. We stopped during our drive to see the remains of an old roman wall, the curious exterior of the church of Les Apôtres, and the Town Hall, where there is a gallery that used to be filled with spectators of lion fights, and is evidently of great age. Also we had the house pointed out to us where Rubens was born and Marie de Medici died, both which events happened in the same house according to the evidence of two tablets on its front. The morning was drizzling wet, so that we did not see even dirty Cologne to advantage, it is certainly a horribly dirty place and the inhabitants do not attempt to deny it, or to make it any cleaner. We returned to dinner at one, where we sat down with about 30 gentlemen, all Germans, and not favourable specimens, as they were very ugly and not at all clean. John brought his writing down into our room in the evening and we made ourselves very much at home here though it would seem odd at home to have our beds and washstands in the drawing room. Here they were so, and looked very unobtrusive along one side of the room, the others being occupied by windows, a very handsome worked sofa, a pianoforte, & stove. We breakfasted in our room and John in his, and afterwards joined company or not, as agreable.

Friday January 29 We did not go out as we had seen all we wished to see, and people can't walk about in Cologne for pleasure. John went to the Post Office and a book sellers and bought some books, and we watched the ferry boats across the river and the masses of floating ice, that had prevented the steamers from running for six weeks and made the poor Landlord grumble sadly. He told us today at dinner that Waghorn[7] had been there the day before, and had told him that the Pacha of Egypt had offered to make him a Bey, but he told him that he would rather be a Lieut. in England than a Bey in Egypt. He says Waghorn hates the French, for they will not assist him in any of his great works, he says he wished Napoleon was there now, he could get on with him.

Sunday January 31 We began the day by having our hot water to wash with brought up in a teapot, the people of this good city do not prize either quality or quantity in their ablutions, one would fancy, from the ancient and fish like smell pervading both towels and water. We saw the boat go at 10, taking a great many passengers, a quantity of cases of Eau de Cologne, two carriages etc. Anne finished a letter to Henry. At dinner mine host asked us to take a walk in his carriage and as the day was somewhat finer we accepted his invitation, and soon after dinner a very handsome carriage and horses and the Landlord's sister were ready and away we went. We drove through part of the city and several pieces of garden ground to a small place, where the good folks of Cologne go in summer to drink coffee and enjoy a beautiful garden and view of the river. We got out of the carriage and our good natured conductress ordered some coffee, and we walked round the garden which in summer must be very pretty, and then we went into a room where some other folks were drinking coffee and smoking, and playing at dominoes, and after ½ an hour we returned to Cologne by a different route. Our kind friend said she hoped we should return from our wanderings by Cologne that we might meet again and we said we should be happy to see her if fate ever took her to England, and so we parted very much pleased at having received such a kindness. The evening of course was spent just as at home in reading.

Monday February 1 We left Cologne by the steamer Ludwig 2nd at 10 o'clock and staid on deck until driven down by the wind and snow, which fell very fast for sometime. There were not many passengers luckily for us, and a nice warm cabin, where we read and knitted until ½ past one when we sat down to the table d'hôte. After dinner we went on deck again to see the scenery, there is nothing much worth seeing for some miles beyond Cologne and we were in time after dinner to see Rolandseck and the Noanenwerth and though the day was bitterly cold we staid on deck until the sun went down, and then went down ourselves and read and played chess until ½ past 8 when we most thankfully arrived at Coblenz and went at once to 'Les trois Suisses' which is close to the quai where the passengers land from the steamers, and just opposite the bridge of boats and the Fortress which looked most lovely in the bright moonlight, the only light we were destined to see it by, as the horrid boat set off again at six in the morning. We went to bed after a capital tea, and slept as well as people generally do who have to get up again before daylight.

Tuesday February 2 Went back to our cabin at ½ past five and made ourselves as snug as we could until it was light, the party on board were pretty much the same as the day before and had nothing remarkable about them as we thought, though one of them we found afterwards was the celebrated French author Eugène Sue[8]. As soon as it was at all practicable we went up on deck and passed through some very beautiful scenery, the mountains, most of them were very snowy, and therefore very different to their usual appearance in the eyes of Cockney travellers, and certainly not so beautiful as when the vines are covered with foliage but it was much pleasanter, we thought, to have the deck pretty much to ourselves, than if it had been crowded as it is in the full Rhine season[9]. We admired the towns as we passed very much, Boppart, Oberwesel, St Goar, Bacharach, Biberich, most of them close to the side of the water and the mountains rising close behind them, surmounted in most cases by one of the ruins, and in some by a large staring hotel, or perhaps a little odious jaunty looking summer house half way up the ascent, the effect of which is to destroy the romance of the place considerably by visions of coffee and cigars etc. The day was dreary and cold and the blocks of ice by the river side were in some places from six to eight feet high, so that when they begin to float they are rather formidable enemies to steamers. We generally exchanged some of our passengers at the towns as we passed them. We dined on board again and arrived at Mayence at ½ past three, and were rather dismayed to find the bridge of boats had been removed to make a passage for the ice to float away and that we must cross in a ferry boat to the railway at Cassel, however we followed our luggage straitway to the boat and got safe across and to the station and there staid in a nice warm waiting room, quite a luxury after our cold voyage, until the train started at ½ past five. We reached Frankfurt in an hour and took up our quarters at the Hotel de Russie and were heartily glad to have tea and go to bed.

Wednesday February 3 We went into a more commodious apartment looking into the chief street of Frankfurt and a very handsome street it is, called the Zeil, and after breakfast we had a very long walk nearly round the town through a beautiful public garden that has been laid out on the fortifications, and a very delightful walk it must be in summer, when it is planted with flowers. There are very fine houses all round the town, the residences of the rich merchants and a very prosperous looking city Frankfurt seems and by far the cleanest we have seen since we left England. We walked through one of the markets, which seemed well supplied with vegetables, spinach, celery, beautiful little carrots in quantities, and salad, and a great deal of sponge which seemed a strange thing to sell among vegetables, perhaps they put it into their soup, there's no knowing. We returned to dinner at one o'clock and met ½ a dozen antique and stove dried Germans. After dinner Anne and I sallied forth in search of wool and other working materials and she thought herself very clever to make the people understand what she wanted though in two out of the three shops we went into the women understood french and a little English as well as German, and they were exceedingly civil in trying to understand what we said to them. We looked at everything in the shops near the hotel and then returned home, in the evening it began to snow again and was very cold.

Friday February 5 A fine bright frosty morning but very cold. We went first to the bankers and while John was transacting his business, Madam La Portière took pity on us for waiting in the cold, and invited us into her parlour where she amused us with the frolics of her little dog Flora until John came and then we went to Mr Bethman's gardens to see Dannecker's Statue of Ariadne[10], which is a beautiful figure certainly, but one sees models and casts from it in all the shops in Frankfurt until it becomes quite tiresome. We had a very pleasant walk round part of the town through the public garden, and as we returned home staid to listen to the military band that was playing at the Guardhouse, they played very well but nothing very pretty. Dined at 1 – our conjectures were correct as to the Englishman who had a Frenchman next him today that would talk, and his Oui, Oui quite settled his native land. We did not go out after dinner.

Saturday February 6 Went to see the Cathedral but there is nothing beautiful about it, or anything particularly curious except the colour which is a dark red, the same stone as most of the public buildings here and some of the private houses and the Statue of Charlemagne on the bridge are made of, so I suppose it is found somewhere in the neighbourhood. We walked through two or three of the markets, and saw plenty of nice fresh vegetables and butter, the butter is not very good which we suppose arises from their keeping their cows shut up in sheds, as sure and except in harness we never saw any cattle anywhere, and at Frankfurt we saw them in carts sometimes by themselves and sometimes paired with horses. This day we crossed the river and walked through part of the old town and got into the country on the other side among the vineyards, which at this season have no beauty whatever, but ascending a steep hill we got a very good view of the city, and then as we were some distance from home and it began to snow we turned back again. The afternoon was snowy and very cold, John went to the post office and to make some purchases, the night very stormy.

Monday February 8 Went in spite of the ground being very snowy and slippery to see the collection of pictures and statues called the Steidel Museum, some fine old pictures among them, but the modern ones very inferior to our English Artists. We spent a couple of hours there and then returned home, as walking was too dangerous a thing to be thought of. In the evening we went to see a new play called Struensee, from the history of Matilda of Denmark and her favourite minister, the play by the brother of Meyerbeer the musical composer, the

Sledge at Frankfurt, 16th February 1847

music by himself[11]. The music was rather pretty but the play very tedious, the Audience might have been English from their appearance, not at all gay or overdressed and we got home a little after ten which was considered very late for a German theatre.

Tuesday February 9 Deep snow on the ground prevented our going out, but we had plenty of work and plenty of employment in watching the gay sledges that made their appearance with gilding and flowers, and horses trimmed with bright coloured ribbons and trappings with small bells fastened all over them so that the street was in a perpetual jingle all day. The boys had sledges on which they were dragging each other about and the poor people had sledges on which they carried their merchandise so that sledges seemed all at once the order of the day, the grand ones had leopard or bear skins to cover the people inside, and the drivers sat behind. They look like pleasant gliding vehicles but rather cold I should think. John had a walk after dinner, but found it very cold and slippery. In the evening drank Wm's health on his birthday.

Sunday February 14 Not out at all, in the afternoon the snow came drifting down in perfect clouds accompanied by high wind, several very handsome sledges were driving about, and among them Mr Bethman's the rich banker, with two very natty looking grooms riding in front on horseback, but it looked much too cold to be pleasant. We were surprised to see the women walking about in such bitter weather without any covering to their heads, no cap, no bonnet, no anything but their beautifully neat hair of which they generally have a profusion.

Tuesday February 16 Snow nearly all gone from the tops of the houses and a brisk wind helped to dry the roads which were in a sad state from the depth of snow. John went to select a voiture to go to Dresden in. A gay wedding breakfast at the hotel today, ladies in pink satin and chasseurs in green and gold, and Monsr. Sarg and his household all in grande tenue. The son of Prince Hohenlohe married a daughter of Prince Wilkinson, so we understood our funny little waiter.

Wednesday February 17 We left the Hotel de Russie in a comfortable Berline at 8 o'clock, said Berline John had engaged to take us to Weimar. The morning was very cold, but bright and sunny and as Monsr. Sarg had packed us up very comfortably with hay for our feet and sandwiches for our mouths, we had a very snug pleasant days journey to Fulda which we reached a little before seven. The country was for the greater part of the way very flat and unbeautiful and only enlivened by a few very wretched, poor, and dirty villages, but we were greatly entertained at their manner of collecting turnpike money, which was by means of thrusting a long ladle into the carriage, from a window, receiving the money, and then poking the ladle into the carriage again with the receipt, which seemed more trouble than coming out, and certainly took much more time, but I suppose they know their own business best. The hotel de Poste at Fulda received us very hospitably and made us very comfortable, except in the matter of noise, which was most terrible all night, as it generally is at the Poste Hotels from the arrivals and departures of the Diligences.

Thursday February 18 We got up before it was light, and set off again at ½ past 7 and rode through streams, and banks of snow, sometimes 8 or 9 feet high where it was cut through for the road, the country we passed through was very hilly, and in some places beautifully covered with plantations of young fir trees. The stage from Marksuhl to Eisenach was most lovely, the road winding between very steep hills covered with snow and in some places plantations of firs or vineyards. It was curious to watch the different colours of the streams that were running in every direction from the hills, caused by the partial melting of the snow and coloured by the different soils through which they run. In some places they were quite a deep red, and others like tea or coffee with or without milk, and sometimes like milk only. The villages we passed were still very poor and horribly dirty, the houses built in general of wood. We did not reach Gotha until long after dark and our last hour's ride was somewhat tedious but at last we were gladdened by a sight of the lights of the town and then by reaching the town itself, we were surprised to find it so large a place, and as far as we could see so pleasant a one. The houses are scattered about with trees and gardens between. We arrived at the Hotel du Mohr at about ½ past 8 and were glad after our long days ride to make good speed with our tea and ham etc and go to bed.

Friday February 19 John went out and just got a peep at the Palace from which our beautiful Prince Albert came, and though in bad repair and an ugly old place it is not one to be ashamed of, of enormous size as John counted 214 windows in one side and there are four sides, it is beautifully situated on a hill, with a very fine garden and pleasure grounds round it, and must have a lovely view in summer. The melted snow had made all places too dirty for walking much so as it was in vain to hope to see anything of the neighbourhood if we staid, we made up our minds to take flight again at 10 o'clock. The Hotel where we slept was the one where Napoleon passed the night when he was flying from the battle of Leipzig[12]. We set off at 10 and rode through a very sloppy country, with streams more or less deep, and along very strait and very interminable roads between avenues of cherry or plum trees, the roads every now and then cut through a bank of snow that we could not see over from the carriage windows. We passed through a very curious old town Erfurt, once the capital of Thuringia, very strongly fortified, and celebrated as having been for many years the residence of Luther. In these railways days they have carried one through the fortifications. We got to Weimar soon after two and having ordered dinner at the 'Erbprinz' we went out to see what we could of the Town, and found it a very clean quiet place with very little indeed to see except Goethe's and Schiller's houses[13] and a pretty walk in the Palace Gardens. We did not walk far, partly because we had not time and partly because it was very dirty, so we returned to the Hotel and had dinner, and were much amused by the admiration the little waiter expressed at the carriage we had come in, which certainly we had found very easy and comfortable, but it as certainly was one of the scrubbiest looking vehicles that one could wish to see, however here we bade it farewell, as the railway between Weimar and Leipzig had been opened about two months.

Saturday February 20 We left Weimar by the ½ past 8 train and were rather disconcerted on a bitter cold morning, by the regulation that passengers were to be at the station ½ an hour before the train started, so at ½ past 7 the Omnibus called at the Hotel and took us and another gentleman to the train, and we got into one of the most soft and luxurious carriages I ever was in, though only 2nd class, as in Germany people seldom travel in first class carriages unless to avoid smoking. We found an old lady in the carriage sitting muffled up in a large cloak, and we had not sat long when there was such a very canine snuffle from under the said cloak, that Anne and I exchanged looks and laughed and the old Dame confessed to having her pet dog in hiding for fear she should not be permitted to take it in the carriage with her. It was a very quiet and well behaved and sleepy little beast, and did not betray its mistress. We had a pleasant ride to Leipzig the only drawback being a ¾ of an hour at Halle where we had to change carriages, and we

Bridge and City of Dresden, from the Neustadt, February 1847

should not have cared for that, only that the railway being an infant there was no decent passengers room and the one where all the passengers waited, and of course as *Germans fed*, had very much the appearance and odour of a zoological collection. However it did not much signify and we got to Leipzig in time for a walk round the Ramparts, very much to the surprise and delight of the natives, who certainly stared in the most unceremonious and rude manner that I ever beheld, we could not make up our minds what there was so very singular in our appearance, but there was evidently something strange, wild and unnatural. Leipzig is a curious old place, especially an old market place, which we were fortunate in seeing on market day Saturday, as on other days it is very quiet and dull. We returned to the Hotel de Bavière to dinner and in the evening John went to the theatre and we were amused by a small concert in the next room to us, which was occupied by three English people, whom they had entered in the hotel list as Sir Tonkin, Lady Tonkin[14] and Mr Batten, and the latter gentleman played most beautifully on the flute, while Lady Tonkin accompanied him most vilely on the Piano.

Sunday February 21 We walked to the place where Poniatowski[15] was drowned and truly if the river was always as we saw it, it was no wonder he was drowned, for it was roaring along and falling in a perfect cataract over a bridge that it generally runs very peaceably beneath. We met a great many of the Leipsigers during our walk, and stopped to listen to the military band, and then returned home. The boys here wear a very sensible sort of winter dress, a pelisse with hanging sleeves, made of blue cloth, braided with black, very warm, very easily put on and off and very good looking. The young children are drawn about in cots upon wheels with little feather beds on the top of them and very droll they look sometimes with a little face looking out at each end of the featherbed. We dined with a very large and very noisy party and sat opposite Mr Batten and the Tonkins and their dog, they were very uninviting looking people, so we had no further communication than the mere civilities. In the evening they repeated their concert, and certainly he did play beautifully.

Monday February 22 We left Leipsig by railway at 2 o'clock and had a very comfortable ride in a carriage to ourselves with a warmer at the bottom for our feet, and reached Dresden a quarter before six, the snow in some places was very deep by the side of the railway, and the waters out to a tremendous extent, covering the land for acres and acres, especially on the banks of the rivers. The approach to Dresden is very pretty and hilly with nice looking detached houses scattered about. We walked from the station to the Stadt Wien where John had written to order rooms, so they were looking out for us, it is in a beautiful situation on the banks of the river just at the foot of the bridge, so that there was always something passing. We dined and then John went out for a walk while we unpacked some of our work etc. We were somewhat rejoiced to find that we had a separate closet for our beds here, as we could not get rid of our English prejudice in favour of keeping bedrooms to themselves. Our room had a beautiful view of the river, bridge, palace and theatre and was a nice sunny light room.

Sojourn at Dresden
February 23rd to April 30th

ROOMS AT THE STADT WIEN HOTEL · DAY VISIT TO MEISSEN · BY CARRIAGE TO MORITZBURG FOR THE DAY · THARAND · EASTER DAY · BROTHER WILLIAM ARRIVES FOR A FIVE DAY VISIT · BY CARRIAGE TO SPITZHAUS FOR THE DAY · BY TRAIN TO LOBAU, BY CARRIAGE TO ZITTAU · TWO NIGHTS AT THE SONNE HOTEL · FRIEDLAND IN BOHEMIA, FOR A VISIT TO WALLENSTEIN'S CASTLE · BY CARRIAGE TO OYBEN · BY CARRIAGE TO SAXON SWITZERLAND · BY PONY UP THE WINTERBERG · TWO NIGHTS AT A MOUNTAIN-TOP HOTEL · DESCENT OF THE WINTERBERG BY PONY · BY CARRIAGE TO RIVER ELBE · BY ROWING BOAT TO THE BASTEI · BY STEAMER ON THE ELBE TO DRESDEN · FIVE NIGHTS AT THE STADT WIEN

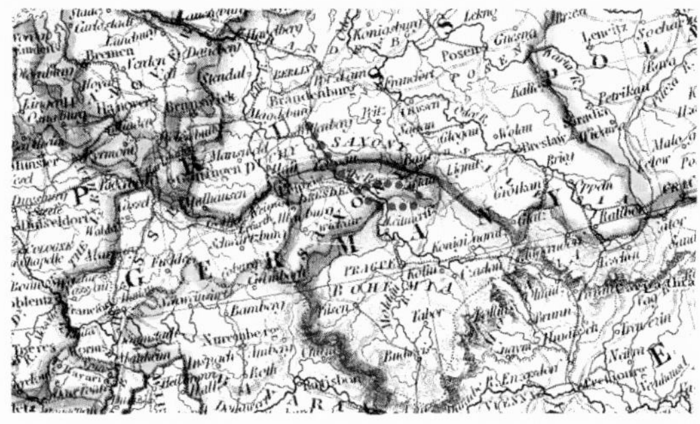

Sojourn at Dresden
February 23rd to April 30th

Tuesday February 23 We went out for a long walk directly after breakfast and John introduced us to the principal buildings in the city, we walked as far as the Grosse garten, a beautiful park laid out with walks and statues and cafes where in the summer they hold concerts two or three times a week. We returned by the Palace and the Zwinger, the most interesting place I ever saw in appearance, though very much out of repair, and only part of a design for a palace built in 1711. We had only time to make a hasty search after some gloves and return in time for the table d'hote which was at one o'clock, the Dresden dinner hour, we were a very small party and as usual we were the only women present. In the evening John went to the Theatre and we worked and read as usual.

Wednesday February 24 John was not very well so we left him at home to nurse and Anne and I went forth to see if we could hunt up several little luxuries such as walking boots etc, a very amusing walk we had. It happened to be a sort of fair such as is held at Dresden once a month, and all the streets and market places were full of merchandise, of every description, quantities of stuffs for gowns, shawls, toys, cakes, tapes and thread, wooden ware such as butcher's trays and shovels, metal pots, and earthenware pans in loads, jewellery which seemed to be very attractive as all the men, rich and poor, wear rings, and sometimes earrings, you may always know a German by his wearing a seal ring nearly as large as his face, on his forefinger. We managed to get all we wanted except the boots, and the shoemaker yclept Auguste Venus, of all the names for the most hideous of mortals, had none that would fit, and as he understood nothing but German, we were obliged partly to give the order in dumb show and leave the rest to the Venus ingenuity to discover. We returned home and were introduced to John's German Master Herr Peters, who undertook Anne as a pupil and made arrangements for beginning operations as soon as possible. In the evening we went to the theatre to hear Tichatschek[1], a very fine singer that John was anxious we should hear as he was about to leave Dresden for a time, we heard Gluck's opera Iphigeneia in Aulis with Madam Schroeder[2] as Clytemnestra. We had very nice places and heard and saw beautifully, the theatre is not very large, but very prettily fitted up and very clean, and the Audience quiet respectable looking people. The King and Queen were there and some of their nephews and nieces, all rather common place looking folk. We were very close to their majesties as we came out, so close as to hear the order to return to Schloss. The whole evenings entertainment consisted of one opera which was over in less than three hours, so that we got home by 9 o'clock, a very great improvement on the tedious performances in the English Theatres. We were much amused as we went in with a little boy and girl who opened a pair of swing doors and bowed in such a fancy old fashioned way to all who entered.

Thursday February 25 Anne busy all the morning sketching the view of Dresden from our window. After dinner we walked to Findlater's, a cafe where the Dresden people go to smoke and drink coffee and in summer listen to the band, we went for the sake of the walk which is a very pretty one and a beautiful distant view of the city from a terrace at the back of the house, the weather was biting cold and snow falling almost all the time we were out, but still we enjoyed our walk very much.

Friday February 26 Did not go out in the morning as for some time there was a mist that looked raw and cold. At dinner met three more Englishers, one old dame and her daughter and son-in-law but very unpleasant. After dinner went into the garden of the Japanese Palace and afterwards along one of the roads out of Dresden, where we heard the juveniles in the military bands learning to drum in the roads, and thought they had chosen a very judicious place for such noisy education. Anne took her first lesson in German. Mr Barnet, a young man that John made acquaintance with last year called and had a chat, he is a pleasant youth from Newcastle, who has been sometime at Dresden, improving in mathematics etc. preparatory to becoming an engineer.

Sunday February 28 Barnet came to show us the way to the English Chapel where we heard the service very well performed by the Chaplain Mr Lindsay, Barnet dined with us and departed and we did not go out again.

Monday March 1 A beautiful sunny day, so we started and had a good brisk trot, first to the Zwinger and then into the outskirts where we saw a bust of the late King put up by his subjects, in memory of the 'Good King' and there is a very fine statue of him in the square of the Zwinger to 'Augustus the Just' so he must have been a worthy old fellow, he reigned in Saxony 56 years. In the afternoon another friend of John's Mr Child called, a pleasant little-talking person. When he was gone we went to the concert room on the Bruhl Terrasse intending to hear an hour or two's music, but we found the room so crowded, that we could not find a single chair as it was one of the days when smoking was forbidden, we came out again and after a strole returned home.

Tuesday March 2 Cold and snowy so we staid at home until the evening and then went to hear the Zauberflöte and very beautifully they performed it. As we came home only just over the bridge, it was so terribly slippery that John had a fall, luckily he did not hurt himself. I fancy he must have got upon a slide as a lady fell in the same place directly afterwards, however except this we got home comfortably and had tea and bed by ten o'clock.

Wednesday March 3 Too wet to go out, the snow seemed inclined to turn to rain which we were rather glad of as we had had quite enough of winter. At dinner the gentleman who sat next me had been in England, so we had a conversation about pigeon pies and Leicester Square and the opera and things in general.

Thursday March 4 Young Barnet called, we went to see a portrait of Napoleon by Delaroche that was exhibited at the Zwinger, a very fine picture supposed to be taken just before he signed his abdication at Fontainebleau, afterwards went to buy some books and working materials that we wanted, stopped at the guard house to hear the band play the overture to Egmont.

Saturday March 6 Staid at home all morning expecting Mr Peters who did not come. At dinner met a very agreable American who asked us to join him to make a party to see the curiosities in the Green Vaults which we did and a very curious collection it is, of immense value with gems and precious metals but more like a set of playthings for children than a museum formed by a King. The ivory carvings were very beautiful and we were fortunate in having a perfect old gentleman to walk through the rooms with us, who did not hurry us but seemed pleased when we took more than usual interest in anything. When we came out of the Green Vaults which are under the Palace, and very cold and damp, we took a brisk hour's walk to warm ourselves, accompanied by our American friend who said he was almost beside himself with pleasure at meeting any lady he could speak English to. John went for a couple of hours to the concert on the Terrasse and we returned home.

Sunday March 7 Anne and I went to Chapel and heard an excellent sermon from Mr Lindsay then returned to dinner and afterwards took a long walk accompanied by our new acquaintance to see the curious old piece of sculpture called the Dance of Death, carved in the year 1534. It is a procession of 27 figures led by death himself, of course, carved in relief on the wall of an old Churchyard. In the course of our walk we discovered our Yankee friend to be the son of Audubon[3] the Naturalist and he gave us a history of his life, past and present.

He and his brother are now employed in finishing a work begun by the father, who is now a very old man, and they all live together with their wives and children somewhere near New York. He was an uncommonly intelligent and agreable person and we thought ourselves fortunate to have seen so much of him. We walked through the Grosse Garten and then Mr Audubon went to the theatre & we returned home.

Monday March 8 We got up earlier than usual and at 9 o'clock went with Mr Audubon to the Picture Gallery and if we had not been so dreadfully cold we should have enjoyed ourselves very much, but it was a bitter snowy morning and the Gallery is never warmed. However we spent three hours in examining what were pointed out to us as the chef d'oeuvres, some beautiful Madonnas & Magdalens and a very fine painting of Our Saviour & St Peter with the tribute money, and an exquisite one of Abraham & Hagar, and among a collection of

2000 of course a vast number of treasures, the subjects principally Scriptural. We staid as long as we could bear the cold and then Anne & I returned home and John and Mr Audubon went to the post office & brought a letter from William. We met at dinner and our friend told us a great many tales of his life in the American forests where he sometimes spends 3 months at once, in search of subjects for illustrating his work, accompanied only by his man & horse, killing his own venison, and washing his own clothes when he meets with a river, which he says is the only chance of washing during these trips. He amused us very much with his anecdotes of the red indians, the way in which they classify mankind. White men first, then redmen, then dogs & then negroes, and the habit that some of the tribes have of getting drunk whenever they have the opportunity, but always as a rule having one man sober to take care of the rest when they are incapable of taking care of themselves, and this one takes away their weapons and separates them if they get to fighting. He told us he had a redman called Black Beaver for a guide, on one of his excursions for 4 months and when he had done with him he paid him his hire & gave him a rifle and very kindly advised him to go back to his tribe without going to New York, where he knew he would be cheated out of his money, but the poor fellow was so grieved at parting from his master that he sat down & cried like a child & there Mr Audubon left him but heard of him afterwards & recommended him as a scout to one of the officers in the American Service which he said would be a very good thing for him. All the afternoon the snow came down in such showers that occasionally we could not see across the bridge, so we did not go out again. John went to take a note to Mr Peters.

Tuesday March 9 Did not stir all morning. At dinner met our Yankee friend and a friend of his, a Mr Vogel[4], a very clever but singular looking old artist. We made an appointment with Mr Audubon to go in the evening to see Madame Schroeder in her best character of Romeo[5]. In the afternoon made an attempt to go out but the snow came down so thick as to make it impossible. We went, however, to the theatre and were very much delighted, we agreed we had never seen better acting or heard better singing than Schroeder in this character, she looked quite like a handsome youth and her song at the Tomb of Juliet was the most touching thing I ever heard, her grief was seemingly so real, not like the usual pumped up stage sorrow that is so common. Juliet was very fair and the other characters all pretty well. The snow was so deep when we came out of the theatre that we could not walk home, pretty rich for the 9th of March. John and Mr Audubon had supper in the saloon and we had tea in our own room.

Wednesday March 10 We took leave of our most agreable friend who left Dresden at 9 o'clock.

Received a packet from William containing kind wishes from all at home & a portrait of my darling Arthur, I wrote home to acknowledge the favours.

Thursday March 11 Worked etc in the morning and after dinner took a long walk through or rather over the snow, which was very thick on the ground though the day was bright and sunny and made us hope that someday it would be warmer. We saw several sledges but quite for use and not for ornament like those at Frankfort. The banks of snow by the roadside are most beautiful, with the tracks of the hares hopping through it in many places. Young Barnet came to tea and play at chess, a pleasant intelligent and good looking youth, who amused us much by the confession, how much he had been improved by numerous school floggings when a boy.

Friday March 12 My birthday, received kind congratulations and remembrances from my two friends, at 11 came Barnet to give John a lesson in Algebra.

Saturday March 13 Sat still all the morning, and then made a vain attempt to get a walk, but the snow came down again and it was so dirty underfoot that we gave up the attempt. John went to the Post Office and on his way there met Her Saxon Majesty[6] trudging across one of the dirty streets most manfully in a beautiful velvet pelisse trimmed with sable, such a dress for such a walk.

Monday March 15 The first day of spring, sunny and mild but awfully muddy, we walked up towards Findlaters and climbed upon a high bank that was raised as a fortification by Napoleon, to see a beautiful view of Dresden. We made ourselves very dirty and splashed, but rejoiced very much in the departure of the cold. Young Barnet came in to tea and gossip in the evening.

Tuesday March 16 Went out but found it too dirty to go beyond the town so returned to hear the band play in front of the guard house, and found much amusement in the numbers of nurses and children assembled there, so different to English ones, the nurses generally dirty and loose looking except their hair which was uncovered and tolerably neat. The children poor sickly wretched looking objects, dressed in all sorts of ugly knitted garments and most of them dragged in their little wheeled bedsteads. We went in the evening to hear Stradella[7], a pretty little opera, very tolerably performed, and were very much pleased especially with the two brigands. Mr Child came to shake hands & we laughed at him for throwing bouquets at Madam Shilee.

Wednesday March 17 We went by the ten o'clock train to Meissen to see the China manufactory, we reached the station at Niederau in an hour and another hour in an omnibus took us 4 miles to Meissen. We walked up to the old Palace[8] where the manufacture is carried on but found the workmen were at dinner and we could not see it until 2 o'clock so we went over the church which was built between the 13th and 15th centuries, but was greatly injured at the time of the reformation when most of the beautiful painted windows were destroyed. There are some very fine brasses in the Chapel at the west end, called the Prince's Vault, where many of the Saxon Princes are buried. We went up to the roof of the church to see the view which is very extensive, and at a better season must be very beautiful, but the vineyards which we saw there were leafless of course. When we had walked round the church we went to dine at the hotel down in the town and then again mounted the steep hill on which the Palace stands and were shewn into the saleroom for the china, we saw some very pretty and a great deal very so so, and then we went into the different rooms where it is made, we saw the process of forming dishes, vases, figures etc and were very much surprised to find the figures were made in separate pieces, the arms, legs etc joined on afterwards. We saw them also making the delicate little flowers for the vases and large boxes of flowers etc ready to stick on the vases when ready, then we saw the gilding and painting and the women polishing the gilding which they do by rubbing it with agates. Then we went through the rooms where the moulds are kept and the kilns for baking it. The old palace is wretchedly ill constructed for the purpose to which it is applied and there is nothing business like about the whole place, it is thoroughly Saxon, the work people looked unhealthy and careless whether they worked or not and the dreadfully hot close smothering atmosphere they are in all day may well account for such appearance. When we had seen all they chose to show us, we set off to walk back to the station, along a flat road and as straight as a line and as we fancied there was a train at 5 o'clock we thought we should get home very nicely by daylight but to our dismay when we got to the station as tired as dogs we found there

Hunting Palace of Moritzburg in Saxony. 18th March 1847

was no train until nearly 8, so there we had to stay 3½ mortal hours at the station house. We had some cake and coffee and were very glad to rest ourselves and for an hour or so were very well amused by the people who came in for refreshments but the hateful smoking at last got to such a pitch as to be almost unendurable, added to which the train was half an hour after time, so we got rather tired of Niederau, but its a long lane that has no turning and we reached Dresden at last and were none the worse for the delay.

Thursday March 18 Mr Peters came to give Anne her lesson and staid to dinner and then we had a beautiful walk in the woods among the young fir trees and by the side of a rapid trout stream, the day was like Spring sunny and warm. We came by chance upon a barrack yard, where the raw recruits were being drilled and in our ignorance of military matters we could not imagine what use some of their evolutions could be, first bending one leg and then the other and then stooping as if they were playing leap frog, however I daresay its all right.

Friday March 19 We went in a very nice open carriage to Moritzburg, an old hunting seat of the Saxon Princes about 12 miles from Dresden. The road is beautiful, almost all the way through a forest of firs and birches, the silver bark of the latter looking beautiful in front of the dark stems of the firs. We went all over the old castle, a curious ugly old place but fitted up with very good taste for the use it was intended for, the rooms almost all furnished and hung with stamped leather and with deers antlers mounted on artificial heads fixed to the walls of the larger halls. The dining hall full of stags horns, one of them with 66 branches, but most of them from 30 to 36, the drawing room or ladies hall was ornamented with all sorts of curiously shaped horns, among them the skull of a horned hare, another apartment had reindeer and elk horns, the most curious thing was a pair of stags sculls so closely locked together by the horns that they could not be got apart without breaking, they were found so in the forest and it is supposed the owners had tangled them in fighting, and died of starvation. There are some curious old views of Dresden and hunting pictures, one by Lucas Cranach, where there are dogs of all sorts and sizes, even a shaved French poodle employed in the chase, the hunting in former times seems to have been like our modern battues for in the picture the King and his court are sitting in a pavilion and shooting all round them. The terrace at Moritzburg is ornamented with curious old stone figures of Huntsmen etc and vases with subjects from fables carved upon them, and the trees are cropped into the most hideous shape possible. There is a fine piece of water on which the palace stands. When we had been through all the rooms we returned to the hotel to dinner and then sallied forth to get some sketches and while Anne was drawing the ugly old castle, John and I tried to find out where the wild swine were fed, the said swine being a breed of animals kept to hunt, and the feeding of them one of the sights of Moritzburg and when the sketch was done we walked some little distance in the forest and at last found the feeding place. We saw some deer and swine feeding at a distance and sat ourselves down to wait until the dinner hour. About ½ past 4 we saw the men come and strew quantities of potatoes and buckwheat and acorns about, and some of the porcine gentry came to dinner, but the herd of something between 50 and 100 that had collected round the place did not seem hungry and after standing and looking at us for a short time they trotted off again into the woods. They are very dirty and ugly grey looking beasts with very long hair and very long noses and when startled or angry bristle up all round their heads like porcupines. When they trotted away we did so too and had a very pleasant ride home again and just arrived by daylight.

Saturday March 20 We staid at home all the morning expecting Mr Peters who did not come. After dinner we walked through the city to the hills beyond and up to the place where General Moreau[9] was shot and where his two legs are buried, and a monument erected to his memory by Alexander of Russia, who had his body conveyed to Petersburg. The view of Dresden from the monument is very good, indeed you cannot get a view of Dresden that is not, the only four steeples in it are picturesque and the city is not large enough to be ugly or clumsy. We took a long round and returned home by the Grosse Garten very tired and the mild sunny days made us begin to find our winter clothing cumbersome on a march.

Sunday March 21 Went to Chapel and heard Mr Lindsay lead the service and a stranger preach a very good sermon, but the latter had the manner of an invalid which is not pleasant. After dinner we walked to the village of Plauen and the valley called the Plauensche Grund, a very beautiful glen where two streams meet and rocks etc are most picturesque. There is a small cafe which is a favourite resort of the Dresdeners on a Sunday and accordingly we met crowds of people going and returning, though I believe the favourite plan is to stay and return by moonlight. As this was the first fine sunny Sunday that we had been at Dresden we had not before seen the population in its glory, and the shoals of people walking in every direction was beyond belief, one would not have believed Dresden could have held them all, they are a respectable looking race but marvellously illfavoured and illdressed.

Monday March 22 John and I went across the bridge to hear the band, after dinner he went to have his hair cut and we went to the Japanese Palace to wait for him, but as he did not come for an hour we got tired and cold and so walked off along the road through the woods, and on our return found John had bought us a large collection of chocolate bonsbons, insects and fruit, vegetables and fish and shells all coloured like nature. In the evening John read us part of his translation from Schiller's history of the Netherlands.

Tuesday March 23 Worked in the morning, after dinner John went to call on Mr Peters and Anne and I went shopping for the warm sun made us almost melt under our winter apparel. All Dresden very unpleasant to the nose, as twice a year the drains are emptied and the contents carried out of the city in carts, and that operation was performed today.

Wednesday March 24 A lovely bright morning, we had a carriage and drove to Tharand, a village distant about one hour and a half. The whole drive was most beautiful, by the side of a

Tharand near Dresden, April 1847

rapid stream, with here and there a very picturesque little fall, the first wild flowers we have seen this year and in passing them in the carriage we could not make out what they were, but when we got to Tharand we recognised them as the blue hepatica, flowering in little tufts on the hills they looked like gems. The village is beautifully situated at the junction of three valleys, the streams flowing through it and the hills covered with beech, birch and fir trees, part of an old ruined castle perched on one of the hills and the village church on another, and the houses scattered by the side of the river, we were quite enchanted with the place and the bright spring day made us enjoy it the more. We got a guide to show us the path up the hill where the best views are to be seen, & found it very hard work climbing up the steep pathway, but were amply repaid by the lovely scenery, and the walk down again through a beechwood was one of the loveliest things I ever saw.

Thursday March 25 Received news of the birth of Gilberts first little child and the well doing of its mother, a very great pleasure to us, the day was like April, sun and showers alternately. We went after dinner to see the collection of Porcelaine at the Japan palace, where they have specimens of china of all nations, and we were sadly ashamed of the English specimens. There are some beautiful biscuit figures and magnificent vases both of Sevres & real china, there is one set of 22 large vases that were given to Victor Augustus 2nd by Frederic 1st of Prussia in exchange for 800 dragoons and their horses fully equipped. I should think there is a specimen of every pattern ever made in China, large animals and birds and teapots enough to satisfy the most enthusiastic lover of old china, there are the first porcelaine vessels ever made in Saxony and the material of which was discovered by an Alchemist in his search for gold, there are then all the gradual improvements until it reached its height and it is now quite on the decline, as the Berlin manufacture is acknowledged to be far superior. The King of Prussia takes an interest in the improvement of the Berlin manufacturers, while the King of Saxony does not seem to take an interest in anything and is letting his china gradually degenerate and his splendid collections of old vases drop to pieces and rot with damp rather than take any trouble to preserve them, a lazy old wretch. We found the day had become damp and cold when we came out of the Palace so we returned home.

Saturday March 27 Anne and I sallied forth to buy gloves and other things that we wanted. In the afternoon John

Plauen, near Dresden, 14th April 1847

and I had a walk and then we called for Anne and went altogether to the Catholic Church to hear a very fine Anthem performed, and returned to keep an appointment with a dress-maker, whom we expected would be a young woman but to our amazement it proved to be a little ugly old humpbacked man, who took measures and orders for our dresses, and we found on enquiry that almost all the Dresden dressmakers are men.

Sunday March 28 Went to Chapel, heard a very excellent sermon from Mr Lindsay and the 100 Psalm played Dresden fashion, not like ours at all. John and I went to the post office where he got a 'Times' from home for which he had to pay 2/6 postage, rather dear. We walked round the boulevards and home by the Brühl terrasse, the Sunday costumes of the nurses that were in attendance on the young fry were some of them very curious, one of them had a scarlet shawl twisted round her head but with a long lace caul hanging down behind, and a huge quantity of coral beads round her neck, and a blue cloth garment like a very short riding habit over a coloured petticoat, then the women with their scarlet petticoats and wadded spencers are funny objects. In the evening we went to the large opera house in the Zwinger to a concert that is always given on Palm Sunday for the benefit of the poor, the performers give their services and there were 400 of them in the orchestra. The room was crammed, and a very fine performance it was, Mozart's Requiem and Beethoven's 9th Symphony, we liked the first best, by far. The King and Queen were present and all the beauty and fashion of Dresden and mighty little of either there was but they are a quiet and well behaved set, are the Saxons, although ugly.

Friday April 2 Good Friday. Went to chapel & were somewhat startled at being asked our name & address. John went to see the ceremony at the Catholic church, where they carried the Host round the church, under a canopy borne by the Princes of the royal family & followed by the Queen, the King being ill, and afterwards placed it in a vault in commemoration of the burial of our Saviour, there to remain until Easter Day.

Saturday April 3 Worked & German exercised, & went to post a letter to Henry & then did a little shopping, & at a little after five went to the Catholic Church to hear a fine 'Te Deum' & see the ceremony in memory of the resurrection, which consisted in fetching up the host again from the vault where it was deposited & again in full procession, Queen, Princes & all carrying it round the church. The procession we saw very little of except the canopy & a head or two, the music was very fine though I do not like the sound of violins – in a church. The crowd exceeded anything I ever was in, the men and women go on different sides of the Church, and of course we were among the latter, but such squeezing & pushing I never underwent, & the people did not seem to care for anything but the mere sight, for they did not listen to the music & were laughing & talking the whole time, at least all those round us were & as for any feeling of reverence towards the ceremony that was being performed, nobody would have fancied that it was one of the most solemn of the Catholic church that they were celebrating.

Sunday April 4 Went to Chapel and on our way were overtaken by Mr Lindsay who spoke very politely to us & explained his asking for our names on the score of having seen us so many times at church that he thought we might have come to live at Dresden & therefore he wished to know, he walked with us to the Chapel & promised to call. After dinner I wrote a long letter to Captn Lowry & took it to the Post & then we had Barnet to tea, & to our great surprise at about 9 o'clock William made his appearance having left home on Tuesday evening & come by Hamburgh.

Monday April 5 William was very poorly all day so we sat quiet until the evening, when we went to see 'William Tell' at the theatre. William was not well enough to go & I dont think he had any great loss for it is a dull heavy piece unless you thoroughly understand german, & the actors & actresses were all hideously ugly. William Tell himself for instance being a great fat wretch with a horrid squint, a person one could not feel any pity for, we left before the last act & found William better & that he had managed to amuse himself without us.

Thursday April 8 William & John went to hear the band play but the weather was so bad we did not go out until the evening when we went to see a piece called the 'Son of the Wilderness', a Tartar chief who is civilised by the influence of love for a tame young lady, a very pretty little piece and admirably performed, we heard also a piece of music very well performed on the flute, by an Austrian flutist, but like almost all solo performances it was a great bore. Mr Lindsay called today & Barnet came in for an hour & some cake.

Plauensche Grund near Dresden, 14th April 1847

Friday April 9 Intended to have gone with William to Tharand but the weather again interfered with our plans, more especially as we had most of us colds and William a tooth that teased him sadly. So Anne & I staid at home & John & William only went to the post until the evening when they went for an hour to the concert rooms on the Brühl terrasse & then we all went to hear Webers opera of Euryanthe and very much delighted we were, especially with Wagner[10] and Tichatschek although the latter, we heard, had so bad a sore throat that there was quite a doubt if he would be able to sing. The overture & chorusses are splendid.

Saturday April 10 At ½ past 9 William took leave of us to return home, it seemed a long journey to have taken for a 5 days stay, but it was a great treat to us, & would be a change for him. The weather was all hailstones & rain & wind, the night had been a most boisterous one so that the prospect for his journey was not very promising but in these railroad days there is not much exposure to the weather. We did not go out but amused ourselves with books & work & Messrs. Peters & Barnet.

Wednesday April 14 Another beautiful day, so after dinner we took a carriage and went in search of the picturesque to the Plauensche Grund, where John & I wandered about while Anne sketched. We were somewhat surprised in the middle of a small wood to find a deserted looking mansion with the name of the Maitre du Ballet on the door, so that I suppose the good people sometimes assemble there to dance, it is to be hoped they choose fine weather. The ground was covered here & there with cowslips, primroses & hepatica & wood anemony, only waiting for a little sunshine to come out in all their beauty, we saw one beautiful & with us uncommon butterfly, the White admirable, which I should very much have coveted if I had been nearer home. We walked home and a very pleasant walk we had but very cold. In the evening Barnet came to make a last appeal in favour of setting off to the Saxon Switzerland, as he was ordered home, & wished very much to go with us before his departure, but he lost his chance, for the weather was too changeable.

Friday April 16 Dull, gloomy & wretched, in the afternoon as it did not actually rain I persuaded Anne to turn out for a walk, for we had staid at home & growled at the weather until we were tired. John would not go, so we went, and had a very cold disagreable walk and returned hoping we were the better for it. In the evening we went to hear 'Don Juan'[11] which we liked altogether pretty well, the music itself is always a treat but some of it was not very well done, the instrumental was the best by far. The end of Don Juan was most amusing, the evil spirits seized him, laid him on his back on a trap door and down he went.

Monday April 19 A very fine bright day, but still cold, we went for a walk into what they call the Reissnitz grund, among the woods & waters, a beautiful walk, but a very tireing one, for the paths were nothing but deep white sand, into which our feet sunk at every step. Anne took a sketch & then we returned home again with rather better hopes of Spring.

Tuesday April 20 Another lovely day, Mr Peters dined with us & then we went in a fiacre to the Spitz haus, a vineyard of the King's, an hour's drive from Dresden, where there is a most extensive view of the City & neighbourhood. We had to climb a hill & 395 stone steps to the top of the vineyard where the view is seen. We were very much amused at the driver of our vehicle stopping as we came to ask his way and telling us that he had been so engaged in looking at the scenery that he had forgotten the road he was going & had passed the proper turning. We sat for some time in a summer house at the top of the hill & then descended again & returned home, the road lay for some distance through a wood of firs & birch or avenues of horsechestnuts, but the trees hardly as yet shewed a symptom of budding or looked more forward than they were in February. The people were all hard at work in the fields sowing & planting, most of the field work being done by women, one we saw dragging a harrow. Poor wretches they seem here little better than beasts of burden, & carry such loads upon their backs as bend them nearly double, & they generally have the worn patient look of a camel, but their scarlet petticoats & white handkerchiefs over their heads make them look very gay & pretty in the fields.

Wednesday April 21 We took courage & in spite of a cloudy looking morning set off by the ½ past 11 train for Zittau. We had for fellow passengers three Saxons that smoked almost all the way, & as well nigh to poison us, they wanted to keep the windows all closed too, but this we really could not stand, we kept the one on our side of the carriage open & so escaped alive. We reached Lobau which is as far as the railway goes at about two, and then had to proceed to Zittau by a conveyance quite indescribable in company with sundry Germans, men & women, thank goodness, we had only one man all the way, inside, for their detestable smoking had almost driven us wild already and as our one man kept it up without ceasing during the 4½ hours we were in his company we found him quite enough. If it had not been for the tobacco and headaches consequent thereon we should have enjoyed the ride & the strange vehicle very much, for the country is very beautiful & the people all busy with their ploughing and sowing, in one field we counted 15 cows & 10 horses ploughing & harrowing. We arrived at the Sonne Hotel about 7 & after waiting an enormous time we got a very greasy dirty dinner, & something called tea, but what the mixture was, is yet a mystery, we were almost afraid of drinking it for fear it should be poisonous, however we got very comfortable warm beds & that consoled us for our grievances.

Wallenstein's Castle, Friedland, on the frontiers of Bohemia, 22nd April 1847

Thursday April 22 John went to call on Mr Rosebach[12] & brought him to call on us, & when he was gone we went in a very nice little carriage to Friedland in Bohemia about 3 hours from Zittau to see Wallensteins Castle[13], a curious old building, given him by the Emperor of Austria for his services in war. The road was very windy, hilly, & beautiful, the weather cold with showers of rain that made it rather gloomy. We went over the old Castle & down into the Dungeons, the place itself is curious & the views from it lovely, but there is nothing worth seeing in the properties, which consist in a few firearms and an immense number of portraits of a family to whom the castle belonged with the musical name Clam Gallas[?], & a few other concerns of no particular interest. After we had been over the Castle we went to the Hotel & dined & then out again, & Anne took a drawing while John & I prowled about. The day was not favourable for sauntering, as it was exceedingly cold & kept continually spitting with rain. We found a very pretty walk through a plantation belonging to one of the manufacturers here, Friedland being a great place for the manufacture of woollen cloths. On our way here we had to cross the frontier of Bohemia, & had a capital proof of the use of passports, the important little person who had to find out whether we were dangerous or not made John get out & go into his office in order to question him, & finding that the passport was not viséed by the Austrian Minister he told him he could not let him cross the frontier, it was more than his head was worth. John offered him a small fee & he thought no more of his head but let us pass without another word. When Anne had finished her sketch, we had another walk & then returned to Zittau, our little horses rattled home in capital style, it rained part of the way, but cleared up at sunset & was very fine.

Friday April 23 We had our swift steeds again & went to Oyben just an hour from Zittau, the weather cold but bright & sunny, the road was a continued village all the way, the inhabitants for miles round Zittau are all weavers as Zittau is the great market of the Saxon linen trade. We arrived at Oyben & went straight up to the ruin, which is situated on an immense rock, and is very curious & interesting, it was built by a band of Robber Knights about 60 in number, who when they had made the surrounding country too hot to hold them used to retreat to this stronghold, where they were quite safe. It was afterwards a monastery and had a highly ornamented church & the monks, who were of the Cistercian order, took so much pride in their edifice & service that they had the solid rock cut away to a considerable depth round the church to improve the sound of the organ. The place was at last

Ruins at Oyben, 23rd April 1847

destroyed by lightening & afterwards again blown up by gunpowder which was ignited during a storm so that there is very little now of the building remaining, but enough to prove that both monks & robbers liked good cellars, & trout ponds and a beautiful view, for a more lovely one never was seen, huge rocks & mountains covered with fir trees & valleys with very picturesque looking cottages scattered over them. It took us a long time to go over the ruin & a great deal of climbing up and down to the various points of view, which were all lovely alike and the hawks were flying in numbers in & out of the ruin, & chasing the wild pigeons, their fellow inhabitants of the ruin. The church is the only part that retains any vestige of what it has been, & there are still the remains of the steps where the high altar stood. We descended the immense steep that the castle stands on and after dining at the little inn went forth to slive[14] for the rest of the afternoon, we did not find the time at all too long in a place of so much beauty. Anne took some sketches & while she was doing one, an old woman who was at work in a field came & squatted behind her to look what she was doing & at last sat down by her side and entered into conversation & talked away at such a rate. Told us what they had to eat & drink, how old she & her husband were, etc etc & wound up by admiring everything we had on, saying we must be very rich to be so well clothed, she could not think how we could walk about in such lovely clothes. Poor old lady we could not return the compliment for she was little better than a bundle of rags. She took a wonderful interest in the sketches & Anne quite won her heart by drawing her too. As soon as it began to get chilly we returned to Zittau & after a walk through the town, went early to bed.

Saturday April 24 We were off by six in our little conveyance on our way to the Saxon Switzerland, we proceeded with the same horses until about ½ past 8 when we stopped to rest them & have our breakfast, & on again for another hour through straggling villages of weavers, apparently of woollen stuffs for the women's petticoats as we saw black & scarlet & yellow wool hanging to dry round the cottages. We stopped to change carriage & horses at about ½ past 11 & had a very beautiful ride up hill & down all the way, our postillon, whom we strongly suspected was not very sober, keeping his horses at a very fast pace which as no accident occurred was rather fortunate, though at the time we thought ourselves anything but safe under his guidance. We stopped at a small hotel on the road to get something to eat & had 2 plates full of rusks & a glass of some sort of spirit & water for John for 4d which we thought a moderate charge enough for a luncheon for three people. At last we came to the place where we were to leave the carriage & either take to ponies or feet, & as everybody said we could not walk, Anne & I took to the ponies, two nice pretty little creatures who in time brought us by a tremendously steep winding path to the top of the great Winterberg where the Hotel is situated. We stopped on our way up to see a waterfall & then Kuhstal, a natural archway in the rock where there is a most extensive & beautiful view, & also at the top of the mountain called the lesser Winterberg where the view is very fine, looking over mountain beyond mountain covered with fir trees & my friends the hawks flying screaming about in all directions. We were not sorry to dismount as it was rather rough riding up & down such steep paths & we found the small Hotel a very nice clean place though very cold, partly from its situation, partly from its not being much inhabited so early in the season but most of all from the still lingering cold of the weather. We had dinner & coffee & were very glad to go to bed.

Sunday April 25 We got up & found to our dismay a cloudy cold morning and the snow falling fast, our civil obliging attendant insisted upon bringing us fresh water from the spring to wash with which we could well have dispensed with, but I suspect she is used to be asked for that luxury by travellers in the summer & therefore offers it in the winter too. Before we had begun breakfast in came Mr Child from Dresden, it seemed curious that one out of the three people we were acquainted with should meet us in this out of the way place, he and his companion only staid to breakfast and then took their departure. We tried to get a walk but the paths in every direction were so wet and covered with snow & the sky so gloomy that we soon turned back again & did not go out any more. Anne made a drawing of the hotel which is a pretty Swiss looking place, the rest of the day we amused ourselves with reading & looking at the beautiful views from the windows, the traveller's books & any thing else that came in the way. We seemed to give unqualified satisfaction to the young mistress who chose to sit in a sort of antichamber next to our room for the purpose of watching us, & she was very much pleased to get up a little conversation now & then about the plants in the room, among them some very nice ones, or anything else that occurred, she was a goodnatured pleasant mannered girl. Two young Scotchmen came in during the day, but as they had German books & did not speak so that we could hear them we did not find out until the next morning what country they belonged to.

Monday April 26 We had breakfasted and mounted our ponies again by a little after seven, the morning was very misty so we were unable to see the sunrise which is one of the attractions to the Winterberg, the morning soon cleared & the sun came out and we had a lovely ride along the winding road down the mountain. We stopped to see several favourite views and another natural arch in the rock & from there walked down to the foot of the mountain along one of the loveliest paths that ever was seen. We met our steeds at the bottom and rode by the side of a rapid stream, through a village & several timber yards until we came to the Elbe, where we took leave of our guide & horses & got into a boat & we rowed down the Elbe for about 2 hours and ½ passing on the way the Lileinstein & Konigstein, two of the other mountains, on the top of the latter stands an impregnable fortress, to which all the treasures from Dresden are conveyed in time of war. We landed at the foot of the Bastei, another mountain in Saxon Switzerland & were met by an elderly lady who claimed the privilege of acting as guide, so up we went & our old friend pointed out all the objects of interest. The Bastei was another of the strongholds of the Robber Knights, & they show where the bars of the gateways fastened in the rock, & where the drawbridge used to be, but there are no remains of any thing like building only excavations here & there that have had names given them in the course of ages. After a long climb we reached the top, & there found a most magnificent view over the surroundings & the river & what was very agreable

Palace of the Zwinger at Dresden, 29th April 1847

also, a very tidy little hotel where we dined, & then began our descent again down a capital path but very steep. When we got down to the riverside we sat down to wait for a steamer that was to take us to Dresden, we waited for an hour & ½ to the great amusement & instruction of an old man who was wheeling stones, & the old dame who had been our guide, who both of them seemed anxious to find out as much as they could. The old man sat down near us to eat his dinner, a large hunk of nearly black bread, & was very curious to know where we came from & then what were the prices of provisions in England, but the old lady confined herself to questioning us as to the length of our stay in Dresden & other particulars of our personal history. At length when we were getting rather tired of waiting the Steamer came up & in about an hour ½ we were in Dresden. We passed the King's summer palace at Pillnitz, a pretty gingerbread looking place close to the river's side & were very glad to find ourselves in our own snug room at the Stadt Wien as we had had rather a fatigueing day.

Tuesday April 27 We went to the Picture gallery until dinner time, then staid at home the rest of the day as we all felt very tired & sleepy & the day was not very fine.

Thursday April 29 Packed together a parcel of winter clothes, books etc to send to England, Anne went before breakfast to take a drawing of the Zwinger, & after breakfast to the Gallery again. John went to the Post and brought a number of letters from home. In the evening we went to see 'Faust' but such a hideous Margaret never was seen, never could I think any where but here, the play very well acted but too long.

Friday April 30 Sent off our parcel to England & anybody would have thought it was the regalia we were sending, if they had seen the fuss the respectable Saxons made about it. Mr Peters dined with us & took a most affectionate leave, & then we went out for a walk but were driven home again by the black clouds, so packed up ready for our journey & went early to bed.

Berlin and the Journey South to the Tyrol
May 1st to May 30th

BY TRAIN TO BERLIN · NINE NIGHTS AT THE HOTEL DE RUSSIE · BY CARRIAGE TO CHARLOTTENBURG, FOR THE DAY
BY TRAIN TO POTSDAM, FOR THE DAY · BY TRAIN TO REICHENBACH, VIA COTHEN, LEIPZIG, AND ALTENBURG
THREE NIGHTS AT DAS LAMM HOTEL (WHILE JOHN RETURNS TO BERLIN FOR HIS LOST POCKET BOOK) · BY CARRIAGE TO HOF
VIA PLAUEN, CROSSING THE SAXON-BAVARIAN BORDER · BY CARRIAGE AND TRAIN TO BAMBERG
ONE NIGHT AT THE HOTEL DEUTSCHES HAUS · BY TRAIN TO NUREMBERG · TWO NIGHTS AT THE BAIERISCHE HOF HOTEL
BY CARRIAGE TO MONHEIM · BY CARRIAGE AND TRAIN TO MUNICH, VIA DONAUWORTH AND AUGSBURG
TEN NIGHTS AT THE BAIERISCHE HOF HOTEL · BY CARRIAGE TO THE MUNICH FAIR · BY CARRIAGE TO THE BATHS OF KREUTH
VIA THE BAVARIAN ALPS AND LAKE TEGERNSEE · BY CARRIAGE TO INNSBRUCK, CROSSING THE AUSTRIAN BORDER
VIA SCHWAZ · TWO NIGHTS AT THE GOLDENEN SONNE ·

Berlin and the Journey South to the Tyrol
May 1st to May 30th

Saturday May 1 What a May day! wet cold & miserable. We were up a little after 4 & taking leave of the owners & dependants of the Stadt Wien & of Dresden & got to the railway before six and were entertained while waiting there by the vagaries of a silly young English Baronet named 'Don' who was going to Berlin to ride a steeplechase against one of the King of Prussia's horses. He had been the talk of quiet Dresden for some time, on account of his dashing appearance with horses & carriages & his flirtation with one of the actresses who I should think will never be silly enough to marry such a young spendthrift, but, on dit. We had as travelling companion a very pleasant Englishman named Smith, who lives at Hastings but has a beautiful farm at Tharand, we had a very pleasant chat with him as far as Leipsig, where we stopped to change carriages & breakfast & then proceeded to Cothen where we had to change again. The day was cold and drizzly & we were thankful to arrive at Berlin by ½ past six. We went to the Hotel de Russie where they were so full they could not give us rooms that we liked but promised better in a day or two, we dined & went to bed very tired indeed.

Sunday May 2 A beautiful bright morning, did not get up very soon & after breakfast went out to see what like a place Berlin is, heard the band play and walked up the Linden avenue to the Brandenburgh gate & into the Thier garten & found a pond full of gold & silver fish & a very nicely planted garden round it with Spring flowers coming into bloom, especially superb beds of hyacinths which grow all round the neighbourhood in such quantities that people gather large bunches of them to put into water for their rooms. Also we saw the rhubarb plant made into beds as an ornamental shrub, they have evidently no idea of making it into pies. We dined at the table d'hote with a large party of foreigners & one Englishman & then went out again, but John had a rheumatic shoulder that plagued him sadly

Berlin

& we did not stay out long, the evening was fine but cold.

Monday May 3 We spent the morning at the Picture gallery, but the Dresden pictures had made some of us very dainty & we rather turned up our noses at the Berlin collection. We spent the rest of the day in seeing the Town and looking at the shops. Dinner today at 4, were promoted today to a better sitting room, a very pleasant one looking towards the Palace & where the sun shone in warm & cheerful all the morning & we had the luxury of a separate closet to sleep in.

Tuesday May 4 Walked to the Brandenburgh gate on which is placed the figure of Victory that Napoleon carried to Paris and the Prussians brought back after the battle of Waterloo. We took a fiacre and drove to Charlottenburg, a summer palace of the Kings designed & named by the Princess Sophia Charlotte, daughter of George 1st of England. She married Frederick of Prussia, & this palace was a favourite toy of her's & it does infinite credit to her taste. It is a most beautiful place most tastefully fitted up, the gardens beautifully planted with trees & the river Spree winding through the grounds in which we saw shoals of fish, some of them of enormous size, 12 or 14 pounds we thought. The most interesting thing at Charlottenburg is the Mausoleum erected by the late King for his wife & containing a most exquisite marble figure of the Queen & also one of the King was placed there at his death, the approach to the Tomb is by a long avenue of Cypress which has a very solemn appropriate effect. The man who went over the Palace with us was in too great a hurry so that we had not so much time to examine it as we should have liked. The ballroom is a very tasteful and splendid apartment, & the last King's bedroom is left just as when he used it, & the last clothes that he wore still hang over a chair, we could not help admiring the evident traces of family affection in the Prussian Royal family. We returned on foot to Berlin which should have been 3 miles but we mistook our path through the Thiergarten & we must have walked considerably more, however, we got home in time for dinner, meeting on our way the Queen & eleven royal folks in their equipages, which are very different in Berlin to the old Saxon Shettesedans[?]. We went in the evening to the Opera to hear Mademoiselle Garcia[1], it was her benefit, there was quite a scramble for places. We heard two acts of 'the Huegonots'[2], & of Robert the Devil[3] & the finale of Somnambula[4] & a Cracovienne[5] between. Garcia is a beautiful singer & pretty good as an actress but personally hideous beyond compare. The house is large & handsome & there was a large party there from the Palace who were supporting their strength by diverse refreshments handed by the royal footmen between the acts, we observed the ladies helped themselves to sugar with their fingers, sugar tongs are unknown. I forgot to mention in the right place, that on our road to Charlottenburg we saw a stork nest on the top of a tree with the little ones inside & the old one sitting by the side, we thought it was a stuffed one until we saw it move.

Wednesday May 5 Went the first thing to the china manufactory & chose a set for a wedding present to Henry, & some other things, saw some exquisite paintings & some of the moulding of the porcelaine, which is just the same process as we had seen at Meissen, but we could plainly perceive the inferiority of the clay to that at Meissen, & as plainly the great superiority of the Berlin painting. We saw some superb vases 5 ft high & painted all over most richly, I think the man said they were worth 1000 dollars, they are only made for royal presents. We went from there to the Kreutzburg, a hill, the only one near Berlin, & more like a small sand heap than a hill, but called so from a monument created by the late King in honour of the battles won by the Prussians & those who had helped him with their 'Gut & Blut' as the inscription says. It is a beautiful gothic cross made of iron & with the names of the battles inscribed on the sides. We had some luncheon in the concert room of the Tivoli gardens close by, which we had entirely to ourselves & then walked back to Berlin along such a road of sand as never was seen anywhere else except the Great Desert I should think, the evening was very wet.

Friday May 7 Up early again & went by the 9 o'clock train to Potzdam a 40 minutes ride. We went first to the Town Palace a very large & royal looking place but with nothing of particular interest about it except the suite of apartments that were used by Frederic the Great & still contain the furniture he used 200 years before. They show his writing table covered with ink & grease, & the satin covers of his chairs & sofas torn & dirtied by his favourite dogs, some of his manuscript music & various other remembrances of him. There was his small private apartment, where his dinner used to be sent up on a table through the floor by machinery, that he might not have servants intrude on him. We next went to Sans Souci another historical remembrance of Frederic, situated in a lovely garden where there are terraces ranged one above another & in the Summer filled with orange trees & a splendid view. The singular old King had his horse & dog buried on one of the terraces & left directions that he should be buried with them, but it was not complied with, they have here a clock that he always wound up with his own hand & which stopped the moment that he died & has never been wound up since. There is a room here that used to be occupied by Voltaire who was a favourite of Frederic, it is adorned with flowers & animals made in china & coloured like nature. We could not of course miss seeing the historical windmill which stands close to the palace. We went from Sans Souci to the New Palace, built by Frederic the Great to show his enemies that he was not ruined by a long & expensive war, it must have been rather a convincing proof for it is an immense place, & superbly fitted up with gilding & every thing that one can imagine that's costly but not with much taste, indeed Frederic's taste from what we could judge both in pictures & other things was rather coarse. There is one immense hall here fitted up with shells & minerals & fountains like a grotto, & deliciously cool in summer. We went now to Charlotten Hof, a very small toy palace built by the present King when Crown prince. It is a model, or nearly so, of a villa at Pompeii and with Pompeian relics, there are also baths fitted up in the same style, very beautifully painted & some lovely statues among the decorations. The day was so hot & dusty that we wished we could have had a bath. We went on from here to the Marble Palace where there is nothing very striking to see except a few very fine statues by Thorwaldsen[6] and lovely views of a lake from the windows,

Berlin, 8th May 1847

but now in good truth we had seen so many Palaces & all so magnificent that we began to feel rather confused, & cry 'hold, enough'. So we drove through the Russian Colony[7], a village built by the present King of Prussia for a number of Russians who were sent to him as a present by the Emperor, & for whom he built a complete village like one in their own country, cottages, orchards, gardens & a church where they might have their own worship, & now being quite tired & very hungry we went to the railway restaurant & dined & returned to Berlin at five.

Saturday May 8 Henry's birthday, went to the Picture Gallery in the morning and then Anne & I went & had a cup of chocolate, as that is what the Berlin people do & we wished to do what was proper. After dinner we were to have seen the Palace in Berlin but the Chamber was sitting so late that we could not be admitted so we went for a couple of hours to a place where there are open air concerts & heard one or two pretty pieces of music & then walked home along the Unter den Linden & were no sooner housed than it began to rain which we were very glad of as the day had been most oppressively hot & close.

Sunday May 9 We went through the state apartments in the Palace which have just been newly fitted up with great & splendourse velvet curtains & crimson & gold hangings on the walls, there are a great many pictures, some of them I daresay good ones but we did not stay long to look at them. There is a beautiful glass chandelier, which they say the King of Prussia expressed his admiration of to George 4th during one of his visits to London, & when he returned home he found it hanging in one of his rooms, a present from his fat friend. We saw the room used for the new Prussian Parliament, which was the ballroom and still unfurnished, but part of it is beautifully painted. We saw also a superb collection of the royal plate, huge gold salvers & two immense beer tankards set with dollars, one of them would hold at least 9 gallons. In the evening we went to a public garden where the Berlin people go to hear music & smoke & drink coffee & beer, we heard some pretty music & saw some gay company, the ladies all hard at work just like a week day, but what pleased me most was a couple of squirrels who were chasing each other from tree to tree, & it was curious to see what leaps they took from one branch to another & how lightly they ran to the very tips of the branches, we returned home early to make ready for quitting Berlin next morning.

Monday May 10 We left gay military, sandy Berlin at ½ past 7 & having taken our seats in the railway carriage were much pleased to hear one of our country-women ask her husband in german, whether they could not get into another carriage, or into their own, a very shabby old concern that was on the line. The good man declined moving, so the poor lady was obliged to ride as far as Cothen with us, & wonderful to relate she survived, it is rather absurd sometimes to see the airs of exclusiveness that silly English people give themselves. We stopped at Cothen at 1 & as we had to wait an hour for another train, we took the opportunity to have some dinner & when we got into the carriage again we had luckily got rid of our important friends. We got to Leipsig about 3 or ½ past & went strait to the station from which we were to start for Reichenbach, on the way to Munich. I ought to mention as a lesson to English railways in hot weather that at two or three stations on the line we had come today, there were trays of ices handed & once we tried them, very refreshing they were for the day was intensely hot, & plenty of dust all the way. When we got to the Leipsig station we were very agreably surprised to find a very nice waiting room belonging to a restaurant & a large sort of verandah filled with plants & tables & chairs where we could sit in the open air, no small gratification in such weather & having to stay there 2½ hours. We managed to pass the time agreably enough & at six were off again & had rather a prettier ride, the country from Berlin to Leipsig being one continued flat, any thing like a hill, however small, was charming as a variety, and the trees looked so fresh & green that when we were cool enough to think of any thing but ourselves, we admired our ride. Besides the scenery, there was a storm of thunder & lightening that we watched all the evening & enjoyed the prospect of its cooling air. Just at dusk we got to Altenburg, a ducal residence & town, full seemingly of handsome buildings, but what we were most struck with was the singular costume of the people. Unfortunately they did not come close enough for us to examine them very minutely, but the women are the oddest looking objects that ever were seen, they have their petticoats only just below the knee & almost tight & a sort of cuirass made of basket work, Murray says, & we did not see them near enough to find out the material of their dress, they have a curiously shaped headdress of black stuff & with their long white legs it is difficult to tell whether they are men or women, until you have seen several. The men wear a black dress with trunk hose, they are a peculiar race & keep up a great many strange customs as well as the costume that has been worn by their ancestors for many long years. It soon got dark after we left Altenburg & we had nothing but the storm to watch until we reached Reichenbach at ten o'clock, an hour after time, & here we got into a diligence higglety pigglety with three germans & after ½ an hours drive got to Das Lamm Hotel and were thankful to get soap & water for our poor dusty outsides & tea etc for our insides & go to bed, the more especially as just before we arrived John discovered that he had

lost his pocket book, containing money etc. He thought he had left it in his bedroom at Berlin so made up his mind to return to Berlin by train at six the next morning, rather hard work.

Tuesday May 11 John departed at ½ past five, & we got up at our leisure & worked until the afternoon, when we went out to see what like a place we had got to, we had a roasting walk & did not find any thing much to admire, either in Reichenbach or the neighbourhood. The town is a manufacturing place for muslins & other cotton goods & of course swarms with very dirty & poor people, & is perfectly overrun with children, healthy little dirty pigs as ever were seen.

Wednesday May 12 Too hot to go out in spite of a thunder storm & torrents of rain in the night, so we sat & worked & wrote letters & watched the passers bye, the women with their singular headdress, not unlike that of Mary Queen of Scots, & nice fresh looking nurses & children, quite a treat after the dingy unwholesome inhabitants of Dresden. John came back in the evening sorely tired after three entire days of railway travelling & worse than all without his pocketbook which he could not hear of, but had had bills posted all over Berlin & hoped it would meet us at Munich, as it was to be forwarded if found by the Master of the hotel at Berlin. John had come as far as Altenburg with the Prince Constantine of Russia, who was engaged to an Altenburg princess, he stopped at Cothen to dine & of course was thoroughly examined by all the other passengers in the train & John did not at all admire him as he said he was very small & sulky & stupid looking. Happy for his bride.

Thursday May 13 Ascension day, kept as a religious holiday throughout Saxony, & before we left Reichenbach we saw the people all in their holiday dress pouring in to Church, such caps & such silk gowns & such crimson umbrellas, & to think that the wearers of such rich attire should the very day before have been working barelegged in the fields doing the roughest & dirtiest work, for we saw the women carting & spreading manure, ploughing, harrowing, sowing wheat & in some places doing the greater part of the work on the railways & generally without either shoes or stockings & to all appearance very little else. We went on our way en voiturier, which in this instance might be well translated biscuit cart, our vehicle being as nearly as possible the shape & make of a London biscuit baker's carriage with the exception of windows at the sides, but we found it a very comfortable conveyance & had a delightful days journey in it, through a beautiful up & down hilly country, that all looked so fresh & spring like that it made us feel young again, & we enjoyed our ride enormously. We stopped to rest our steeds at a small place called Plauen, but as the weather was cloudy & heavy we did not deem it wise to stray far from the Hotel so just took a short strole through the little town & then returned & amused ourselves with some bread & butter & coffee, and as soon as our steeds had finished their breakfast we proceeded through a very richly cultivated country. The corn looking most thriving, and very large crops of something in full bloom that we fancied was rape seed which is grown here for oil, fields of clover & to our surprise large fields of common hearts-ease in full bloom & we could not imagine what it was grown for, the villages we passed were wretchedly poor & dirty & the inhabitants also, though all keeping the holiday in a rational & respectable manner. We passed the boundary between Saxony & Bavaria & slept at Hof, the first Bavarian town we came to, & a very pretty town it is, & tolerably clean which may partly be accounted for by its being nearly new. It has been burned down ten times & I should think may very likely be ten times more as the houses are roofed & principally built of wood, therefore a fire spreads rapidly. We dined & then John & I had a walk in the cool of the evening, a very pleasant one by the side of a beautiful river close to which the town stands, there is a curious old bridge. The main street is very long, and along the middle are a number of fountains with large basins where the inhabitants wash their vegetables & fetch water to supply their houses. We were introduced at dinner to a new dish, though looking like an old friend, asparagus, which we were rather surprised to find was cold, but still more so, on finding that it was dressed like salad with oil & vinegar, decidedly not an improvement.

Friday May 14 We left Hof at six and proceeded in our biscuit cart through a rather more desolate & dreary country than yesterday, the crops on the hills not being even sown or the ground ploughed, which we began to animadvert upon until we came to two or three patches of unmelted snow, and observed that the trees were still quite wintry & then we forgave the Bavarians for not putting in their crops sooner. At about 11 we came to the place where our horses were to breakfast & where we had made up our minds to breakfast too being by that time pretty ready for it, but oh woe, woe!! as the Germans say, such a prospect of breakfast, such a dirty place & such a dirty man. He said we could have coffee so out we got & then we waited until we had seen & heard them go thro' the operations of lighting the fire, roasting & pounding the coffee & then making it, but such coffee as it was when made, more like tobacco water a great deal, so we did not drink a dangerous quantity of it & having satisfied our hunger with bread & butter & hard boiled eggs we were right glad to escape from our dirty quarters & be on the road again. We soon arrived at the station, where we were to take to the railway & leave the biscuit cart, which we did with much regret for it was a comfortable & wellbeloved vehicle. We waited about ½ an hour for a train & then went on for four hours which were principally spent in stoppages as we stopped every ¼ of an hour for some minutes while our numerous conductors and guards discussed beer & things in general. At last after a most tedious ride we reached Bamberg & went to the Deutches Haus, a very comfortable clean Hotel. We ordered dinner & then with a valet went to see the Cathedral, founded in 1004 & finished in 8 years. Bamberg was originally the capital of a small principality governed by a race of Bishops & there are 130 monuments to them in the Cathedral also the Tomb of the Emperor Henry 2nd & his Empress Cunigunda beautifully carved in marble & in excellent preservation, the Bishops' monuments are mostly of brass & have been removed from the floor of the Cathedral & placed along the walls of one of the chapels to save them from being worn away. Bamberg is still a Catholic place & there are still two or three Monasteries existing there, we saw the Palace where the Bishops used to live & some of the other lions of Bamberg, but were too tired & hot to walk about much & went very early to roost, there was a stork's nest on a chimney opposite the hotel.

Saturday May 15 John got up early & went to the top of a hill a mile & a half from the town to see an extensive view which he was very much pleased with, in spite of its raining all the time he was there & his coming home very tired. We breakfasted & left Bamberg by the railway and in two hours were at Nuremberg, & took rooms at the Baierische Hof & then had a valet de place & a carriage & went first to the Bankers to get some money but it was just dinner time, so we could not get any though we saw the banker himself, one of the richest men in Nuremberg, who told us if we would come after two, we could not only get the money, but he would shew his collection of curiosities to us. So we promised we would & went to St Sebald's Church, formerly a Catholic Cathedral but now used as a Lutheran church, the only very remarkable things about it being the carved doorway & a monument to St Sebald, a beautiful shrine in bronze, the masterpiece of Peter Vischer[8], which took him & five of his sons 13 years to complete. The remains of the saint are enclosed in a chest encased in silver & covered by the bronze canopy, there are 12 figures of Apostles, 12 of fathers of the church & 70 others with a rich lacework of foliage & flowers. Our tiresome old valet took us to some places that we did not care much for, as there was no particular history attached to them we voted them rather a bore. The old Castle, where there was really nothing to see but a parcel of old china stoves, the house where Albert Durer the idol of Nuremberg lived where we saw his painting & sleeping rooms & his kitchen & then he took us to an old house curious enough for its age & singular antique galleries, but at present used as a manufactory of what we call dutch toys which are almost all made at Nuremberg & we suspected we were only taken to see the house that we might buy the toys, but as we had no intention of carrying dolls & such gear about with us we soon beat a retreat. Then we went to a gallery of paintings, quite rubbish, then to some private house to see a head of an old man by Albert Durer, where we felt as if we were intruding and were glad to get away. Then to the Catholic church where there is nothing very remarkable except the gaudiness with which it is decorated, then to the Rathaus where we saw the great hall & the Council chamber where all the business of the town is transacted & the portraits of the late & present Kings of Bavaria, two very unpleasant sensual looking faces, and a very curious representation in stucco of a tournament held here in 1434, the figures are the size of life & it forms the ceiling of a long gallery, the helmets & shields of the Knights all covered with the different heraldic devices. Then we went to the church

of St Laurence, the largest & finest in Nuremberg, a most magnificent building with some very fine painted windows ancient & modern. It was originally Catholic & the principal ornament of the interior is the repository for the sacred wafer, a spire of gothic openwork 64 feet high & most minutely carved & ornamented, it is supported by three kneeling figures, the Sculptor, Adam Kraft[9], & the two apprentices who assisted in the execution of it, there is a beautiful stone pulpit in the same style recently erected. We went next to our friend the Banker's where after giving us the money he conducted us upstairs into his 'Curiosity Shop' & showed us his treasures. Not all of them thank goodness or we should have been there for weeks, but his chief pets consisting of the room where he kept them, which had not been painted, nor I should think cleaned, for 300 years, a beautiful silver filigree cup 2ft high & most exquisitely wrought in imitation of flowers & insects, lizards etc & which was evidently the pride of the old man's heart, some very curious old illuminated books, some engravings by Albert Durer, among the first engravings ever executed, & what I thought a great curiosity, a tortoise that had been in his family 70 years & 20 years before it died it layed several eggs. There were the eggs & the tortoise under a glass case. We bowed ourselves out at last & were very glad to have some dinner & sit still the rest of the evening.

Sunday May 16 We did not go out until after the one o'clock table d'hote & then just sauntered through some of the curious old streets into the outskirts but it was so hot we turned home again & had just arrived when we had such a whirlwind & storm of thunder & lightening, such banging & smashing of open windows, & such a shower of hail, however it cooled & sweetened the air & we were glad we were not in a public garden that we had seen all the people going to. We saw a very curious funeral go by in the morning, three women walking in front, one carrying a large bunch of artificial flowers, another a tray with all sorts of wreaths & coloured ornaments & all with a lemon in their hands which is a constant custom at German funerals. The coffin was carried on an open hearse covered with a black & white pall strewed with flowers & white satin bows. The customs here are some of them very curious but the old streets are much more singular than the people, such oriel windows & gable ended houses & dragon water spouts & statues of Saints or other things put up at all the corners & the people are families descended from the old merchants that have lived like the old banker in the same houses for hundreds of years, like the toads that are sometimes found in stones. Nuremberg has been strongly fortified & there are a great many towers & old gateways left still.

Monday May 17 Up at ½ past 4 and set off at six in a voiture for Munich, we stopped to breakfast at ½ past 9 & dinner about 1. The country was almost all corn land & rather flat until the end of the day when we had some very steep hills, the villages poor dirty & deserted looking, not a creature to be seen except occasionally a shepherd with his flock or an old man herding a few cows, the greater part of the life we saw was geese and a great many young oxen, & the few people were wretchedly poor looking, the roads throughout Bavaria are bad. We got to a small

Nuremberg. 16th May 1847

village called Monheim about 7 and as our driver had planned that we should sleep there we did, in a very dirty unsweet little inn. Here again we saw the storks sitting on the roof of a curious old gateway, they were just busy building their nest.

Tuesday May 18 Off again at six and had a very pleasant up & down ride through flourishing looking cornfields to Donauworth, where the railway runs to Munich. We were in time for the 9 o'clock train & had got our tickets & were just wandering about the station, when we came upon a sheep washing, & were so engrossed in the operation that we stupidly let the train go without us, & had to wait for another until ½ past 12. So we walked back to the nearest Inn for some luncheon & back to the Station after taking one first look at the Danube, which runs through Donauworth. We sat at the station until ½ past 12 & an hour & a half took us to Augsburg, and as we wished to see it we stopped there & had a walk of a couple of hours about the town. It is a curious old place, the chief street is considered the finest in Germany, the houses many of them painted in fresco & ornamented with carving etc but the desolate uninhabited look of the city is most striking. There were a very few people crawling about, but nothing like the stir & bustle one expects to see in a large city like Augsburg. There are not many lions at Augsburg, 3 beautiful bronze fountains in the principal street are well worth examining, we saw the outside of the Cathedral and walked into one of the large churches where we saw them dusting the faces of the disciples on a large painted piece of carving with a dusting brush, just as anyone would sweep a staircase. It gave one a very fair idea of the real solemnity attached to such things. We soon had seen all that seemed worth any trouble on a broiling day, & so walked back to the railway station, where there was a very good restauration & had a dinner & sat still until 7 when the train took us in two hours to Munich to the Baierische Hof, a very large hotel looking out upon a square, planted with trees, & after our long hot day we were really thankful to find ourselves in such good quarters.

Wednesday May 19 We did not get up very early & then had divers odds and ends to do, so did not go out until 12 and then just sauntered up one street & down another, which was all the heat would allow us to do & found our way a little about Munich. We saw the King driving about & went into two of the churches & into the English garden which is a little like Kensington gardens with a very chalky river running through it. Anne & I hunted up some caps & John some books & then returned home, dined at the five o'clock table d'hôte & met only one Englishman & his wife & 4 Scotchmen, very stupid & disagreable so we did not try them again. Storm in the evening as usual.

Thursday May 20 Went at 10 o'clock to the Leuchtenberg gallery of paintings, which is open to the public every Thursday from 10 to 12, they were collected by Eugène Beauharnais[10] who married the sister of the King of Bavaria & lived here, there are only two rooms, one of old pictures & one of modern, some very good. A very fine portrait of Josephine, his mother, and a very bad one of Napoleon. We staid there an hour & then went to the church where Eugène was buried but found it closed, so we went to see the old gateway called the Isar Thor which has been newly decorated with frescoes & statues & looks like a duck in borrowed feathers. We went through a part of the old city of Munich which reminded us of Paris, & the people looked just as dirty & withered as the french poor look. We returned home in time for the 1 o'clock table d'Hôte & met a mixed party of English & foreigners, the former unpleasant as usual. The afternoon was a mixture of extreme heat with wet & storms so, except John, we did not go out.

Friday May 21 We took a valet from the Hotel and a carriage preparatory to a long days lionising & went first to the Glyptothek, a gallery of sculptures formed by the present King when Crown Prince & paid for out of his own income. It is divided into 12 rooms or halls all paved with marble & painted in fresco, one Egyptian, one Etruscan & the others distinguished by the names of some favorite group or Statue, as the Hall of Apollo etc. They are not such miserable remains as our old marbles but have been repaired & the missing parts restored by Thorwaldsen, and therefore gave one a very much better idea of what they once were, than the headless &

legless trunks in our Museum[11]. There is one room filled with Thorwaldsen's & Canova's[12] works, very few but exquisitely beautiful. We went next to the Church of St Lewis the same we had looked into the day before, it is very beautifully adorned & painted & has an Altar piece of the last Judgement, 64 ft high, & a splendid circular window, thence we went to the library said to be the second in the world, only surpassed by that at Paris. It contains about 540,000 volumes & 18,000 manuscripts, of course we did nothing more than walk through most of the rooms, but we had pointed out to us some very curious old illustrated books in glass cases, some of the first books printed in Germany & England, Albert Durer's prayer book illustrated by himself & Cranach, Luther's bible with portraits of himself and Melanchthon[13]. Among the autographs were Luther's, Frederic the Great's, a letter from Charles 1st of England to his sister, very well written & easy to read, also Talleyrand's & many others of great interest. From here we went to see a church that has some very fine painted windows, there are now 4 new churches in Munich, two built by the King & 2 by the City, this is one of the latter & is yet unfinished. There are 19 splendid windows containing the history of the Virgin Mary, made in Munich, it is the parish Church of Maria Hilf. We then returned to the 1 o'clock dinner which we much preferred to the exclusives at 5 & at ¼ to 3 went to see the new palace which the King is building, the lower story being yet unfinished, we went through several suites of apartments beautifully painted in Fresco from subjects by the Greek poets & others from german authors, the floors inlaid with different woods. We were not very enthusiastic in our admirations until we came to the throne room, which certainly surpasses any other place we had seen, it is entirely white & gold, along the sides are placed 14 statues of the Victors & Princes of Bavaria, 10 ft high, in the costumes which they wore, made of bronze & gilded, they each cost £2000. On one side there is a gallery resting on 20 caryatid statues of white marble, the throne & canopy are as usual of crimson & gold & the tout ensemble is unrivalled I should think in taste & grandeur. There are two rooms in the palace filled with portraits of the beauties of the Bavarian court, among them the English ladies Erskine, Milbanke & Ellenborough, also Lola Montez[14] who has lately made such a sensation at Munich. We were greatly amused at a very nice smell of raspberry jam in one or two of the apartments as we came to them & at last we came to one with a table laid & a napkin put over the whole, & we made up our minds if we could but peep we should find the puffs the King was going to have for lunch. We had a number of people to go through the rooms at the same time with us & were not struck either with the cleanliness or good manners of the Bavarian Canaille. We went now to the Basilica of St Boniface, one of the King's churches, & most splendid it is, resembling the Basilica of St Paul at Rome, it is supported inside by a double row of marble pillars, 72, each 20 ft high, the pavement was not finished. The frescoes are considered the finest of modern times, & represent the history of St Boniface from his leaving Britain as a child, until his interment at Fulda, having been made a Pope & resigned his dignity to retire into the cloister, the roof is painted blue with bright gold stars, it is much too gay & splendid for a church I think & only fit to be admired for its beauty as a building. We were now quite tired of sight seeing so returned home, on our

Fair at Munich, 25th May 1847

way stopping to buy shoes & we were surprised to find the lady shoemaker spoke excellent English, they say a great many English pass the winter in Munich on account of the cheap living as you may have a set of apartments nicely furnished consisting of 2 bedrooms & sitting-room for £3.0.0 a month & provisions etc generally speaking equally cheap, this year of course being an exception here as elsewhere.

Saturday May 22 We thought better to spend rather more quietly as it was immensely hot and sightseeing rather a fatigueing amusement, so Anne & I did not go out until the evening, when we all went to hear the band play in the English garden. We had a beautiful walk & some very pretty music & saw the King & Queen who came in a green & gold open carriage, the King driving, & stopping now & then to be admired, & 4 of the young princes & princesses in a carriage like the Isle of Wight bedsteads[15] only larger, who kept bowing like Mandarins, poor wretches. The King is a horrid withered looking old skeleton, apparently eaten up with conceit at his own taste & cleverness, however we were glad to have a good look at him, the Queen is a very plain old woman, the young things rather fair & good looking. We staid for an hour & then the music & royal party being gone, we went away with the rest of the audience who were most of them very common dirty disagreable looking people, the women very ordinary in appearance & the men looking like dirty dissipated artists, I don't like the Munich people at all. I should not forget to mention a most entertaining person we met at dinner, he told us a funny story of a friend of his who had been in Australia, & had written him word that when they played whist there they played sheep points & a bullock for the rubber, because they had no ready money.

Monday May 24 We went to see the other church just built by the King & which he attends, it is quite as richly painted as the Basilica with subjects from the old & new testaments at each end of the church & a dome in the middle containing the figures of our Saviour & the four Evangelists, it is well worth seeing but I do not like going into these places where the Catholics are praying, for one cannot but look with horror at the mockery that is going on and at the same time feel that they must dislike us for looking at what they consider so holy with mere curiosity & admiration for its outside shew. At ½ past 3 we set off in a carriage to see the Whit Monday fête at a beautiful wood an hour & ½ from Munich. It was very hot & dreadfully dusty, but the scene was so unlike anything we had ever seen that we were very glad we went. Thousands of people sitting as happy & contented as possible in different parties either on benches or the grass as it might happen, eating & drinking and chatting & under a sort of rotunda where there was a band, the peasants were waltzing & polking as if for life & death, some of them with their singular dresses beautifully embroidered with gold & all sorts of gay colours in their handkerchiefs & a sort of small full cape like a grenadiers, they did not look much figures for dancing but really they seemed to enjoy it in such a simple happy manner that we were quite pleased to stand & watch them. The King generally goes to this fête but he was ill & therefore the Crown Prince & his wife went, we met them in a narrow pathway & had a bow from him & one of the pleasantest smiles I ever saw. We returned home in the cool of the evening, the dust was dreadful, I never saw it worse at Epsom. In the evening there was a beautiful halo round the moon which we hoped might betoken wet.

Wednesday May 26 Went to the Picture Gallery from breakfast to dinner, then to buy stockings, gloves & in the evening to a shop where they sell the beautiful coloured glass[16] where John made some purchases & then we staid to hear the band play in the Hof Garten for an hour & then we had a short walk in the English garden to find Count Rumford's[17] monument which we could not & then home. Our company at dinner here are most entertaining, one old man with a beard ½ a yard long who they say is a Bavarian General & who dresses & behaves in the most extraordinary way, yesterday he was drinking wine & beer mixed because he said it was the best thing to cool him & today was dipping his napkin in his wine & washing his eyes with it. Another old creature that eats his fish as other people do cake, takes it up in one hand & breaks it into pieces and puts it into his mouth with the other, not using his fork at all, another was evidently destitute of shirt except a front, which had unfortunately for his vis a vis become considerably misplaced, but some of them are quite dandyfied & come out very powerful in jewellery & cravats.

Friday May 28 At six o'clock our carriage stopped the way & we left Munich, the country was for some time rather flat but very green & spring like, & full of crops of various kinds, the corn rather poor looking, the villages few & far between. We stopped at a small place at 11 to dine, & as we had to rest the horses for two hours, we strolled out in search of a subject for a sketch, but there was nothing inspiring & the sun so hot as to drive us back again to the Inn where we dined in the village post office, our repast at one end of the table & all the official concerns at the other. At one o'clock we were en route again & had a beautiful up and down hill ride & soon got among the Bavarian Alps & to the banks of the Lake Tegernsee, where the King has a palace that he comes to in summer, a curious ugly old place that was a convent, & is beautifully situated. We wondered he should stay in nasty Munich when he could live here, for the lake is one of the most lovely scenes imaginable, the road we travelled lay so close to the edge of the water for some miles that we could look down into it, and see the swarms of fish & the beautiful clearness of the water. About 10 miles from this & through a beautiful valley are the Baths of Kreuth, a fashionable Bavarian watering place & a more lovely scene it is impossible to dream of, a little nest of houses quite surrounded by very high mountains, covered to the tops with trees except in one or two instances, where the tops were bare rock with patches of snow still remaining here & there. Here we halted for the night & every thing looked so fresh & cool after dusty hot Munich, that we felt sorry at the idea of quitting again the next day, but our man & coach & horses were hired to take us to Innsbruch by a certain time, so to Innsbruch we must go. We had tea & ham & very nice cakes supplied by a curious little dwarf not more than 4ft high but fitted up with moustaches & all complete. Anne went out with her sketch book & John & I rambled about among the numerous paths that wound in all directions & amused ourselves by collecting the different wild flowers that were in bloom, &

The Achen See in Bavaria, 31st May 1847

which had been a sourse of admiration to us during our day's ride. We collected 31 distinct sorts and all except 2 blooming in profusion, there were several we did not know the names of, but among those we did was a most beautiful small gentian, heartsease, strawberry, globe flower, two or three kinds of cistus etc. We walked about until it was nearly dark & then went to bed by moonlight.

Saturday May 29 At ¼ to five our dwarf tormentor called us & at 5 we were again on our way & were amply repaid for the early rising by the beauty of our day's journey, such a succession of lovely scenery could not be surpassed in the whole world. The road for many miles wound in & out among the mountains & for six miles close over the edge of a lake, the most lovely clear green, with the mountains rising strait from the water on the opposite side of the lake, covered with trees while the rocks on one side were as far as we could see up covered with wild flowers, the large blue gentianella, heaths & a cistus like a briar rose & the large purple clematis climbing among the shrubs. It is impossible to imagine anything more beautiful than the whole ride & we had it completely to ourselves which was another charm, the morning was fresh & cool & we did enjoy it very much indeed. The numberless little mountain streams that came rushing either across the road or ran along the side of the winding road we passed along when we quitted the lake, I do not know which we admired most. We saw the Kaiser's Klaus, a gigantic water dam used for penning up a mountain stream until there is a sufficient body of water collected to float trees down, which are felled in the mountains & then floated down the rivers to Munich. Soon afterwards we passed the Austrian frontier, & as we had heard them abused for going through such a very strict search of travellers luggage, we were most agreably surprised & pleased at being permitted to pass, without any examination, on merely giving our word that we had nothing contraband as it saved us much time & trouble. Certainly our valuables had not a suspicious appearance for they were very small for a party of three, but we have as yet been subjected to no trouble or incivility in any respect & all through Bavaria were not even once asked for our passport. At the Austrian frontier they made John fill up a paper stating his name, age, whether married, single, or widowed, his business, what he had come for, & when he was going away & who he had with him. The road by the side of the lake Achensee is only a ledge cut in the rock, it has lately been widened sufficiently for two carriages to pass but the rock overhangs the entire road for some part of the way & you look quite down into the lake, the water in the lake is said to have sunk 4ft at the time of the great earthquake at Lisbon[18] & did not recover its height until 24 hours after, which seems a very singular natural phenomenon. On leaving the lake we descended by a tremendously steep winding road into the valley of the Inn, one of the most beautiful valleys in the Tyrol. We kept along the banks of the roaring Inn until we came to the small bridge across it leading to the small town of Schwaz, where as our steeds were to stay two hours we were to stay too, & a dirtier unsweeter spot we could not well have staid in, we had a very nasty dinner & then went out until such time as our man & horses were ready & during that time saw a funeral procession. The priest & two or three attendants bearing the crucifix went to the house to fetch

Baths of Kreuth in Bavaria, 28th May 1847

the corpse, & then returned followed by 30 or 40 women chanting in a low kind of howl, the marks of the romish faith through the Tyrol are most disgusting, you cannot go into a little road side inn but there in the common drinking room hangs a large crucifix & figure, painted in natural colours, but so exaggerated as to be a perfect caricature, & the same thing meets you at every corner or turning in the road. The people generally take no more notice of it than if it was a sign post, but if a canting hypocrite wants to beg, he will turn up his eyes & go through a series of contortions as soon as he thinks he has attracted your eye, in every small road side Inn we went into there was a small vessel of holy water nailed up just inside the door. Altogether there is more to disgust good sense & proper feeling in Bavaria & the Tyrol as far as regards Images & superstition & priestcraft than ever I saw in France or anywhere else, otherwise the people seem a decent wellbehaved set, enough, but we always noticed that where there are most priests there is most poverty among the people. The afternoon was showery & wet but still the ride to Innsbruch was beautiful all the way. We arrived there about 7 and went to the Goldenen Sonne, in the chief street. The costumes of the men & women varied when we got into the Tyrol, the men & women wear high crowned hats like witches, the men black velvet jackets etc & white stockings and their ladies generally dark stuff gowns & bright coloured handkerchiefs. The Tyrolese houses are like Swiss Chalets with flat wooden roofs apparently only fastened on by rows of large stones and carved wooden balconies all round & outside staircases. The crops were mostly wheat, Indian corn & beans planted together, & hay, & here & there a larger field of different sorts of vegetables, but the fields of wild flowers exceeded any garden I ever saw in brightness. Innsbruch is quite surrounded by mountains & before we arrived there we saw the clouds gathering considerably below their peaks. We had a storm of thunder & lightening & some heavy rain, but as our vehicle was comfortably covered in, it did not signify & we got to our quarters safe & dry.

Sunday May 30 Was so wet & stormy that we could not go far, we ran to the Franciscan church to see the monument of the Emperor Maximilian 1st, a marble Sarcophagus with 24 bas reliefs of events in his life most exquisitely carved, so minutely that in one of them even the pictures on the walls of the church were carved & the embroidered figures on the priest's robes, the faces very beautiful & very perfectly preserved. But the most splendid part of the monument is a complete arcade of bronze statues of the Ancestors of the Austrian royal family & other historical personages, of gigantic size and most interesting as models of the costumes worn by the said persons, most of them of the 16th century. Among them is one they call King Arthur of England, but the man who described them to us told us it was really Edward the black Prince which we thought it was not, but did not say so. The Emperor was not buried here so he need not have made himself such a splendid tomb, there is a fine monument of Hofer[19] who really was buried here. The rest of the day we spent in reading, writing & watching the people & their strange dresses. The women wear black hats, or the same fur caps we saw at Munich or a sort of wooley looking cone like Robinson Crusoe, we had after dinner preserved medlars & grapes both very nasty, I never heard of preserving either before.

Over the Alps and Across Lombardy to Genoa

May 31st to June 20th

BY CARRIAGE TO IMST · ONE NIGHT IN 'ROOMS' · BY CARRIAGE TO NAUDERS
ONE NIGHT AT THE POSTE INN · BY CARRIAGE TO TRAFOI, ON THE ROAD TO THE STELVIO PASS
ON TO BORMIO, OVER THE STELVIO PASS, ACROSS THE ITALIAN FRONTIER · BY CARRIAGE TO SONDRIO VIA TIRANO
BY CARRIAGE TO VARENNA VIA MORBEGNO AND COLICO, AND ON TO LAKE COMO · TWO NIGHTS AT THE ALBERGO REALE
BY BOAT TO BELLAGIO FOR THE DAY · BY BOAT TO COMO · BY CARRIAGE TO MILAN · FIVE NIGHTS AT THE HOTEL DE VILLE
BY CARRIAGE TO PAVIA, WITH A VISIT TO THE CERTOSA · ONE NIGHT AT THE ALBERGO DELLA LOMBARDIA
BY CARRIAGE TO NOVI, VIA MARENGO · ONE NIGHT AT THE HOTEL L'AIGLE NOIR · BY CARRIAGE TO GENOA
SEVEN NIGHTS AT THE HOTEL DE VILLE

Over the Alps and Across Lombardy to Genoa
May 31st to June 20th

Monday May 31 We were up, had breakfast & were ready to go by six o'clock when our coachman came up with a doleful face to say he could not go for there was a mistake in his pass ticket, & he must go to the police office which did not open until 9 o'clock. We found on enquiry that he had only just bought the carriage & horses & the license was not properly transferred to him, & another coachman who I suspect was rather jealous of his having so good a job, had informed against him, so just as the horses were in & the boxes packed, up came a police officer & said we could not go, however as John had made all his arrangements with the man & we rather liked both him & his equipage, which had brought us most comfortably from Munich, & moreover as we suspected it was a trick, we determined to wait, & at 9 o'clock our Jehu[1] came & asked John to go with him to the police magistrate which he did, & when the case was inquired into & the man had made a piteous complaint of an English family having been detained for three hours, the officious gentleman who had done the deed was called up & reprimanded & the magistrate very politely apologised to John for the delay & we were allowed to depart at 10. We were rather in the dumps at having been delayed 4 hours for nothing and with nothing to do, as it was too wet to walk and our bags & work & all were tied on the carriage & we did not think it worth while to have them unfastened again. However at last we were free & soon got into such lovely scenery that we forgot our woes, the road wound round the foot of the mountains & almost all the way by the side of the river Inn, one of the most 'ranting roaring Hades' that ever was seen & every here & there a beautiful waterfall or stream rushing down from the mountain into the river. The valleys, wherever there was a piece of level ground, were rich with crops of Indian corn, beans, peas, barley, buckwheat, wheat, flax, hemp & grass, the latter not at all like our grass land, but like a beautiful flower garden, one blaze of all sorts of colours, a kind of blue salvia, yellow single chrysanthemums & buttercups & dandelions

Trafoi
2d June 1847

& two or three sorts of bright pink flowers name unknown, they were I should think much more beautiful to look at than valuable as food for cattle, but that may be only my ignorance. The people were very busy hoeing & weeding & the land generally seemed much better kept than any we had seen elsewhere. We stopped to dinner at a nice little tidy inn in a small village and were surprised to find such a variety of provisions, positively asparagus & oranges & potatoes & beautiful fresh trout, & salad besides numerous other delicacies. We were dodged all day by Lord Stamford[2] who though he had four horses & we only 2 did not get on any faster than we did, at night we had the rural felicity of meeting the peasants returning home with their troops of funny little cows. The cattle are all very small and generally the same colour all through the Tyrol, a sort of ash colour & with bells round their necks, it was a pretty sight to see the large parties of them winding along the roads long before we came up to them & the bells sound very musical at a little distance. We got to Imst at about 8 and were told at first that there was no room for us at the only hotel in the place, a pleasant prospect, but afterwards they agreed to take us in if we would be satisfied with the accommodation they could find us, as they were unusually full owing to a rifle match in the village. They found us really very decent rooms, & good coffee & bread & butter & honey & about 5 sorts of cake & burnt almonds & we did very well. They have a most terrible practise all through Bavaria & the Tyrol of putting aniseed into the bread which makes it most offensive & occasionally almost too bad to eat, we asked why they did so and they said, to make it wholesome for travellers, which is rather kind of them but I, as one of the said travellers would have preferred it unwholesome. The old landlady gave us a long history of herself and daughter before we went to bed, how the latter was at a french school learning French & English & a great deal more, we slept like tops and were up again the next morning before 5.

Tuesday June 1 On leaving Imst, received from our amicable old hostess a bunch of flowers, peonies & iris & stocks, & a piece of something which she called Kitten cheese but which we found was very good quince cheese. When we were overtaken by a five hours fast on the road, we passed my lord again when we stopped to dine, we hoped for the last time as it is tiresome to be so dodged. We travelled all day through the same scenery as yesterday, John & I walked a great deal which is a much more agreable way of seeing the scenery and the fresh air & beautiful turns in the road seem to keep up ones vigour & spirits so that one can walk twice as far as along a level stupid road. We saw again our friend the gentianella and quantities of my favourite cornflowers & scarlet poppy, & the large purple clematis. The villages were dirty & untidy & the cows such dirty little brutes, quite a pity for they are naturally very pretty little creatures, almost like toy cows they are so small. We got into a sad scrape at night by going to the wrong inn, we had walked on and very far outstripped our vehicle & did not choose to wait for it so turned into the first inn we came to, & ordered coffee & beds, & when our man arrived he was very angry[3], what for we did not seek to know, & as we had by that time snugged ourselves down in a curious little old room we did not much care. We found in the travellers book the names of our friends

Avalanche Gallery on the Stelvio, 3rd June 1847

the Morleys & Overburys & went very tired to bed at the Poste at Nauders.

Wednesday June 2 We were called at 5 by the male attendant on the horses coming to our door and calling out 'Auf' & vanishing so up we got & made as good a breakfast as we could on very indifferent bread & butter & atrocious coffee, & were rather disappointed that there was no raspberry jam as we had had some very good the night before, & it helped down the other viands amazingly – they have a custom in these parts of wishing you may eat well when they bring you your dinner and when the dinner is at all tolerable you smile graciously & think how kind they are, but when it occasionally happens to be very nasty, you think what a cruel mockery of your woe it is & can hardly force out a ghastly grin. We had a beautiful wild ride though not a long one in distance, as the horses were hardly beyond a walk the whole day, on account of the steepness of the road. In the morning we travelled through a beautiful fertile valley containing 3 lakes of considerable size, & soon came to the river Adige near its source, & a turbulent young thing it is, dashing along over the innumerable masses of rock in a perfect white foam all the way. We went through two or three celebrated passes today and yesterday, especially the one where the destruction of the French & Bavarian armies took place in 1809, 10,000 men advancing against the Tyrolese were allowed to proceed until they got into a narrow pass where the rocks almost met over their heads, when the Tyrolese rolled down huge masses of rock upon them & fired upon them from all sides, so that hardly any escaped. We had a good opportunity of seeing the ravages the storms make in winter, for the road over the Stelvio is only just opened & we were almost the first people that had passed since the winter, & in many places the large stones & earth that had been washed down were still lying on one side of the road, which had been just cleared to make a passage, & in one place the road was actually washed away & the river gushing through the gap it had made. Luckily it was a place that was apt to misbehave itself & there was therefore another road for some distance, but the heaps of snow still unmelted through which the storms had made a passage & the large uprooted trees lying in all directions and the immense slips of earth & stones gave one a fearful idea of the destruction a winter causes in these mountainous passes. The people were very busy repairing the road where it had been destroyed. John & I had a delicious walk of about an hour up to Trafoi, our resting place for the night, it was so steep that we had extra horses, indeed the whole days journey was one continued hill, & we met waggons with 12 & 16 horses and a man to each pair, & it seemed wonderful even then how they contrived to get such loads up such hills, one small team we saw consisted of 4 cows & a horse & funny enough they looked. We got to Trafoi about 4 & after some refreshment which a very nasty dinner had made very requisite, to say nothing of a long walk & a most keen cold mountain air, Anne went out to get a drawing of the beautiful peaks covered with snow, among them the Ortler Spitz, the highest mountain in Austria, & which we were to ascend the next day. Anne was soon surrounded by the young population & a very dirty set they were, & most indefatigable starers, for they never took their eyes from us so long as we staid out of doors, which was only until Anne had finished her sketch for it was cold and bleak. We saw the men fetching home & housing their large flocks of sheep & goats & cows, & then retired to our rooms & it was so cold there that we sat for the hour or two of evening with our cloaks & great coats on. Trafoi is only a nest of ½ a dozen huts and a miniature Inn with only 8 beds so we were lucky to have it all to ourselves. Their supplies are very limited, they only get bread once a week, the landlady told us if we could stay till Saturday we could have some fresh bread, but strange to relate the inducement failed to make us postpone our journey even for three days.

Thursday June 3 We left Trafoi at six o'clock & began the ascent of the Stelvio pass & were soon out of humanities reach & looked down upon the little village where we had passed the night from an immense height. John preferred walking so we parted with him at the Inn & did not find him again until after we had passed the summit of the mountain, about 5 hours, he got to the top before us as though we had 4 horses we only went at a foot's pace. The road is a wonderful construction of a series of easy slopes winding backwards & forwards & is kept in admirable repair though the damages of the past winter were still very apparent & in some places where the sides of the mountain had been loosened & fallen it looked like an immense heap of brick rubbish & whole trees. We gradually lost all signs of vegetation & at last came to the region of eternal snow as the guide book calls it, & here are wooden terraces to keep the snow from the road, which in two instances out of ten they had failed to do, & these two were so completely filled with snow that there was no passage through them at all & we were obliged to go outside which was not pleasant. The others had a passage through but the snow piled up to a great height in front, & generally a great mass on the sloping roofs which had begun to melt & run through the roofs & hung in huge icicles, some of them 7 or 8 ft long & looked like a beautiful stalactite cavern. John had knocked off a great many as he walked through but we were still very destructive as we passed, the top of the carriage came in contact with them & down they came with a crack like broken glass & rattled off the roof to the road behind us. We reached the summit about 10 & there dismissed our extra horses, there was nothing to see for the road was cut thro' the snow to the depth of 10 or 12 ft so that we could not for some distance see out of the windows any thing but a white wall on each side. We passed a small obelisk that marks the boundary between Italy & the Tyrol & began to descend, which was much more speedy than the ascent. At about an hour from the summit we came to the Cantoniera or house of refuge for travellers of which there are five on the pass, this one called Santa Maria, here we were thankful to find John after the wet cold walk he must have had. We joined him regaling on bread & cheese, having ordered something more spicey for us on our arrival, in the shape of a stewed black cock. The day was a holiday so every body was gone to church except the master of the inn, a very dirty old Italian who could not speak either English, French or German, so he & John had had some difficulty in coming to an understanding, & he had produced 4 different sorts of game that they find in the mountains for John to choose which he would have dressed & when we arrived he took Anne into the Kitchen to see the choice morsel stewing. The old man was cook & every thing else & in a

Santa Maria, on the summit of the Stelvio, 3rd June 1847

short time provided us with a very good dinner, most excellent bread, which is a rarity. While Anne & I were dispatching our black friend in came the lady hostess and her attendant from church & two such free & easy damsels I never saw, they stood & stared at us until they were satisfied & then burst out laughing, & then asked us all sorts of questions as to what we were & where we were going & to our astonishment took an immense interest in the affairs of Ireland[4]. We parted monstrous good friends & they presented us each with a china rose, no small favour I expect as in a place where the snow never melts flowers must be rather a treasure. In descending the road passes through 7 tunnels bored in the rock, they are some of them of considerable length & are lighted by holes like loop holes. We reached the bottom about 2 o'clock & thus completed our passage of the Stelvio, the highest in Europe practicable for carriages, being 8850ft above the level of the sea, it was constructed by the Austrian Government, to open a better communication between Vienna & the centre of Lombardy & was finished in 1824. The whole days ride was beautiful, the gradual ascent from trees & plants & to the summit where there was nothing to be seen but bare rocks or immense tracts of snow & the most lovely cascades & waterfalls dashing down in every direction from the mountains & roaring along the bottom sometimes making a tunnel for themselves through the snow, which stood over them like a bridge, the ranges of mountains one beyond another all above description so I shall leave it alone. We got to our halting place Bormio at a little before three and intended going to a nice new hotel that is recommended in the traveller's book but it was not yet opened for the season so we were forced to take up our quarters in the dirty town & equally dirty Inn & after securing rooms went out to take a walk, but found the whole place so unutterably filthy & disagreable that we returned home & made ourselves as comfortable as was possible for the evening, our greatest consolation being that we should get away in the morning. It was curious to see the difference ½ a days journey made in the people, on one side the pass we leave the simple boorish Tyrolese & on the other find the cunning dirty idle Italians, whom we heard playing their favourite game with their fingers all the evening.

Friday June 4 Most willingly did we bid farewell to dirty ruinous disgusting Bormio, and if any thing could make one forget or forgive the horrible filthiness of the Italian houses it would be the beauty of the country between. We rode today through a succession of such lovely valleys as it is impossible to describe further, than to say they were full of vines running over trellises, with crops of barley & indian corn & flax & grass, which in some places they were cutting & making into hay, in others the hay was already carried, & in others still growing & full of wild flowers. We changed the toujours fir trees of Saxony & Bavaria for Walnuts, Chesnuts & Mulberries which they cultivate for silkworms & gather the leaves off the trees into sacks, completely stripping a tree of every leaf & then cutting it down to the old wood where it sends up beautiful new shoots with enormous leaves. The trees were so loaded with the young fruit that it quite went to the heart of such lovers of mulberries as we are to see such destruction but what will not people sacrifice to finery. The people are thoroughly dirty & picturesque, the women with their long ragged looking black hair fastened up with large silver pins like spoons or when working in the fields with the white headdress folded square like a towel, they seem to work for an hour or two in the morning and again in the evening & take it remarkably easy in the middle of the day. We stopped to rest the horses & dine at a small village called Tirano or rather a small town, & such a room as we went into would astonish anybody, setting aside newcomers into Italy, the utter & extraordinary dirtiness of it nobody would believe, it had originally been painted in fresco but now looked more like a very old dirty decayed cheese than any thing else I can compare it to. We sat while we waited for dinner, consulting how it could have got into such a state, I called into our council a very pleasant English traveller who was waiting for a conveyance to Bormio, & dined at the same time with us, but we could not come to any verdict and therefore suppose it is a peculiar disease that Italian houses are subject to. The gentleman I spoke of had been a great traveller, in the Holy Land, Greece, Hungary, more than once in Italy & Germany so that he gave us some very useful information concerning our future route, & entertained us most pleasantly with his descriptions of the Turks & Constantinople & the scorn & disgust with which the Turks & particularly the women treat Christians, abusing them & their *Mothers* in no measured terms & he described very amusingly the quiet half dosy lives of the Turks who, he says, never read or in fact do anything when they can avoid it but take their carpet & spread it under a tree & smoke, & if anyone speaks to them they say 'God is great' & take no more notice, but smoke away & this is their life for day after day & year after year. We had a pleasant ride of 3 hours to Sondrio, another small town & really rather a decent one, the Inn very tolerable, it is in a beautiful situation surrounded first by vineyards & then by very high ridges of mountains, some snowy & some beautifully clothed with trees, which look now in their full freshness. We had some coffee & then a strole through the town, to the great wonder & no doubt admiration of the inhabitants, Anne got a drawing & we soon returned as we thought a storm was brewing or else the lovely scenery would have tempted us to stay out longer. We made the acquaintance today of baggage mules & saw several with casks of wine slung over their backs & now & then one with a fair lady astride on it.

Saturday June 5 Left Sondrio at six, in a state of great indignation at the exorbitant charge for one night's entertainment, the landlord here is notorious in Murray & all the traveller's books as a dreadful cheat, & we found him so. We had a lovely ride through similar country to yesterday's as far as

Morbegno where the horses stopped to rest & John got out to walk to the next stage, Morbegno is a horrid dirty little town where we had to ride through the market place & all the market people selling their Parmesan cheese & the raw silk they had saved from their small collections of worms. The people here are dreadfully afflicted with goitre. From thence we went along a succession of strait dusty roads to Colico where we staid to dinner, and after dinner asked to be introduced to a room where there was a silk worm menagerie, we went into a loft where the worms were lying in trays made of wicker work like hampers, these were covered with paper & then strewed with mulberry leaves, upon these the worms which were now nearly at full size and were expected to spin in three days. They live just a month and spin in twigs placed upright between the trays on which they feed. I was very much pleased to have seen them for they seem quite the staple commodity of the neighbourhood, nearly a third of the trees had been stripped completely bare for their food. When we left Colico we came almost immediately upon the shores of Lake Como, & had a lovely ride along its banks to Varenna, the afternoon was very hot and the lizards were running about the rocks, we passed by hundreds. The Hotel at Varenna is close to the Lake & with the most lovely view imaginable across to Bellagio which we sat & enjoyed all the evening with the windows open, for the weather was very close & stormy.

Sunday June 6 We breakfasted at 8 for we had got into such early habits that we could not lie in bed any longer, at 11 o'clock we had a boat & crossed the lake to Bellagio, a point of land on which is situated a small village & an estate[5] belonging to a man who has spent a great deal of money in beautifying it & laying it out in terrace walks & making caverns in the rocks through which you see the different views of the lakes Como & Lecco, & most exquisite the views are from every point. The grounds are a beautiful wilderness, no attempt at tame flower gardening at all but roses climbing as they like over trellisses & up poles & in full bloom as high as 14 to 16 feet, white & pink & crimson all with such clusters of flowers as never were seen but we were only just in time for they were many of them quite on the decline. There was one little warm corner where aloes & cacti & the banana & other tropical plants were growing & in bloom, orange trees evidently grew all the year round in the open air & the olives were full of bloom with a little delicate white flower. In the course of our walk through the grounds we met 9 peacocks strolling about, & yet in contrast to this paradise of a garden the house looked like an old tumble down stables. We rather hurried out of the grounds to see a religious procession that was to parade the village as it was a saints day, we got into a very good place for seeing without being seen, & a very curious & disgusting sight it was, the whole way through which the procession was to pass was hung on both sides with table linen, sheets, sails, shawls, carpets, & every thing that could be hung up & the path was strewed with flowers. At last came the procession, first a woman carrying a crucifix then a long train of women who chanted at intervals, then a large number of men with white surplices & scarlet capes & long lighted tapers, who took turns with the women in singing & a horrible noise they made, then came a band of music, who played all sorts of tunes, not sacred

The lakes of Lecco and Como from Varenna, 5th June 1847

music by any means, between the singing, then followed another crucifix & then a canopy under which walked the three priests, & the boys with the censers by the side. At different places along their route temporary altars were erected with canopies over them & tapers lighted & we happened to be close to one of these & were very curious to see what ceremony would take place on passing it, the women & men who went first took no notice except that those whose tapers had gone out tried to light them again at those that were burning on the Altar, & if they lighted easily it was all well & good & if not, it did not seem to signify. When the priests came in front of it they all knelt down and chanted some short prayer & then the two inferior priests fumigated the superior with the incense, lifting up his robes in every direction which had a most absurd effect & then he fumigated the Altar & then away they walked again, the band striking up a good quick tune & the crowd following & as soon as they were passed a woman walked off with the tapers from the Altar in the most unconcerned manner, & the people took down their table linen & sheets & we went back to our boat, wondering there should be such hypocrites as Catholic Priests, or poor ignorant foolish people to be led away by sweet smiles & embroidered robes & wax candles. The sky looked so threatening when we got back to the boat that we thought it wiser to return home than to cross to see a beautiful palace belonging to the Princess of Prussia. The lakes are not pleasant in a storm so we returned to the hotel, the rowers here stand up with their faces towards the place they are going to, which looks very odd & must be much harder work than English rowing. After all we had only a few drops of rain & one or two claps of thunder &

lightening so we need not have been afraid but the better part of valour is discretion & if we had had a storm we should have been rather in a mess. We had half an hours walk in the afternoon but the dust was rather unpleasant so we returned & sat writing or reading the rest of the evening.

Monday June 7 We watched all the morning with some anxiety for the passing away of some very stormy clouds which we feared might rather interfere with the pleasure of our aquatic excursion to Como, the wind rose very much & the lake got rougher & rougher & we had a few peals of thunder & I began to think how very nice it would be to stay where we were instead of tempting the stormy waters, but we had appointed one Jehu to meet us at Como & so it could not be. We had a capital dinner & when we left the comfortable Albergo Reale at Varenna we had each a most beautiful bouquet presented to us of oleanders, verbena, roses & I do not know what else, but they were very large & very lovely & very sweet, & very soon died poor things. We went out in a boat to meet the steamer which was to come from Colico & a tossing, pitching row we had for an hour &½ & two of our boatmen very quietly laid down & went to sleep quite Italian fashion, then at last came the steamer much to my delight, as I had begun to think whether I should mind being drowned. We had a very pleasant trip of two hours to Como, the mountains & lake most lovely all the way & innumerable villas & palaces along its shores, among them Pasta's[6], Taglioni's[7], and the Queen Caroline's[8], a beautiful place close to Como, we were right glad to find our coachman & equipage waiting for us, & in a few minutes were on the very dusty road to Milan. The road between Como & Milan is very flat & uninteresting especially to people who have been feasted with scenery until they have become dainty, we saw crops of lupins growing & could not imagine for what purpose, the corn turning quite yellow. We met several travelling carriages making their escape from the heat & dirt of Italy during the summer & congratulated ourselves that the more we met, the more room there would be for us. We were six hours getting to Milan in which time it was dark, & we should have disliked this more if it had not afforded us the novel pleasure of seeing the fireflies darting about like bright sparks in all directions, the glow worms were shining brightly in the banks. We were closely questioned at the gate of the city & the man seemed to have rather an inclination to examine the luggage, but he didn't & we got to the Hotel de Ville a little before 11 & had very nice rooms & tea provided directly which was quite a new thing, for they seemed in most of the Hotels to take time enough to light the fires & boil the water & I believe in most cases they did so, but the mistress here was an Englishwoman & knew English people have a predilection for tea, which the foreigners laugh at us for, we did not go to bed until midnight.

Tuesday June 8 John went to the post office & brought quite a budget of letters from home which were most welcome after our long absence from news of any sort, when we had read them we went to the post again with a letter to William, where we were warned to beware of the pickpockets of Milan, they have more ways than one of picking pockets in Italy. We went next to the bankers to get some money, then to the Duomo which we only just walked round, then to the triumphal arch[9] on the road to Paris just outside Milan. It was built by Napoleon to commemorate some of his victories but left unfinished & the Austrians have finished it with bas reliefs from their own history, very beautiful but rather ridiculed from their absurdity in introducing the Ministers Metternich & Talleyrand etc in Roman dresses, it is a splendid arch & had a very fine group of Victory etc in bronze at the top. The walk was very hot & dusty so we only sauntered quietly back again through some of the streets to the hotel & as our windows looked into one of the best streets, the Corso de Servi, we did not want for amusement, the people seem to come out in swarms just as the sober sleepy Germans would be going to roost. The men go and sit in parties outside the Cafes, the women here wear a black lace veil like the Spanish Mantilla over a high comb but the countrywomen stick innumerable silver pins in their hair behind & with large oblong ends like spoons & it is somewhat absurd sometimes to see all this weight of ornament attached to such a dirty uncombed looking head as one never sees among the very lowest & dirtiest in England. Milan has apparently very well supplied shops & the streets are in one respect a great improvement on any we have seen since we left home, there are generally 4 rows of flat pavement along them, two for pedestrians & two for the wheels of carriages to run along & rough pavement between for the horses to run along, a very good contrivance. We had only a very small party at the table d'hote at 5 o'clock, but a very good dinner including peas, & beautiful cherries & wood strawberries & really after our long absence from fresh fruit & vegetables they seemed doubly welcome, in the evening I had one of my great treats, an orchestrina[10] to play under the windows.

Wednesday June 9 We went soon after breakfast to the Cathedral & climbed quite up to the top from where we had a very fine view of the country round & of the city, & an enormous city it is, but our principal idea was to examine the exquisite beauty of the Cathedral itself, which is finished so richly with statues & every kind of decoration in white marble with such exceeding minuteness & taste & variety, that you might spend a life in finding out all its beauties, which are always receiving additions & the breakages & accidents repaired. After we had spent some time on the roof we descended & requested to see the Shrine of St Carlo Boromeo[11], which is in a chapel under the centre of the Cathedral, one of the priests was called away from the service to go with us & he lighted his taper, & preceded us into the Shrine where he pointed out the entire lining of the chapel of solid silver chased & worked with the events of the Saint's

Genoa, 20th June 1847

life & ornaments in the corners consisting of cornucopias pouring out real Spanish coins. The Shrine is almost covered with votive offerings, the case in which the body lies is gold & silver gilt & our reverend attendant after deliberately lighting a row of candles pointed out all the beauty of the workmanship & then he explained that if we wished to see the body there was five francs more to pay, & as strangers sometimes refused to pay after they had seen the sight he liked to have a regular understanding. Of course we agreed to his terms & he very leisurely lowered the front of the Shrine by a windlass, undrew a crimson curtain & exposed to view the inner case composed of rock chrystel of very large size set in gold & richly ornamented, & there lay the remains of the Saint reduced to a mummy with only the face exposed. Dressed in full pontificals, mitre, cope, gloves, ring, & the crozier by his side all most resplendent with large gems, besides a complete heap of jewels lying on his chest, a small crown of gold suspended over his head, a most superb diamond & emerald cross & a small figure of a baby in gold, all votive gifts from Sovereignes, the latter from some Queen or Empress as a thank offering for the birth of an heir & in the midst of all this splendour is constantly carved the favourite motto of the Saint viz. 'Humilitas' which the priest pointed out & seemed to think very good fun, I believe if we had at all encouraged him we might have got up a good laugh over the nonsense but we didn't. The whole time we were in the Shrine the service was going on just over our heads & it seemed much more like a scene in a Theatre than any thing real, the Shrine is only shewn to strangers, the true believers are never allowed to go any nearer than the chapel outside, which is opened & lighted up for that purpose once or twice a year. When we had examined all the riches of the tomb the good priest wound up the side again, put out his tapers, & led us to the upper world again, first shewing us an embroidered portrait of St Carlo, & stopping at the entrance & bowing very low for his five franc fee, took his leave & we walked out in search of the church of St[a] Maria di Grazia & at last found it or rather the building near the church which was originally the refectory of a convent but has since been used for a military stable & is now nothing. Here are the miserable remains of Leonardo da Vinci's fresco of the 'Last Supper', said to be his finest work, & if one could see any of it one might give an opinion but there is now scarcely a trace of any thing except mould & damp, the plaster has cracked off in large patches & altogether it is in such a deplorable condition that I could not but think it absurd to expect any one to go to see it. We went into two or three other churches, St Ambrogio & others whose names I do not recollect, but they were mostly remains & dirty old places with nothing very remarkable about them. Milan swarms with Catholic Priests & dirty churches, I think there are 53 of the latter in the map John has bought as a guide. The streets are full of beautiful fruit & vegetables, cherries, currants & apricots, but none of them good, one might as well eat turnips, we seem to have come at once from the blossoms to the ripe fruit without any degree between, for the cherries we passed on our road were not at all ripe.

Thursday June 10 Went to the Brera Gallery where we saw first a very good copy of Leonardo da Vinci's picture & a very poor collection of specimens of new manufactures etc & then the

Gallery of paintings, many of which we recognised as old friends among the prints to Hewletts Bible[12] but altogether were disappointed with the collection. We then walked through a very pretty public garden to the Lazaretto[13], which was used at the time of the plague, but has been since allowed to go to ruin & is now let out in beggarly little shops, we should not have gone to see it but for that misleading book of Murrays, which is complete rubbish. We went next to find some remains of a roman temple, consisting as usual of a straight row of dirty crumbly old columns which I confess I found neither beauty nor interest in, & as we had now been a very long round we returned home. We had mostly English at dinner & one man annoyed me by asking an old lady next him, evidently a perfect stranger, if she knew that 'Mr Cobden[14] had been here?' a horrid Manchester wretch I'm sure, who cares where Mr Cobden goes? John went in the evening to see some horsemanship & wrestling & was very much pleased, the Milan people are quite different to the Germans in their hours, they never seem to come out until about 8 o'clock & then the streets are thronged until 11, in the daytime the streets are made very gay by the different colours of shop blinds, mostly a sort of orange colour, they hang down to the ground across the pavement & are embroidered & vandyked & very gaudy.

Saturday June 12 We left the comfortable Hotel de Ville en route for Pavia which is only 5 hours from Milan, we stopped on the road at the 15th mile, to see the celebrated church of the Carthusians called the Certosa of Pavia built at the end of the 13th century & still in most excellent preservation, as it well deserves to be, for the richness of its decorations is unequalled. The exterior is of marble beautifully carved, & the inside full of small chapels, each ornamented with an altar of fine mosaic of precious stones & the walls painted in fresco from the history of the particular Saint to whom each chapel is dedicated, & a very fine painting as an altar piece in each. The worst of it is that women are forbidden to be admitted except into the body of the church because it is dedicated to St John Baptist & a woman was the cause of his death, so that it was quite bo peep with us, & the lay brother who was within the pale with John, a poor little pale faced thing with his head shaved & a white surge scull cap, the rest of his dress was a Carthusian monk's of some sort of thick white material, he was very civil & said he was sorry he could not admit us, but that the rules were very severe. So he went over the whole with John & left us to a very intelligent old man who shewed us all the Pope considered proper for women to see, I suppose, but we got a great deal of information out of him, which somewhat repaid us for the punishment of our curiosity. The Monastery used to be very rich but was despoiled by Napoleon & is now a mere subsistence for a superior & 12 fathers & a few lay brothers. The fathers live in small houses each one by himself & are not allowed to speak except on Thursdays, they are never to touch meat, but have each a small piece of ground where they grow vegetables, & John's little guide bitterly lamented the disease having made its appearance again already in their small crops of potatoes. They have to perform service from 12 to 2 every night within Church & rise again at six, & look as if they were as nearly reduced to ghosts as they well could be to be alive. We only saw one of the fathers at a distance gliding about the church like a spirit. The little brother kept John such a time

Peasants in Lombardy gathering mulberry leaves for silkworms, June 1847

showing him the Monk's houses etc that we began to fancy we should see him come back in white flannel & with his head shaved, but he didn't, & we continued our journey for another hour to Pavia, the Albergo della Lombardia, the road was terribly dusty & the swarms of flies most annoying & the country not at all exciting, being a strait road with flat fields on one side & a canal on the other all the way. We dined & then went to see the Cathedral of Pavia, a curious ugly old building but containing a beautifully carved monument of St Augustine in white marble & under the slab on which the figure of the Saint lies, they shew the actual bones in a glass coffin. We next walked to the old church of St Michelle supposed to have been built in the 6 or 7th century & where the early Lombard Kings were crowned, the front has been curiously carved with things almost like Egyptian figures, but time has worn away the stone so that they are very indistinct. There is a very curious covered bridge over the Ticino river but the most national thing we saw was a scene at the hotel door, which we conveniently looked down upon from our windows, three men were sitting on a bench and two of them were picking the small deer out of the head of the third with a dinner knife, a nice idea for the visitors at the hotel. We had changed our voiture & driver at Milan, & our present Coachman must have been the original of Eugène Sue's Chourineur[15], I only hope we shall get safe to Genoa, but he is an unpleasant looking person.

Sunday June 13 We really could not stay in Pavia & were therefore obliged to stretch a point and go on, so we left at six & travelled along a flat dusty road until 10 when we stopped at a small & very dirty place to rest the horses & our new man proposed staying 4 hours which we rather resisted and got off ¼ of an hour sooner, having had some lunch & for two hours after had nothing to do but to watch the very Italian manners of the travellers who stopped for the same purpose. We passed very near the field of Marengo & curiously enough on the very anniversary of the battle, we continued along the same sort of country & had a desperately hot ride with very little incident except here & there, the people up in the mulberry trees & the women gleaning where the corn was cut & carried. We passed very few villages but all so wretched & dirty, & the people such nasty looking wretches, one old woman I was amused with, a dirty old pig without any stockings but carrying her fan in her hand, fans being very much more used in Milan & the neighbourhood than parasols. We got to our resting place L'Aigle Noir at about six & found it a much cleaner place than we expected to find in a small town like Novi, we had coffee & were passing our time in watching the people assembled in the market place, when we saw a long procession coming down one of the streets. It was called the Corpus Christi & was all by torchlight, every one in the procession carrying a lighted candle. First came two boys bearing white banners, then a great many men & women in white dresses with black capes & most of them leading a child, some of them had couls drawn down over their faces & some not, then came the Crucifix & canopy & boys bearing incense for Priests under the canopy, & then a band playing very merry tunes considering the solemnity of the occasion & lastly came the whole disengaged portion of the population of Novi, the spectators in the market place excepted, who all went down on their knees as the procession passed & I thought much good might it do the said knees in any Italian town, fat Italian knees do not mind dirt. They have plenty of priests in black & monks in brown in these parts, the latter looking like dirty bad old women slouching about, with ropes round their middles & their heads shaved.

Monday June 14 We were awaked a little after three by the pleasant & cheerful singing of mules & donkeys in the market place & soon after such a gabbling & chattering as never was heard, so up we got and a very curious sight we saw, the first silk market of the year in the middle of the silk country. The small dealers brought the cocoons in large baskets or small according to their stock, but some brought them in large panniers on a mule & the silk merchants came to buy for spinning. At first we thought the cocoons were some small kind of eggs as they were quite white and larger than the schoolboy production we had seen at home, so we asked the waiter for an explanation & found that the white silk of Novi was highly prized in other parts of the world. We left at six & got into a beautiful hilly country in an hour or so, the road winding in & out among the hills beautifully, we stopped for three hours in a comfortable little Inn in a beautiful situation, & then on again nearly all the way by the side of the dry bed of a river, which was rather uninteresting but as we approached Genoa the fine houses and the hope of catching a glimpse of the sea revived us. At last we came to Genoa itself, first coming in sight of the fortifications which encompass the city 7 miles round, then an immense & dirty suburb where we first saw the pig skins used for wine, such nasty looking things that look as if they had only cut off the head & legs of a pig and not cleaned or done anything else to it, with all the bristles on. We passed the lighthouse, entered the gate & then the view of Genoa the city of palaces burst on us & a splendid city it certainly is, the long ranges of palaces, for they can be called nothing else, with marble balconies etc running all round the shores of the bay, the bay itself filled with shipping & a splendid marble promenade between the houses & the water, under which is a piazza with warehouses. The Hotel de Ville where we were recommended to go, looks out on the promenade & into the bay & at first we were rather aghast at being shewn into rooms that only looked into a back yard, which large size & the splendid painted ceilings & gilding did not seem to compensate for, so after dinner we rebelled & got rooms in front which though much smaller had a fine view of the sea, & then John & Anne went out for a walk on the terrace & I staid & looked out at window, though there were not many people out & they who were, were principally composed of my favourites in

Genoa, 20th June 1847

Genoa
June 20th

black & brown. I must not forget the old friends we saw growing wild on the hills during our days ride, everlasting pea & what we in England call Canterbury bells, but in Genoa we can hardly call them so, the trellises covered with vines & the lovely oleanders in full bloom, white & every shade of pink, were growing in profusion round the houses as we entered the city, & quantities of a small bright scarlet carnation & china roses & pomegranates.

Tuesday June 15 I did not go out all the day but Anne & John went out to find their way about Genoa, and get some cake for lunch, the weather intensely hot, so that again we were wishing for a storm which however did not come, and the great event of the day was getting rid of a gentleman & lady and noisy child out of the next room. We dined with a party of foreigners & had some very foreign fruit, almonds brought up fresh from the trees, the kernels of which are not a bit better than our common hedge nuts, & a sort of fruit that we thought were golden pippins, but found they had a stone in them like a tamarind. We asked the waiter what they were but he said they were a kind of pear which they certainly were not, Anne asked a woman the next day at a fruit shop but she said they were hasponys[?] & as we could not find anything like it in the dictionary we must wait for time to develope the mystery. There was no want of entertainment for the street was a very busy one and the noises innumerable, in the first place the entire basement of the houses are occupied as workshops by black & copper smiths, who are banging & hammering all day, then there are all the curious noises incidental to the near vicinity of shipping & the landing of goods, then the long trains of loaded mules 12 or 14 in a string with the uncouth noises of the muleteers & the discordant roar or bray of the animals themselves, & all this mixed with perpetual chatter & shout & organ playing & church bells ringing make the sum total a very overwhelming one. The terraced walk is quite deserted during the day, on account of its being quite too hot to hold anyone, I suppose, but in the evening people crawl out a little and these some few made their appearance there.

Wednesday June 16 Directly after breakfast we went out for a walk & walked up one street & down another until we came to the ramparts where we got a very fine view of the city and port, we stopped once or twice to rest when we could find a little shade, but the heat was most overpowering. The streets of Genoa are very convenient in one respect, they are so narrow and the houses so high that they are generally shady, they are so narrow that there is only just a narrow rough stone way for the mules along the middle & for walking bipeds at the side, and the muleteer is often obliged to shout to you to let his beast & his load pass or you would get a bump with a wine cask or a scratch with a load of wood. The curious fact of it is that the houses in the narrow streets are complete palaces many of them marble, large halls with marble pillars & painted ceilings & fountains & the outsides beautifully ornamented with statues & carving, & yet in these halls you see generally a cobler seated with his stand of trading materials or a trunkmaker or a flower seller or some other small trader, & from the windows above you see different articles of wearing apparel that have been washed & hung out to dry, even in the hotel where we are & where the balconies are all of carved marble, there are stockings & gowns etc perpetually hanging over the said balconies which to our English eyes has a very strange look. The houses have most of them evident marks of having been built & occupied by princes, & though they are let quite alone as to repairs or anything of that sort, from the durable quality of their material & the purity of the air they do not look so ruinous as bricks & mortar would at half their age. There seem to be no broad streets at all & the shops in the best streets are funny little concerns about the same size as those in the Burlington Arcade & all open to the street, no doors, no windows but sometimes a curtain to keep out the sun. The back streets are horrible, dirty & unsweet & with inhabitants equally nasty, children deformed in every horrible manner & nearly naked, that is literally with nothing on but a shirt, but the novelty of both place & people is most striking to us, & the beautiful sea & immense quantity of shipping in the bay quite a treat.

Thursday June 17 Again went out directly we had breakfasted & walked through the streets where the gold & silver workers live as they all herd together, & keep their wares in small stores open to the street, gold & silver filigree ornaments are among the principal manufactures of Genoa, & it is somewhat remarkable to see very poor dirty looking women, perhaps without stockings with a beautiful worked pair of ear rings. They sell a great many pins with ornamented heads for the ladies to pin their veils to their hair with, as a white veil over the back of the head & reaching below the waist like a scarf is the common walking attire of the women of all classes & with their pale goodlooking faces & fine dark hair it is a very becoming head-dress. We went up an immensely long hill, between two walls which is the usual style of the outskirts to the city, the walls enclosing the gardens of either private houses or convents of which there are a great many, we came at last, nearly melted, to the fortifications, where we found a beautiful view of Genoa. We then descended again & perambulated for an hour or two in & out of the curious narrow and crowded streets looking at the wares exposed for sale, consisting very largely of provisions, pickled & dried fish, & quantities of fine looking fruit & very stale looking vegetables for the latter flag as soon as they are gathered in this hot climate, in fact nothing looks very fresh, for the people only seem half alive, & towards the middle of the day are lying about in every direction asleep. We walked about until too hot & tired to see any more & then returned home for the rest of the day.

Friday June 18 We had a valet & summoned up all our courage to knock off all the sights of Genoa, we went first to the royal palace, where there is nothing remarkable except perhaps the general shabbiness of the place, then to the Palazzo Durazzo to see a beautiful suite of apartments & a small gallery of very fine old pictures, among them portraits by Vandyk, of several members of the Durazzo family to whom the palace belongs. The furniture was very old & curious tapestry, & the hall & staircase of marble ornamented with some fine statues, but it looked like one of the deserted enchanted palaces one reads of in the Arabian Nights. Next we went to the Palazzo Serra to see a Saloon which is one mass of gold & white marble & lapis lazuli &

Genoa, 20th June 1847

looking glass, & the eating room adjoining where the furniture was of crimson silk velvet & gold bullion fringe & the chairs covered with gold & silver brocade. We next went into two of the churches which were very richly painted & adorned, in one of them we saw the covered pew where the Doge used to sit. We just entered the court of the Jesuits college which used to be one of the Doria Palaces but came out again very wretched to think that the nasty Jesuits should have the fruit off one of the finest fig trees we ever saw, which is growing in the garden. We went over part of the old Doges Palace & saw the two halls where the Council used to meet, with the raised dais for the Doge & members of the council, & as we came out we saw two of the councillors who still wear scarlet dresses. Next we went to the custom house to see a very curious old hall, that is now full of desks & clerks, but round the sides are the statues of the nobles or citizens who had benefited the city by their munificence, the Dorias, Spinolas, Grimaldis etc, they are in two ranges, the upper ones standing, the lower sitting, all the size of life & in the costume they wore and an inscription to each recording his particular charities, one had founded a hospital, another had bought off a tax on provisions that oppressed the poor & all had done some noble thing to benefit his city. It seemed a great pity this curious old place should be full of wooden enclosures, so that it was impossible to see it to advantage or indeed to see the lower range of figures at all, we seemed now to have seen all that had much interest so we dismissed our attendant, had some ices & returned home, we saw the people in the streets cooking macaroni & grilling large snails, which did not look nice.

Saturday June 19 A wet morning kept us indoors until about three when we tried to get round the bay as far as the lighthouse but had not got above half way when the mud became quite impassable and we were obliged to return. We saw the outside of the Doria palace which must have been indeed a palace in its palmy days but is now a school. The oleanders in some of the gardens were quite dazzling, with their many blossoms, large size and rich colour. We sauntered about the curious narrow streets & saw an immense deal of hair dressing & 'picking' going on in the streets, from which we inferred that it was a Saturday operation & that there were travelling professors as neither men nor women seem to do their own, I suppose they cant see to catch the game & that seems to be the principal part of the entertainment.

Sunday June 20 A pouring rain all the morning, in the afternoon it cleared up, so that some of the natives came out for our amusement, but it was too dirty to allow us to walk. We saw some Turkish & Egyptian sailors who look the more picturesque the further you are removed from them, as when they are near they are dreadfully dirty.

Steamer to Naples, by Diligence to Rome

June 21st to July 4th

BY STEAMER FROM GENOA TO NAPLES VIA LEGHORN AND CIVITA VECCHIA
ARRIVE NAPLES · NINE NIGHTS AT THE HOTEL VITTORIA · BY CARRIAGE TO VISIT THE GROTTO OF POSILLIPO
TO POMPEII AND CASTELLAMMARE FOR THE DAY · BY CARRIAGE TO THE GROTTO DEL CANE
AND THE LAKE OF AGNANO (THE PHLEGREAN FIELDS) · BY DILIGENCE TO ROME, VIA MOLA DI GACTA, TERRACINA,
AND THE PONTINE MARSHES · ARRIVAL IN ROME

Steamer to Naples, by Diligence to Rome
June 21st to July 4th

Monday June 21 John & I went out for an hour & just looked into the Cathedral & one of the other churches where mass was performing, the former was very gaily decorated with crimson & gold hangings & the priest in very gay robes. We went & had some ices at a cafe & then walked about among the shops, inhaling the rich various, & most offensive odours of Genoa, & then returned to the hotel & prepared for departure, we dined at ½ past 3 & at six went on board the steamer 'Maria Christina' & took our places for the night & then went on deck to watch the arrival of the other passengers. We set off at about 7 & I speedily descended to the cabin leaving Anne & John to make acquaintance with a very pleasant Scotchman & an American & his wife who also proved very intelligent pleasant people, there were also a Count & Countess from Neufchatel with 4 servants & a dog & a carriage, who were the entertainment of the whole ships load. The Countess gave herself such airs & the poor old husband pottered & fussed over his treasure to such an extent, fetching down her nightcap trimmed with pink, himself, & perpetually pressing her hand & smiling at her in such an irresistible manner as to make good sport for all the observers & the lady was so decked too with such an embroidered cape trimmed with point lace, & such innumerable bracelets & rings & other things that one would fancy encumbrances on board a steamer for three nights passage. We had a smooth voyage the first night & when we got to Leghorn we all went on deck & one of our companions in the ladies cabin of whom ourselves included, there were luckily only 4, went on shore never to return thank Heaven for the spitting was not at all agreable. The other a nice kind quiet German staid on board all day with her husband, but every body else landed & all except ourselves went on by railway to Pisa, but we did not feel lively so had only a dejeuner at one of the hotels and a strole through Leghorn & a nastier place or nastier people I never wish to see & the heat was almost unbearable. The principal trading seemed to be done by hawkers who were

Civita Vecchia, 23rd June 1847

selling every thing that could be imagined between fish & English cotton handkerchiefs which seemed the two chief articles of sale, we were soon ready to leave Leghorn again, stopping before we got into the boat to see a Statue of Ferdinand I, Grand Duke of Tuscany, the figure itself being nothing worth, but supported by 4 very fine bronze figures of African slaves larger than life, likenesses of a father and three sons who were taken prisoners by the Duke. We saw the galley slaves[1] at work in the boats as we returned to the steamer, & they positively had the impudence to beg for money, rather odd objects for donations. The poor German lady and her husband we found on board very hot, & rather displeased at having had no breakfast provided for them, as an exhorbitant charge was made to all the passengers, for berths & the use of the table & the table was seemingly nothing but the table as with the exception of a feed at 6 o'clock there was nothing to be had except tea & coffee & dry bread, wretchedly bad all of them, except what was paid for extra, & as the dinner at six was after the boat had started many of the passengers were hors de combats by the time it was ready. So we & the Germans sat & grumbled together for a little while & then the rest of the passengers came back & the boat set off & down I went again into the cabin which I should have had pretty much to myself except that it was a sort of storeroom for the bread & linen etc & some of the mens clothes so that we sometimes had three or four men in & out all the time we were dressing & there was no Stewardess, there was only a negro faced ugly little Italian wretch as femme de chambre. The Germans called him & he ran in & out quite at pleasure, that is to say at his pleasure, not ours.

Wednesday June 23 At about 8 we got into Civita Vecchia & as I could not stir until the boat stopped, the people were all again dispersed before I got on deck. The only thing in the place of any interest was a Brigand prisoner & his band of men, also prisoners for life, & as the steward told us there was literally nothing else to see & we should find it a very dirty place, we staid all day where we were, that is until half past one when the boat sailed again. The Americans gave us a description of the Brigand, he has been there 20 years and is accused of having murdered 230 people, he only confesses the 30 & says he killed them all except one in self defence and the one for love, that he has been very penitent for many years, that he gave himself up to the Pope by promise of free pardon which he did not get, & so now he consents to be made a shew & dresses himself for the purpose quite in Brigand style, & is very glad of a five franc piece when silly Americans give it to him. They say he is a very handsome man with black hair & grey beard, & was very civil & communicative & he said, very penitent & that he would not do anything wrong again if he were let loose, but I fancy he will not be tried, the band were very unpleasant & clamorous for money, they were most of them knitting, what a Brigand occupation, the lady said she was very glad to get away from them. The Count had been on shore to be shaved as he told a fellow passenger when he returned & as the fragile countess went with him we supposed she was a necessary part of the performance. She got on board again with the assistance of her lord and three servants & dog, & immediately there was a great stir made. Two mattresses were brought on deck, & two pillows besides the private pillow of her ladyship which never left her, these were covered with a quilt then spread with divers cloaks & then a large dining table was turned up on edge to preserve her from the sun & a large umbrella spread for the same purpose, & in a short time she was placed on the couch & her devoted spouse sat close to her, patting her hands & holding a smelling bottle to her nose, & after all poor creature I believe she was very ill, & would have been better & more decent down stairs. But as I was down there myself I saw & heard no more, but they say she made a most unearthly howling for some time & would have been wiser to have confined herself to her own cabin & her maid & her husband if he liked it. Nancy was not long before she turned in requesting the Lord of the Bedchamber not to admit any body but himself which he kindly agreed to. The passage to Naples was rather a rough one & we did not arrive until about ½ past 10.

Thursday June 24 We were all ready to go on shore long before we were permitted to stir, as the police had to come on board & give us a permit to land and get our passports which had been taken from us at Genoa, so there we sat very hot & very impatient & a great many people came on board to stare & lounge away their time. The steward very much pressed our smuggling some shawls on shore for him on our shoulders, but as we did not choose to smuggle on our own account we declined the honour of doing so on his. At last we were permitted to land & we gave ourselves up to a valet from the Hotel Vittoria, where we meant to go, & really if he had not been an active decent man I think we and our goods would have been torn to pieces in the Custom house, where we had to land & where everything was torn open in the most rude & uncivil manner possible. We had nothing contraband except 11 cigars which John shewed them at once & which they immediately appropriated I expect to themselves, his dictionary was wrapped in paper which they tore off and threw on the floor and every thing was dragged open in our portmanteau & such a fuss made about my scotch shawl that we expected they would have taken it, as the man smelt it carefully all over & perhaps liked the smell. We only wished we were Italian enough to give them a setting down but we were not & were therefore obliged to take it quietly, & after all their incivility they positively mobbed John & would not let him pass without a fee, which he resisted for some time, but was at last obliged to give way & a five franc piece, & we got out of the custom house, but we were not safe yet, for the porters had rushed off in all directions with our luggage & the valet had to look out quite sharp to get it all together again & then there were about a dozen wretches got round us & the carriage, fighting & swearing & elbowing & making such a clamour that really we were very glad to drive off & find ourselves out of reach. We got beautiful rooms looking over the lovely open sea, & tiled floors so cool & nice & quiet, that we soon began to laugh over our misfortunes, especially after a good wash & a very clean nice breakfast of bread & butter from the Kings dairy at Portici & tea, very good & very quickly served, & there we sat looking at the sea & the few copper coloured natives that made their appearance, two of whom great big boys were stripped quite naked & jumping in and out of the sea, & then coming on shore & either dancing about or hanging themselves over a rail to dry, & such coffee coloured snips as they were. In the evening we went to the Villa Reale, a beautiful public garden planted with all sorts of trees & shrubs that were unknown to us, the cactus & oleander seemed to grow almost wild & the beautiful Erythrinum or coral tree as large as a moderate sized apple tree & full of blossom & the orange & olive trees quite as common as laurels in our gardens. The day was a fête day on which occasions a very good military brass band play in the garden & all Naples either promenade inside the iron railing or drive in very dashing little open carriages just outside the said railing all the evening until quite dark, we staid until 8 & then went home & dined, & very soon were glad to go to bed, & for the first time were surrounded by a transparent mosquito curtain.

Friday June 25 A very fine & plentifully hot morning, John went the first thing to the banker's & post office, & while he was gone our American fellow passenger called to ask if we would go up Vesuvius with them in the evening, & told us how he had managed to escape having his luggage examined, by feeing them, which partly accounted for their being so offensive to us, as no doubt they often drive people into feeing them to get rid of them, like other beggars. We did not mean to climb Vesuvius unless our Valet insisted so declined the invitation. We went in the middle of the day for a very lazy promenade into the town, that being a piece of hardihood that the Neapolitans would not have been guilty of, for they, especially the ladies, never stir out until about 7 in the evening & then drive out in their carriages with their unnaturally bleached faces looking like ghosts & not one half as beautiful as the deep brown faces of the lower orders, who are some of them when young very lovely, the children have such little bright intelligent faces, & sometimes literally no covering but a shirt, & frequently not even that. We took our strole & thankfully crept along any little strip of shade that we could find for the heat was awful, we were agreably disappointed in the streets which were all well paved with good flat pavement

& filled with small but well supplied shops of all sorts, a great many with carved ornaments of coral or lava from Vesuvius. We walked along the chief streets, saw the exteriors of the palace, the principal Church, & theatre & the numerous street trades of lemonade, fish etc, the former is sold iced at little ornamented stalls at the corners of the streets, decked out with branches of orange & lemon trees with the fruit on, & large heaps of oranges & citrons for sale, the lemonade is in swinging buckets, which they constantly rock backwards & forwards to cool in the ice in which it is placed. But the most striking feature of Naples is the beggar population, they are in perfect swarms, especially on the steps of the Churches where they lie down & sleep & then wake up to scratch either themselves or each other, scratching being the chief amusement or indeed occupation of the lower orders of Italians. We saw a man scratching an old woman's back down I cant say how far, but there was an enormous expanse of brown material visible as we passed, & he seemed doing it quite con amore, & in right good earnest. The annoyance of the beggars if they see you receive any change is perfectly irritating, they thrust themselves before you so that you can scarcely move, & if you once give one of them a trifle, woe be to you, you'll have no more peace, they beset you thick & threefold, bringing forward all the deformities & horrors they can collect, & if it were only for their entomology they are not pleasant near neighbours, we walked until we could walk no more & then returned home. We were amused before we went out by a sight that would rather horrify eyes that had not been gradually broken in to such enormities, a man on horseback going into the sea for a bath with no article of drapery between them but a bridle, they were evidently enjoying their bath very much and were swimming about together very comfortably, & when they rose a little out of the water they looked so shiny & fresh. We dined at 5 & then had a carriage to go to the Grotto of Posillipo, on our way we stopped to see a place belonging to an old Italian Colonel, who is very rich, & spends all his money and time in adorning the garden, which is laid out in winding walks & planted with huge geraniums, cacti, aloes, & orange & lemon trees, covered with fruit & flowers, Oleanders & a great many trees that were quite new to us. There was a most lovely view of Naples, across the bay, & pretty little ornamented buildings scattered about the grounds, in one of these there was a very good collection of stuffed birds, animals, reptiles, & insects, in another only a statue on a fountain, in one a giant eel, a tremendous fellow in a pool of water, with relics from Virgil's tomb surrounding his home, to make him poetical, then there was a collection of live creatures, gold & silver pheasants, white & coloured peacocks, guinea fowls & a few animals, small fowl etc, a porcupine, an emu & a stag all living together very amicably. There was a sort of cavern or grotto close to the edge of the water, this was hung with coloured lamps & ornamented with statues & I know not what, in this romantic place the old gentleman not long ago gave a very large party, inviting all the elite of Naples but making the proviso that the gentlemen were all to be dressed like English sailors and to come in boats, whether there was any peculiarity about the ladies dresses or mode of arrival we did not hear, but it must have been a very pretty sight when the lamps were all lighted and the dancing going on. The greatest curiosity of the place however was a small pool, in one corner of the grotto, where there was a preserve of

Italian lemonade stall, July 1847

the most unnatural looking fish that ever were seen, their shape was that of small dolphins, their fins like large wings with a border round them of the most vivid blue & a large spot in the middle like the eye in a peacock's tail, they were most lovely when they expanded their fins & as they rose out of their dark pool they looked like spectral things, we asked the very uncultivated young lady who was our guide what their name was & where they came from, but could get no further information than that they came a long way & were very expensive, & made very good soup, they seemed very happy & thriving & were from 1 to 2 ft long. As we climbed up from the cavern close to the water's edge, to the entrance of the gardens which was a considerable height above, we encountered the old gentleman possessor of the domain, in a cap & loose dressing gown superintending the watering of his garden, he bowed most politely, which we returned in same manner, & then took our departure from his beautiful place, & could not wonder at any one making a sort of idol of so lovely a place. As we proceeded we passed the residence of Lablache[2], a sensible quiet looking small white house surounded by a garden & with a magnificent view over the bay, & one could not but confess that he had spent his english earnings very wisely, & still more strange, for an Italian singer, respectably. We had a delightful drive round by the Bay of Baia & along a road where the vines were hanging in festoons from tree to tree & such magnificent bunches of grapes, and when we passed through a village the population seemed all out of doors, & great curiosities they were, the men looking like labourers resting after their days work, & the women spinning or nursing their baby bundles. We returned home through the Grotto of

Posillipo[3] an immensely long & lofty tunnel through which the road runs, it is supposed to have been made by the Romans but the time is unknown, it is a magnificent work, & very dark, and I was very glad when we got out of it again as I was afraid we should run foul of somebody, there were a few lamps but only sufficient to make darkness visible. When we got into Naples again the valet recommended our driving about a little to see the streets when lighted & we were very glad we took his advice for such a bustling scene as it was never was seen, all Naples seemed either walking or driving except the shopkeepers who were all lighted so that we could see into the shops, which are generally very small, & have universally a painting or figure of the favourite saint with a lamp burning in front, hung up in some part of the shop. The people drive & walk just as pleases them without any absurd prejudices about left or right sides of the road, & the marvel to me is that crowds are not killed every day as they generally drive at full gallop where they can, & there is no curb pavement to preserve the lives & liberties of poor walkers. The fish & lemonade sellers were busier than ever & the people were sitting about the streets eating parched beans & the heads of indian corn which were stewing in large pots in the streets. We met a large party of soldiers just entering Naples from a march with band & colours etc etc, the officers on horseback. We went through the same streets in the evening that we had walked along in the morning, and the wide awake appearance of the people after sunset was most striking, they are a terrible late set at night for their theatre does not open until 9, & then is not worth visiting according to all accounts. After our drive we returned to tea & thought we had done rather a hard day's work, we soon retired to our net which answers two purposes, it keeps mosquitoes out & keeps fleas in. Oh! the fleas of beautiful Italy!!!

Saturday June 26 We had a carriage and a valet, a very decent well behaved man & at 6 o'clock started for Pompeii, going early to avoid the heat in the middle of the day, both on our own account & the horses. The road from Naples to Pompeii was very terribly dusty when we saw it, the towns of Portici, Resina, Torre del Greco, etc that we passed through, all dirty & in ruins & people equally dirty & looking as if they were too lazy ever to be any better. There are many remains of what must have been very splendid palaces along the road still bearing the names of the families to whom they belonged, but most of them look now as if they were let out in apartments, to all sorts of people from Ladies & gentlemen to lazzaroni & mules. In about 3 hours we reached the entrance to Pompeii & a guide having produced himself we commenced operations in form, with the Villa of Diomede, the entrance, dining room, bathroom, with the remains of the stove, & flue for hot air, the cellars under ground where the family were supposed to have taken refuge from the ashes at the time of the eruption, as parts of several skeletons were found fixed by the ashes to the wall, & there are two or three distinct shades of profiles on the wall where they were found. The wine was kept in large brown earthen pots which stood upright in stands made for them along the walls of the cellar, we went into several tombs where the vases containing the ashes of the dead were still remaining & one of the stoves used for burning the bodies preparatory to burial was very perfect. The villas seem all built pretty much on the same plan, a

Vesuvius from Castell' a mare
June 26 · 1847

square entrance court surrounded by pillars, with a pool of water or fountain in the middle & the rooms all round, the sleeping rooms quite open to the air, no doors, no windows, all more or less ornamented with frescoes on the walls, & mosaic pavements but really there is so little remaining, as every thing that was moveable has been taken to the Museum at Naples, that I was very much disappointed with it. We saw two or three bakers shops, where there still remained the huge grinding stones for the wheat, the vessels in which the bread was mixed & the oven, exactly the baker's oven of the present day, we went over the temples of Isis, Bacchus & I dont remember how many more, & then walked along a dreadful path of dust, the remains from the lava, & what is just like our small dust from ashes, to the Amphitheatre the most perfect of all the buildings as the seats are there & the pit where the beasts were kept for the combats. The old pavement of the town is very perfect still, shewing the ruts which were worn by the chariot wheels & the large stepping stones laid across some of the streets to enable the people to avoid the burning lava that used to flow along them occasionally, but altogether we found it rather a disappointing place, there is still a large part of the city buried & the King gives permission to any person of importance who visits Naples to excavate, the last person who availed himself of the permission was the Emperor of Russia but he discovered nothing of importance. I must say I should be very sorry to live so near Vesuvius for it has very considerable eruptions still, occasionally. Eight years ago it buried a small village, & only two months since the sea was so hot with the burning ashes that boats could not go upon it, & yet no sooner is one village buried than the people build another over it, & use the lava for materials, one thing is to be said there is generally time for the people to escape with their lives, but then it is not agreable to have your house & property destroyed, it has kept continually puffing out smoke since we have been at Naples, & our American friend saw flames as he was returning from the theatre in the darkness – so that I should not wonder if we hear of an eruption before long. We wandered about Pompeii for three hours in such a burning sun, & in such burning dust that we were most thankful when our guide conducted us out of the city & we found ourselves again seated in our comfortable carriage on our way to Castellammare, a small watering place that the Neapolitans frequent when Naples is too hot. We got there in an hour & were soon supplied with hot water & towels, the greatest luxuries in the world after a hot dusty walk or ride, & there we staid to dine & wait for the heat of the day to pass, we had a beautiful view of the sea & Vesuvius & sat watching a party of eleven merry little brown snips, who were running in and out of the sea & diving like ducks & then spreading themselves on the black sand in the sun to dry. We took a very short strole through the town which is a dirty little place & we were too tired to walk far into the neighbourhood which is said to be very pretty, so at six o'clock we began our journey homewards & had a rather cooler but detestably dusty ride home again. It was the fete day of the patron Saint of one of the churches that we passed, so the church was illuminated all over with little oil paper lamps of various colours & several of the houses near were decorated in the same manner & in one place there was a very grand illuminated arch over the road which looked very gay & pretty as it was nearly dark. The streets were crammed with people either sitting at their doors or walking or riding in the public conveyances, carriages with two wheels & one horse, which they fill as full as they can, & then hoot & scream the horse into going at full gallop, very often you see three men sitting on each shaft & four standing behind. We counted from 7 to 15 as the allowance for one poor wretched horse, the people are as black as indians & generally dressed entirely in white. In the morning as we went we met them coming into Town with their mules loaded with fruit & vegetables. Whole panniers of cucumbers & apricots & a very long thin sort of gourd & quantities of very large onions, tomatoes & capsicums & baskets of large green figs & curiously small mealy pears, cherries defying all description & many other vegetables. We saw several quite young children as we rode along with what we supposed to be their breakfast, a cucumber so big that they could scarcely grasp it with their little hands, but they seemed munching away very perseveringly without any fears of its disagreeing with them, though they had no pepper or vinegar. The colours of the buildings at Pompeii are most unpleasing, especially in a burning sun as we saw it, the favourite colours were a glaring red & an equally glaring yellow, and all the walls of the houses are painted either with red or yellow.

Sunday June 27 We did not go out until between 6 & 7 when we just sauntered into the Villa Reale for an hour, the band was playing & an immense number of people walking & sitting about but it was dreadfully close, so not agreable & the people are not pleasant to look at, they are either like bleached Negroes or very black ill looking Jews, they have most of them very large black eyes but very bloodshot looking as if affected by the heat, & such fine colours as the ladies indulge in resembling negroes in their taste for finery, such a number of amber coloured gowns, & pink & scarlet shawls & feathers of all colours & short sleeves & bracelets & frippery. I have not seen for a long time I think never such vile taste, & the men are all just as dandified & I thought looked very much like swell mob & perhaps they were a good many of them for they say Naples is celebrated for pickpockets. We were amused by the valet telling John as if he thought it would be very bad news, that the English Ambassador was not at Naples now so there would be no services, I daresay he thought we should be very sorry. I must not forget an acquaintance I made today that rather proved the retirement of our apartment, we were sitting quietly reading or writing in the middle of the day when out came a mouse, & for some time we were very much entertained to see the little beast make its way to the table & sideboard, at least the floor under them, in search of crumbs. Unfortunately for him there were none, so he was obliged to wait. At luncheon I put him a piece of bread under the table, but he did not return so suppose he was tired of looking in one room, but the little thing was so tame I quite took a fancy to him & put a piece of bread in a drawer that he might not find Mother Hubbard's cupboard bare if he came again. One of the prettiest things in the evening is to see the fishing boats rowing about on the sea with a flambeau to attract the fish, the reflection in the water as it moves along is most beautiful.

Monday June 28 We took courage & summoned our protecting spirit to attend us to the Museum or anything else very well worth our seeing at Naples, so at ten he & a carriage

Vesuvius from Castellammare, 26th June 1847

were waiting and we went first to see the church of St Francois de Paule, a very beautiful building, the interior of which resembles the Pantheon at Rome, it is most richly adorned with fine marbles & round the central part of the church stand 8 colossal figures in marble of the Evangelists & fathers of the church. We went next to a small chapel St Maria de la Pieti[4], built by a noble Italian family as a Mausoleum, & ornamented with marble monuments etc, the most remarkable of which are allegorical portraits of two of the family, the woman as modesty, covered by a veil, and her husband represented as a man struggling to get free from a net in which he was entangled, but what the difficulty was that the real character had had to contend with we could not make out, as our Valet was not acquainted with the history. The third & most beautiful figure by the same artist, was a recumbent figure of our Saviour with a loose drapery thrown over it, so exquisitely wrought that you might see every feature as distinctly as through a thin muslin covering, the face & figure all wonderfully beautiful, the chapel has unfortunately suffered to fall into decay, almost ruin, partly caused by an earthquake & partly by the poverty of the Da Sangro family whose property it is, but it is now under repair. Next we went to a church the name of which we could not understand, a curious old place with a very fine old carved marble pulpit, & two columns that they say were part of the temple at Jerusalem, very beautiful they are too but very much smaller than I should have pictured the columns of the Temple, we had a proof here of the sanctity in which all their ordinations are held, for while we were examining the columns a monk who was sitting there got up and spoke to our Valet, who asked us whether we would like to see the Nuns at prayers, as this was a Jesuit's church and the chapel where they were at prayers was at the back of the High Altar. Of course we said 'yes' so the old brown creature, upon receiving a fee, unlocked a gate and we went to the back of the Altar & through a grating got a glimpse of the Nuns in their black and white dresses, we could not but be struck by having such a prohibited sight proposed to us by a person set there to keep order & propriety. Last & not least we went to the Cathedral dedicated to St Janvier, built to replace two temples to Apollo & Neptune, it must be very old as it was seriously injured by an earthquake in 1456, the most curious part of the visit to us was to see how busy all the reverend gentlemen were, there was mass performing in two or three places & the confessionals all as hard at work as they could be, no doubt clearing off old scores before the fête of St Peter's which was the day after, some of them were shaking their heads as if the disclosures were very shocking indeed & twice we saw the penitents kissing the priests hands so I suppose they had been let off easily. Never was there a place that so swarmed with priests and friars as Naples, you do not see them in 1s & 2s but in 6s & 7s marshalling about schools of young ones that are perfectly horrible to think of & they wear the strangest dresses, some of them all in black with black silk stockings & tights & others with purple stockings & gloves, & stock & a cord of the same colour around their hats, some have scarlet stockings & a scarlet cord on their hats, some have a purple cassock with red buttons & button holes, the monk's dresses are generally brown or black, but some of them wear white capes etc which gives them very much the appearance of old women. We did not stay long at the cathedral but went to the Museum where we saw the

Naples from the Villa Reale, 28th June 1847

very valuable collections of Antiques from Herculaneum, Pompeii & Rome, the vases, mosaics & bronzes from Pompeii were very interesting to us, & of course are all the best that have been found there, & very perfect they are, but it seemed to me rather absurd to find uses for all the relics, for instance some small carved ivory things, they called shirt buttons, & several other things they have given names to, perhaps very far from the truth & as I believe it is not actually known who the inhabitants of Pompeii were at the time of its destruction it is rather ridiculous to button their shirts with ivory studs. There are several sorts of provisions that were found, bread, corn, flour, dough unbaked, except by time & Vesuvius & several kinds of nuts & fruit, there is a very fine collection of statues and a gallery of very poor pictures among them a portrait of Masanielle[5], & a picture containing a sort of history of his revolution, a very valuable collection of gems, & gold & silver ornaments from Pompeii & several other collections that we got too tired to see, more especially as in Egyptian treasures & one or two other sorts of collections our own Museum is superior to most others. So we staid until the Museum closed at two, & then stopping for some ices on our way we returned home, & there we staid until 7 when the carriage came again to take us for a drive & we went to the Cemetery about 2 miles from Naples, a beautiful place very nicely kept like a flower garden, a little in the style of Père La Chaise[6], but not so full of sentiment & frippery. It was laid out by Murat when King of Naples & nobody is allowed to be buried nearer the town, the rich folks have family chapels & vaults & there are catacombs for those who cannot afford a chapel & the very poor are buried in pits of which there are 366, one of these pits is opened every morning, the bodies are thrown in and in the evening it is closed for a year. We saw one of the yards where these pits were, all covered down & paved but with a trap door to each pit, but our curiosity did not lead us so far as to look into the open pit, the gardener who went over the place with us gave us a beautiful bouquet each, of white china roses & fuchsia & we staid as long as our time would allow looking at the splendid view & enjoying the pleasant freshness of the gardens, for we had had a tremendous shower of rain in the afternoon and it had made every thing fresh & cool. We had the pleasure too as we returned to see Vesuvius shooting red flame several times. We went on our return to a curious little theatre San Carlino, where the beauty of the performance consists in the Actors close imitation of the dialect & gestures of the lower orders of Neapolitans, but as the Natives they say, cannot always understand them it was rather Heathen greek to us, however as we got a private box for 4/- it was not an expensive amusement, it was a nasty dirty little place of course, & another disadvantage at Naples is that none of the Entertainments begin before 9 or half past, which does very well for people that sit up all night & sleep all day.

Tuesday June 29 It was the fete of St Peter & all business was suspended for the day, shops closed & every body making holiday. In the evening the band played in the garden & all Naples & the neighbourhood were driving & walking about in such gay colours as even negroes would have envied & the shouting & singing & noises of all sorts nobody can imagine, the unearthly howls that the men make at their animals when they are driving, which they do at such a pace as to be perfectly frightful. We treated ourselves to a little music from one of the Piferari[7] who walk about carrying their pipes & a bench to sit upon & a couple of puppets that they cause to dance by means of a string tied to their knees. The instrument is something like the bag pipes but far more musical, & the tune I suppose the same that the old woman's cow died of.

Wednesday June 30 We had a second visit – close in shore – from a huge fish, porpoise or shark that was hunting the smaller tribes & jumped quite out of the water now and then, I was in hopes the fishermen would pursue him but I supppose he was not worth the trouble, John went in the morning to find a manufactory of porcelain like the Etruscan, we did not go out but worked & wrote, I wrote a very respectable long letter to Gilbert. We dined at 4 & then had a carriage & went to see the Grotto del Cane[8], so called from their amusing the visitors by putting in a dog to be smothered by the fumes of Carbonic acid that rise from the ground. It is a very small hole & we just crept in & waved the vapour up into our faces to try its effect which was most singular, they say ten minutes would kill a man & I should say five would be quite enough, as the dog was not in ½ a minute before he was quite stupified, & reeled about when he was brought into the air as if he was tipsey, the guide lighted a torch several times which was instantly extinguished by the vapour which lies along the bottom of the cave & at a little distance looks like water. We went afterwards into another part of the rock where there were fumes of ammonia which the guide told us was as good as Champagne & a capital thing for the appetite, we tried it in the same way as the other by waving the hot fumes into our faces but did not discover the Champagne properties. We next went into a series of small caverns full of sulphurous vapours & so hot that it was like going into a stove, the inner we really found too hot to venture into, the rock had several apertures & when the guide held a light to them it seemed to tempt out a perfect cloud of vapour, there is a sort of bath that he says is much used by people affected with rheumatism. We were not sorry to get out of these nasty places without being suffocated or any further injury than turning a glove red that had been exposed to the fumes of sulphur. The lake of Agnáno is situated in the midst of these volcanic caverns & is quite hot 4 feet below the surface, & quite unuseable as water & any body sleeping in the air near it is affected with violent illness, it seems to agree with the frogs for I never saw such myriads & all of a beautiful green colour. There is said to be a villa of Lucullus[9] under the lake but it has always been a mystery what the bottom is, as the water is frequently in a boiling state & bubbles up continually, they say some time ago there were 8 or 10 men made up their minds to dive & see what there was, but they were never seen again, & any thing thrown in sinks & never rises again. The Prince of Capua has a small hunting seat here, very small for I think there are not more than two rooms and his Chasseur a very handsome man in a very shabby dress was our conductor. We had a beautiful but rather dusty ride home again after sunset, we passed again through the grotto of Posillipo on our way, John presented us with a beautiful bouquet of carnations, hydrangea, geraniums & verbena & I dont know what else but it must have been two feet round, for which the man asked 2 carlini, but was quite content with one, 4d the cheapest nosegay I ever saw & so sweet. The country round Naples is very well cultivated & the crops when we saw them were principally maize, wheat, haricots, hemp, & the palma christi or castor oil palm, which is a very beautiful crop, the potatoes they say have been plentiful & good all the year, & there is no sign of scarcity now, for a great many of the poor seem chiefly to live on them, & they are cooked in huge caldrons in the streets & sold by weight and must be very cheap, as the poor labourers here do not earn on an average above a penny a day & out of that have to pay for wine, which they will not any of them do without, they cannot even afford salt to their potatoes, it is both dear & bad here. At night while we were at tea as a specimen of the delights of an Italian life, a flea hopped from my head into the butter & there stuck, what should we think of such an event in England, yet here it only caused amusement, not surprise, I could not even rejoice that I was rid of an enemy, for I had plenty left, more to my sorrow.

Thursday July 1 The whole morning a pouring rain with thunder & lightening. Notwithstanding we went after breakfast to Rothschild's the bankers & then to the Etruscan manufactory, where we saw a variety of beautiful things, John ordered a great many, among them some tiles for the passage at Shirley, & then we returned home. The evening was close but fine & we walked up a tremendous steep to the fortress of St Elmo that overlooks Naples, thinking we should get a beautiful view of the bay, but when we got there the view was only landwards. John got up on the elevation on which the fortress stands to see what he could from there, but a sentinel called out to him in an awful manner from the fort, to down so I suppose he thought John was going to take his castle away from him, & it did not seem very easy either, the walk home again was not very pleasant, as the streets are so thronged in the evening as to be quite disagreable, & the carriages drive at such a pace, & have no curb stone to keep them in their proper ranks, so that there is no protection for foot passengers but shouting & that is heard to perfection in the streets of Naples. John treated us to a sight of

the legitimate drama today, viz: Pulchinella, the original Punch being a native of this city, it was much the same as the English version except that there is no baby killed & Punch is dressed all in white with a black mask.

Friday July 2 We walked directly after breakfast into the Villa Reale or public garden & walked nearly the whole length of the beautiful avenue of olives the like of which is not I should think to be met with elsewhere in the wide world. John left us to go to the post office, & Anne & I staid while she took a couple of drawings, we were hurried home by fear of storm for the clouds were very threatening & the showers of Naples are no joke, we sat at home the rest of the day which was the festa of St[a] Maria della Grazia & only the 4th holiday in one week that all the

From the Villa Reale at Naples, looking towards Posillipo, 28th June 1847

shops had been closed & no business done except by my favourite priests. Part of my entertainment during the day was watching two little coffee coloured boys that had established themselves on the curb stones opposite the windows & were at all sorts of tricks, begging & whining out their appeals for bread & money, & saying perhaps they should die of hunger, & then bursting out into such a merry laugh that I could not help laughing too, & then one of them proposed singing a barcarole & forthwith commenced & at last when he had fairly gained a trifle of money out of us, he set off with such a caper as was perfectly irresistible, they are a funny set the lazzaroni, for if they fail in whining a coin or two out of you, they generally grin & set your mind quite at rest as to the risk of their starving & yet except the Irish[10] never were a set of such half naked tatterdemalions seen. We did not go out any more that day as we had seen all we thought was worth taking the trouble to see.

Saturday July 3 Got up at five, & at six a man came for the luggage & at 8 we set off in a pouring rain in the Diligence for Rome. We had a coupé to ourselves & were thankful to find there were very few other people going & most thankful that the rain would cool the air & lay the dust, we passed through Capua a curious dirty old town but only staid there to change horses of which we had five when we started & either 4, 5, 6 or 7 during the journey according to the road. The country all the way was rich beyond imagination, vines trained in every possible festoon either from the trees or high poles with crossbars at the top for the plants to trail over, whole orchards of orange and lemon and pomegranate trees as large as our moderate sized apple trees, & the latter in full bloom, the most beautiful things that ever were seen, then there were long tracks with olive trees not by any means so beautiful, & then chesnut & almond trees, then perhaps all together, the crops generally speaking maize, or lupins the latter quite ripe or stubble where wheat had been growing and where the women were carrying the sheaves away on their heads & large quantities of hemp which is a rich beautiful crop. The people too in this part of Italy are most exceedingly handsome, tall well shaped figures with the most beautiful intelligent faces that ever were seen, & with more of the national costume than we had met with before. We were sadly plagued with beggars every time the coach stopped to change horses, but they did it very quickly and indeed the whole travelling so far as speed & roominess were concerned, was much better than we expected, the great drawback is the entire want of accomodation for travellers in respect of refreshment. We were ten hours before we stopped anywhere & then we had ¾ of an hour allowed for dinner & then no more than ¼ of an hour during the remainder of the journey of upwards of 30 hours. We staid to dinner at Mola di Gacta, a dirty little fishing town, but in a lovely bay of the sea, we had some very tough lamb and fish dressed in very rancid oil & one or two other delicacies that we managed to satisfy our hunger with and then proceeded again through a fine hilly country as long as we could see, for it gets dark much sooner in Italy than it does in England. The hedgerows were bright and beautiful with all sorts of colours, the pink everlasting pea & a very large white convolvulus & a few wild roses, mixed with the green of the vines & huge olive trees, many of them in bloom, and the cactus & fig, the acacia & pomegranate & bright scarlet berries of the wild arum. After dark we some of us went to sleep & with the exception of waking up when we changed the horses when we sometimes saw a curious sight of the natives at mess, & smelt a curious & unpleasant odour of their favourite garlic, we got on very quickly until we reached Terracina the scene of Fra Diavolo[11] & where I expect a few years back Banditti was a more common word of fear than it is now. We stopped here just at midnight as this was the Roman frontier and we had to proceed in a Roman carriage & have our luggage examined which was a mere form in our case and only intended we thought to give John the opportunity to offer a bribe, which he did not choose to do. In about ¼ an hour we were again en route and again we were fortunate enough to get a coupé to ourselves, the only other passengers being a quiet old German and his daughter who had come all the way from Naples. We again betook ourselves to slumber which lasted until daybreak when we found ourselves nearly across the Pontine marshes, at six we stopped to change horses & were allowed ¼ of an hour for breakfast but such a dirty hole of a cafe, the only place we could find open there, the coffee & bread produced were hardly useable by us, but a little wretch of a boy, a true Italian, (thief to the backbone) while our backs were turned rushed into the place, pocketed the bread we had left & stood looking as unconscious as a statue. We continued our route, for some time rather hilly & winding through fine shady avenues & at last came to the plain on which Rome stands, we passed the Monument supposed to be that of the Horatii and Curiatii, a hideous old concern, & at one part of the road some men and women were threshing their wheat[12] & the Diligence drove right through it, I should fancy the road was not much frequented or the corn would be high flavoured when done. We at last came in sight of Rome which is situated on a plain surrounded by hills so that you see it lying before you for miles before you come to it, we came first to one old ruin & then another, all more or less rubbishing looking, until as we got nearer the city we came in sight of an immense aqueduct which has still remains of beauty. As we entered the city we saw the Colosseum & then went to the temple of Augustus to be searched again, just as if we could have furnished ourselves with any quantity of contraband goods between Terracina & Rome when we had never left the Diligence for one moment except to breakfast, by courtesy so called & then were never out of sight, it made us rather rabid to be detained again & more so to be at last obliged to pay a bribe to be let off easy, but the man here asked straight forward for it, & as if it had been refused we should most likely have been made to suffer in proportion, it was paid & we were suffered to depart with our packages all unopened save one. We were thankful to be received very politely & comfortably provided at the Hotel d'Allemagne, and spent the rest of the day in as quiet a manner as possible. John had a ½ hour's strole but we did not go out.

Sightseeing in Rome

July 5th to July 12th

THE VILLA MEDICI · THE VILLA BORGHESE · THE BASILICA OF ST PETER · THE CAPITOL · THE COLOSSEUM · HIS HOLINESS THE POPE · ST JEAN LATERAN · BY CARRIAGE TO TIVOLI · THE VATICAN GALLERIES · THE PANTHEON · THE SISTINE CHAPEL · SANTA MARIA MAGGIORE · THE TARPEIAN ROCK

Sightseeing in Rome
July 5th to July 12th

Monday July 5 After breakfast John went to the post office but there was such a crowd that he got tired of waiting & came away without his letters & then we all went out together and found our way first to the gardens of the Villa Medici. The house has been most highly ornamented with bas reliefs & is still in very good preservation, but such a deserted quiet looking place, the gardens are long straight walks almost like a labyrinth enclosed by box hedges 14 or 15 ft high & ornamented with statues or fountains, all out of repair, very shady & delightful for a walk in very hot weather but entirely without any beauty whatever, the Villa is now used as an academy for the Beaux Arts, belongs to the French Government & the pupils are sent from Paris. The Villa Borghese, the grounds of which we also walked into, is still inhabited by that family, there was very little beauty in these grounds, but in our wanderings about we now and then got a peep into something like a garden & saw some splendid magnolias & the double pomegranate as big as china roses & so full of bloom, but nothing at all like flowers did we see, a few poor drawn up french marigolds & a few very bad dahlias were the best we saw, no sweetpeas, no mignonette, no nothing. We now made our way into the city passing through the Place du Popolo, an immense square with an Egyptian obelisk in the centre & statues all round, the people were very busy taking down the stands that the illuminations had been fixed to, during the great fête of St Peter which was just over. We passed through the Place Navona where there is an immense group in bronze forming a fountain and also a fruit market, & the immense heaps of apricots were quite a sight, the vegetables never look fresh in the Italian markets & generally have a stale unpleasant smell, they keep them constantly watered which with the heat of the sun naturally produces very speedy decomposition & makes the markets any thing but sweet. At last we found our way to St Peter's & no description can give any idea of its excessive richness of decoration & yet without the grandness of many of the churches we had seen before, the inlaid marbles & splendid mosaics, the latter copied from celebrated pictures with figures larger than life but so finely executed that we were discussing whether one of them was a painting on canvas or a fresco, when we discovered on a close examination that it was mosaic, the Altars are almost all mosaic in beautiful arabesque patterns & the immense marble statues of Popes & Saints are without number. We were too tired & hot to examine the church properly, so we sat down on a bench until we were a little cooled & rested & then just walked round the Cathedral & looked at some of the statues & monuments & among them found a very beautiful one by Canova to the memory of the three last members of the Stewart family or as they were here called the sons of James 3rd of England. There are three bas relief profiles of the princes & at the bottom of the monument two most exquisite weeping figures at the door of a mausoleum, opposite this monument is one erected to their mother, the wife of the said James 3rd. The church was so deliciously cool that we felt quite unwilling to turn out again into the broiling sun, but we could not starve, so were obliged to seek for food to sustain our fainting natures, & we had to seek a long time, for the Roman pastry cooks are by no means nice looking, however at last we met with some cake & very nice lemonade which gave us strength to reach home[1] once more. In coming out of St Peter's we passed the staircase of the Vatican & there we saw two of the Pope's guard, such objects as I never saw, their dress seemed entirely composed of shreds of scarlet & yellow & all hanging loose like a fools dress, their hats black with a long scarlet horsehair feather on one side, they were both seated half asleep as Italian guards always are so we could not fully estimate the beauty of their appearance, but hope for a nearer & better view. We dined at 4 quite alone though called a table d'hote and then Anne & I went into the Corso to buy some things we wanted, & John staid at home writing & battling with the flies & fleas which exceed every thing one can imagine at Rome, its no use catching them at all. In the evening two of us were in bed & the other preparing when we were all roused by a great noise in the street & on looking out, we saw a tremendous crowd of men carrying flambeaux & shouting & then we noticed that many of the houses were illuminated, one opposite had a bust of the Pope with a row of lamps & tall candles burning in front of it, the crowd stopped & shouted below this house & then proceeded to the end of the street, where there was a fountain[2] which they paraded round & then extinguished their torches & returned again hissing & hooting at the houses that were not lighted up. We found on enquiring the next morning that the Pope had been establishing a national guard, which he had long wished to do in opposition to the Cardinals, & at last had done it on his own responsibility, & the people were accordingly making a fuss with his Holiness.

Tuesday July 6 We had a carriage & valet at ½ past 9 & went to see some of the Antiquities, first we went to the Arch of Septimus Severus, & if we had not been roasted alive we might have admired it very much, but the Sun was shining full upon the spot & verily it was hot. We went next to see the Mamertine prison where St Peter was confined when the Angel opened the prison doors, we had to descend two flights of dark steps into the dungeon, on the rock by the side of the staircase they shew an impression of a face, which they say is that of St Peter whom the gaoler struck against the wall & his face left its likeness on the rock. He must have been a hardfaced mortal, & people must be rather softer than him now, to listen to such nonsense with common patience, in the dungeon they shew the pillar to which he was chained & a spring of pure water which they said miraculously appeared at St Peter's bidding when he wished to baptise his gaoler, 'another tale for the Marines'. We went next to the Capitol where there is a museum of very fine antique statuary & some very ordinary pictures, two or three of Guido's[3], very beautiful, & a very interesting collection of busts of Italian poets & other great men by Canova. On the top of the principal staircase of the Capitol are two huge figures with horses, the statues supposed to be Castor and Pollux, the horses, from their being out of all proportion, we supposed to be favourite Shetland ponies belonging to the aforementioned worthies. There is a magnificent Statue of Marcus Aurelius[4] on horseback, but the abomination of all these things is that they none of them stand where they used to do, but have all been moved by the munificence & stupidity of one or other of the Popes, I do wish they had let them alone, that I do. There is a curious old Palace shewn in the Capitol, full of old inscriptions & statues & hung with very curious old tapestry. We did not go to see the Tarpeian rock, as the Valet said it was not worth seeing & it was so excessively hot that our energies were well nigh exhausted. We next went through the Arches of Constantine & Titus & past the columns of Trajan & Phocas to the Colosseum, & there we got out, & as well as the heat permitted examined the immense place, the size of which one can hardly imagine even when on the spot, it is very much more ruinous than the one at Pompeii, but must have been once a perfect wonder. Now, with the usual bad taste there is a crucifix put up in the centre & stations for pilgrims to pray at all round the interior, just as if there were not enough churches in Rome, but they must needs pray in the remains of an old theatre. Our guide now humanely proposed that we should return home on account of the heat, & we were very glad to accede to his polite proposal, seeing in our way a splendid fountain[5], we dined at 2 in order that we might go in the evening to see the Pope go out for his drive, which we were all most anxious to do. At 4 we set off in our voiture once more & went to the Baths of Titus, a curious collection of large vaults & high brick walls, very beautiful brickwork certainly & with here & there very slight remains of painting & other ornaments, the history they give of this building, is that originally Mecoenas had a villa on the same spot the only remains of which is a piece of black & white mosaic pavement, this villa was burnt in the time of Nero, who built one for himself on the ruins, which Titus added to. It has been entirely buried in earth & is now being excavated by degrees, the celebrated group of the Laocoon was found here. We had to go twice over this immense place, first with a stupid old dolt that knew nothing about it & then with a proper guide, who was absent when we first arrived, many of the places were quite dark & we had wax tapers to light us about & to light up the paintings. We now found it was time for us to go & watch for his Holiness, so we went to the Palace on the Quirinal Hill where he lives, & here just as we arrived the carriage drove up to the foot of the staircase & the guard who always accompany him, composed of young Roman nobles on

Pope Pius IX entering his carriage at the Quirinal palace, Rome, 6th July 1847

horseback in uniform & with helmets on. The carriage is crimson & gold & the livery purple & crimson, the carriage a large old fashioned coach & the Pope's seat is like an armchair on the back seat of the vehicle & his two attendants sit opposite, but I must put back a little. Soon after the carriage came the body guard & two of them stationed themselves at the foot of the staircase & we took our places close to them & there we stood for about ½ an hour anxiously watching every symptom of approach, & first the coachman a fat rosy looking old fellow put on his gloves very leisurely, then the carriage was drawn up quite close to the steps, then a man came down with something like a large umbrella in a case & which I suppose was the canopy they hold over him when he walks, then when we were all on the tiptoe of expectation down came a reverend old priest who had been getting some medals blessed, to be either given away or sold. Our valet asked him to let John look at them which he very goodnaturedly did, then presently the footman opened the door of the carriage & some more of the guard came down the staircase & at last, the great man himself, dressed completely in some sort of white woollen stuff, made in the same shape as the priests black dresses and a small white cap on his head. He is a remarkably sensible intelligent goodlooking man & seemed to take a glance round & see everybody and everything that was there, looks like a perfect gentleman, very elegant in his manner & a most pleasant smile, for as he drove away he gave the assembly his benediction, & the expression of his face was most agreable. He had two priests in purple dresses in the carriage with him, & was most warmly cheered by a great many people who had assembled in the streets to see him pass. We were most delighted at having seen him so well, for he will some day assuredly make a noise in the world, the people even now appeal to him as he drives out not to give way to the Cardinals or Priests, & he is very much beloved because he will listen to the appeal of the meanest or poorest person, he looks like a good man but if he is he will not long remain Pope[6], for no good man would consent to carry on the trickery & deceit necessary to that office. I forgot to mention that before we went to see the Pope we went into a small but very richly ornamented chapel to see the preparations for the funeral of the Mother of the Cardinal Barberini, the whole building was hung with black velvet with broad gold lace, & the altar with black velvet lined with gold coloured silk & gold lace several inches broad, the coffin stood in front of the altar on a very high catafalque surrounded by lighted tapers. We went into two or three of the smaller chapels, which were all very highly adorned with marbles & fine mosaic altars, & under one of them was a figure in a glass case that they said was the real body of St Victoria, with a large gash in her throat & a very handsome blue silk dress, & flaxen wig. We said we thought it was wax, but they assured us it was the real body & shewed us the bones inside one of the hands & sure enough there were the bones of a hand, but it was some artful popistical trick I'm sure. We went when the Pope had driven off to the church of St Jean Lateran, the oldest in Rome, & one of the most profusely adorned, but we did not go so much to see the church as to see a ceremony performed only once a year when the Senator of Rome goes in state to pray before the heads of St Peter & St Paul which they profess to have enclosed in a chrystal case & raised on an ornamented shrine in front of the high altar, there are two heads there, no doubt, but the doubt is, whose? When we entered the church the shrine containing the relics was lighted up & there were processions of priests in red & white dresses with their cowls over their heads parading the church and praying in front of the altar. The procession arrived in about 8 or 10 carriages with a great many walking footmen in all sorts of strange dresses, the carriages very gaily painted & gilded. The senator was the Count Orsini & he was accompanied by five gentlemen, all the five were dressed in a loose robe of cloth of gold & behind them were 4 pages in crimson & gold, they all walked into the church & prostrated themselves before the relics & remained praying for some time, everybody that liked kneeled down, but very few liked, as the pavement was rather hard & when the grandees had finished their devotions they all went out of the church again in the same order & got into the carriages again & away they went. We went down under the church to see the cloisters which are still very magnificent, they are supported by fluted columns which have been beautifully inlaid with mosaic, the columns are tolerably perfect but a great deal of the mosaic has been picked out. They show here 4 columns with a slab over the top, which they say is the exact height of our Saviour, also several columns from Pilate's house at Jerusalem. The large equestrian Statue of Marcus Aurelius on the Capitol was found in these cloisters, I suppose buried under the earth. Near this church stands what they call the Holy Staircase, said to be the stairs of Pilate's house, which our Lord ascended, the holy steps are all now cased in brass, & nobody is allowed to ascend them except on their knees, they only lead to a small altar at the top & as there are steps on each side of them, we went up one side & down the other, but we saw two people going up the holy staircase on their knees, a poor man & a very respectably dressed woman, and a very awkward operation it seemed, of course there were contributions to be made by the true believers. We now returned home very hot & tired, & delivered ourselves up to the mercy of the fleas & Roman fleas have no mercy and are numberless.

Wednesday July 7 We at six o'clock mounted a Roman chariot, very shabby & of a singular boat like shape, to go to Tivoli, three hours from Rome. The ride is hideous & unpleasant, country like a desert & nothing beautiful except the lizards, the cattle with their large wide spreading horns & the occasional banks of wild flowers, close to the road side, the scarlet poppies, the bugloss, yellow celsia, bindweed & many others in profusion made a lovely variety of colours, we stopped half way to see the deposites of a volcanic lake, & very curious shapes it took, like sticks & weeds petrified. The first thing we went to see at Tivoli was the site of Adrian's Villa, an enormous place that the Emperor made a plaything of, it was 7 miles round & enclosed his own imperial palace, two or three temples, a large space for his guard & their horses & a piece of ground for them to exercise in, but the most amusing part was a miniature street with shops that he built & called Alexandria, where they sold wine & water & ices etc for the amusement of himself and friends, who used to sail to it in boats, across a river or lake that was constructed on purpose. There is little now remaining but bare walls & an immense sort of tunnel that was originally the entrance to the imperial Palace, there are still remaining the walls of the temples of Venus & Minerva which stood close together, but very few remains of painting or other ornament. We did not go the circuit of the 7 miles, but saw quite enough to give us a good idea of the size it must have been & the views on all sides were lovely, looking over a valley rich with olives and other trees & bounded by mountains. We had to go three miles to the small & dirty village of Tivoli where there is a small dirty Inn, the traveller's only refuge, where they put up with what they cant help. Here we had some lunch, bread & figs, & then John mounted a horse & we mounted donkeys & set off to make the tour of the cascade, we first descended to the grotto of Neptune, an immense cavern where the water rushes & roars down what looks like the bottomless pit, a dreadful place where the guide told us there were generally one or two travellers lost every year by being too venturesome, next we ascended to the tunnel that has been cut for the principal fall, the bed of which has been turned into quite a different direction to prevent its washing away a part of the village which stood just above it, they have rather spoiled the fall by their contrivance as it has now a more artificial look. We made the complete tour of the falls, of which the largest is called the cascade, the next in size the cascatella & two or three lesser ones the cascatellina, the latter used to ornament the villa of Mecoenas, but are now used in iron works, the Villa having departed this world.

We had a beautiful but burning ride of some two hours, the principal trees here are olives of immense age, as we returned to the Inn we stopped to see the Villa d'Este which was painted in fresco with representations of the history of Tivoli. It belonged to the Cardinal d'Este who was the last occupant, & when he died it came into the possession of the Duke of Modena who never took the trouble even to go and see it, & the present duke his son has followed his example, so there is the beautiful place going to ruin, the frescoes all perishing from damp & the pleasure grounds & fountains innumerable that adorned the villa are all falling to pieces & choked up with rubbish, it seems a great pity, but every body knows his own business best, & except the beauty of the country round there is nothing enticing in its situation for Tivoli is a very poor looking wretched place. We returned now to the hotel and were very glad to dismount from our steeds as the harness was not of a satisfactory nature & kept us in a state of doubt whether it would last until we got to the end of our ride, Anne took a sketch or two of the Cascade & then we had a very nasty dinner which thanks to the 4 dogs belonging to the Hotel we made a respectable hole in, the poor brutes looked quite starved and I should think do not often dine on beef steak & maccaroni, but they did that day owing to the entire nastiness of both those preparations. We dined in the open air under the remains of the Temple of Vesta & just in front of the cascade, so what could we care for eating, luckily the dogs did, so we spared the feelings of the providers of the feast & our own at the same time. At five we returned home, the evening was very close & hot & the country as I said before little else than a bare plain, dotted with the miserable remains of buildings, several traces of the old roads, which were composed of very large masses of stone very rough to ride over.

Thursday July 8 We sat at home in the morning except John who went to take our places for Florence, 48 hours at a stretch, in such weather, very dreadful to think of, but better than 4 days Vetturino with the filthy ruins to sleep at, would we were out of Italy. In the afternoon we went to see the antique statue galleries at the Vatican, which are only open on Thursday from 4 until dusk, we walked through the numerous rooms and saw some very fine mosaics from Adrian's Villa at Tivoli, and other places, the celebrated group of the Laocoon found in the baths of Titus, the real Apollo Belvedere, & Antinous & innumerable other statues & vases & baths & also some very fine pictures, Raphael's 'transfiguration', which is considered his masterpiece, a most beautiful picture by Guido of the Madonna, St Thomas & St Jerome, & one by Guercino of the 'Incredulity of St Thomas'. The principal painter of the Vatican was Raphael who was employed expressly by two of the Popes for that purpose, & painted many of the apartments & outside galleries, unfortunately the latter have been, in the course of ages, very much injured by damp, but there are still remains of beautiful arabesques & figures, there are copies of Raphael's cartoons in tapestry very much faded & rubbishing looking, but it is useless to try to describe the innumerable treasures in a place that contains 12,000 apartments & 200 staircases. We staid until we were tired & then returned home & John went to see a performance at a daylight theatre which he was very much pleased with. We were very lucky in our valet de place, a most intelligent spry old gentleman, the merriest for his age & size that I ever saw I think, for he trotted about in the heat like a perfect salamander & would not agree that it was so very hot, when we were all but baked. He told us a great deal of the present state of feeling respecting the Pope, that he has perpetual battles with the Cardinals, because he wishes to abolish the observance of so many feasts & festivals & says the people cant afford to keep so many idle days & that it is far better that they should work for their families, he also talks of making some of the numerous communities of priests & monks herd together & give up their houses & properties for the use of the poor, and of course his clergy do not like all that sort of thing at all so I think there will be some fun one of these days, John saw three of the Cardinals going in state to the Pope's levee. Our old guide was a great admirer of Napoleon who, he said, had made very fine plans for the improvement of Rome if he had lived to execute them, at any rate he was very unsparing in his improvements for he intended pulling down all the streets that stand on the same side of the river as St Peter & the Vatican, & he did pull down two churches that stood over Trajan's forum, excavated the forum, & so opened a space round Trajan's magnificent pillar, which must have been nearly buried before.

Cascade at Tivoli. 7th July 1847

Friday July 9 At 8 o'clock we went to the Church of St Pietro in Vinculo where there are some fine works by Michael Angelo, one of them the full length figure of our Saviour with the foot cased in bronze to prevent its being kissed away. Then we went to St Stephano Rotunda, where we did not linger long, for it was decorated all round with the most disgusting pictures of Martyrdoms, in the centre was a small marble model of a church, which they said contained the ashes of St Stephen. Next we went to the Pantheon which is used as a church and is in very good preservation, as good as the Goths & Vandals left it, for they took away the bronze doors & ornaments of the Portico. Here Raphael & Annibal Carracci are buried, the bones of the former were found about 6 years ago very perfect, there were 4 priests performing the service in the different altars, but nobody seemed taking any notice of them, there is a statue here which was once a Vestal but is now called the Madonna, what's in a name? We went next to the Vatican & saw the Sistine Chapel which is only used at Easter, which they call the Holy week, when very grand ceremonies are performed there, here the Last Judgement by Michael Angelo & several more of his paintings are seen. They tell a curious story of him, that when he was painting the Last Judgement there was an old priest that used to go & talk to him & tease him so much that to punish him he painted a likeness of him in Hell, at which the priest was so angry that he appealed to the Pope to have the portrait altered, but the Pope told him that as a priest he ought to know that no prayers could deliver him from Hell, that if he had only been in Purgatory he might have been able to get him out by his prayers. We went over the Popes apartments in the Vatican, they are now never used as he always lives at the Quirinal, there was nothing remarkable about them except his little dining table, for the Pope always dines alone. Next we went to see a few valuable manuscripts in the library of the Vatican, they have some very old illuminated works & Poems in the handwriting of Petrarch, Tasso, Boccaccio etc, the library is an immense place in very good order, the galleries all ornamented with frescoes & one of them contains a splendid Malachite vase from the Emperor of Russia & a very fine Sevres vase, a present from Charles 10 of France. They have a collection of curiosities found in the Temples, among them some instruments of torture that our valet told us were used to Martyrdom the Christians, some very fine cameos & a great many other works of art that would take a twelvemonth of cool weather to see. We returned home, taking ices in our way, for a rest of a couple of hours, during the midday heat, which nobody who has not felt it can possibly imagine, neither would anybody be likely to imagine a tolerable decent clean old lady having the fleas perpetually hopping out of the sleeves of her dress into the butter or anything else that happened to be in the way, but travellers see strange things especially in Italy. We passed the celebrated remains of the statue of Pasquino[7] the satirical tailor, the place where all the Satirical effusions of ancient Rome used to make their appearance, there is only a small part of the figure left now at the corner of one of the streets. At two o'clock we went to the Doria Palace to see the pictures, some very fine ones, some very much the reverse, the Princess Doria is the daughter of the Marquis Shrewsbury & her sister married the Prince Borghese, & died at the age of 22 very much respected for her charities & good works in Rome, it was pleasant to hear a country woman so spoken of, though she was a papist. We went next to the Villa Spada which was laid out in the 16th century, it has been now for 40 years the property of an Englishman who is now spending a large sum in adding to & adorning it, from the grounds there is a good view of part of the ruins of Rome, & the villa itself is built over the remains of the palace of Augustus, whose dining room we looked down into like a well in the garden. We went afterwards to the Church of the Capuchins where there are some fine paintings, the Church of St Jean en Fonte or Baptistry of Lateran where there is a very valuable font which is always used when a Jew or Heathen is baptised into the Romish faith, a ceremony generally performed with much state on Easter Eve or as they call it Holy Saturday. Then we went to St Pierre in Vincoli, where they profess to have the chains with which St Peter was bound at Rome & Antioch & which chains on being brought to Rome miraculously joined together of themselves, they are kept in a closet of which the Pope keeps the key, & they are shewn with much ceremony once a year, in this church is Michael Angelo's celebrated Statue of Moses with the tables of the law, under the Chapel in a vault is the first Christian altar that was erected at Rome. We looked into two or three other Churches & then went to the museum in the Palais Lateran containing some antiques in the statuary line that had been rejected at the Vatican, & among the other dusty old relics that are kept on the shelf here, is a huge portrait of that vain old wretch George 4th in his coronation robes by Lawrence which he sent as a present to the Pope, & which the Pope evidently didn't want. The great curiosity here is the mosaic pavement from the Baths of Caracalla, one piece is very beautiful, an interlaced wreath with groupes of fruit, but the other is curious only, or rather disgusting, portraits of his gladiators, the size of life & perfectly naked, except two of them & such horrible looking wretches, it gives one an idea of the taste of the worthy gentleman who could love such toys, some were full length portraits & some only half length & divided by a border into square compartments, so that there is no beauty to recommend it at all, but it is very perfect & a very large size & we had to go up into a gallery & look down at it. After this we were too tired to go any where else, so we returned home to dinner & rest for the evening. One of the curiosities of the day I must not forget, a scorpion that was crawling over the pavement of one of the churches, it was black & just the shape of a small lobster, it was running very fast & I stopped it with the end of my parasol & asked the man what it was & he said it was a bad beast, we proposed that it was a scorpion & he agreed that we were right.

Saturday July 10 John was not well so would not go out in the morning but Anne & I wound up courage to see as much as we could & at 8 o'clock we had a carriage, for walking was impossible in such excessive heat & went to the church of St[a] Maria del Angeli, which was built on the site & with the remains of the baths of Dioclesian. There 8 only of the ancient columns remaining, of a sort of brown porphyry & above 40 ft high, the others are made to match them as nearly as possible, there are some very fine paintings, also a valuable fresco that was removed from the Pantheon & is kept carefully curtained, our guide could not find any one to draw the curtain so did it himself, but the noise of the rings brought out a couple of pale faced monks from

a side door who came gliding in & did not seem at all pleased at our having unveiled their picture, however a small donation had the usual soothing effect, Salvator Rosa & Carlo Maratta are both buried in this church. We went now to St^{a} Maria Maggiore near the ruins of Juno Lucina, they say that two of the Saints were commanded in a dream to build a church on the spot where they should find snow the following day, August 5th, the hottest month in the year, & the next day there was a fall of snow that just covered the space where the church now stands, such is the tradition of the building of St^{a} Maria Maggiore[8], it is partly built of the remains of the temple of Constantine, there are 4 rows of magnificent columns & a great part of the ceiling is composed of exceedingly rich mosaic, but the most costly part is the Borghese Chapel of which Canova said there was not a single foot, that was not priceless for beauty and rarity. It is a perfect mass of sculpture & precious marbles & stones & in the middle is a raised altar on which is the Sacred Host, under the Altar is a small shrine where lights are kept constantly burning, there is another chapel almost equally rich belonging to the Doria family & they are the burying places of the two familys who have numbered many Cardinals & several Popes whose monuments are here. I should like to have staid here to listen to the beautiful music but time would not wait, there seems much less service going on in the churches in Rome than in the other cities where we have been staying, here & there we saw a priest in one of the small chapels moving about his properties as if he was performing some culinary business, but generally the churches were quite deserted. We next went to the Palazzo Rospigliosi ornamented most richly with bas reliefs & busts & statues from the baths of Constantine, there is a beautiful ceiling by Guido, the subject is 'Aurora' & in the picture gallery there are a series of half length pictures by Rubens of Our Saviour & his twelve Apostles, that are very beautiful indeed, it is a very small collection of paintings but I should fancy a very valuable one. The entrance to the palace through the garden, a long walk under a trellis 10 ft high covered with lemon trees with the ripe lemons hanging through in quantities, was one of the most beautiful things I ever saw. We afterwards went to the Palazzo Spada to see the Statue of Pompey at the foot of which Caesar was killed, they shew a red mark on the leg that they say was made by Caesar's blood, but that is rather absurd, there is also a small gallery of pictures here. Next we went to the Corsini Palace where there is a large gallery of very fine paintings, Raphael's Fornarina, & several by Guido, very beautiful, especially the daughter of Herodias with the head of St John, the face of the woman is most lovely. We had now been looking at pictures for 4 hours & were so tired that we begged to return home, so we only stopped to see two very fine sarcophagi from the baths of Caracalla & one or two of the fountains, the aqueduct of Dioclesian still partly supplies Rome with water which is thus conveyed a distance of 35 miles, the pleasantest things in Rome are the innumerable fountains & quantity of good fresh water, it is the only redeeming quality the nasty hot place has. At 4 o'clock we went to the Palazzo Sciarra, but the keeper of the gallery was ill or said he was, and we could not see it, so we went to the Villa Borghese just out of the town, & here there was nobody answered our attack on the bell, so I suppose the man there was ill too, we had a pretty ride through the park belonging to the palace, which was once the property &

residence of Pauline, the sister of Napoleon, famous for her beauty & bad character. As we could not make any one hear or care, we went on to the Palazzo Colonna to see a small collection of pictures & two very fine cabinets, one set with precious stones the other with most exquisite ivory carvings, one of the subjects the Last Judgement by Michael Angelo, the figures quite perfect though the largest are not an inch long, the gallery itself was the most princely we had yet seen, & gave us an idea of what the Roman nobles may have been in times past, now I believe that they are many of them little better than beggars or gamblers and obliged to let their palaces in floors to get a living, the French Consul has the first floor of the Colonna Palace. We saw the remains of the temple of Janus, the small arch of Septimus Severus & the Cloaca Maxima or ancient drain which is still used as a sewer to drain Rome into the Tiber. We went next to the Baths of Caracalla built in the year 212 when they say 1600 people could at one time bathe at once, beside the baths he had libraries & sculpture galleries, a theatre and dining hall, it was here that the fine mosaics had been found. The Pope is still carrying on the excavations of these baths which have been completely buried by themselves, they were partly destroyed by fire, & still more by the Goths, & the immense roofs have fallen in & buried every thing to the depth of many feet. We saw some very perfect mosaic pavement still left, but otherwise there is little perfect enough to be admired, one or two heads of statues & a few bases or capitals of columns, & a very flourishing family of guinea pigs belonging to the man who has the care of the ruins, & he being a wit, told us they were modern, the guinea pigs, I mean. They have found some very fine basalt vases & marble baths in the ruins, some of which are in the Vatican & others in the squares of the city, which are mostly ornamented with antique vases or columns or fountains. We next went to a place that had been a palace to see a view of the city & river, we stood on the Aventine Hill & looked over the Tiber, with the remains of the ancient bridges, to St Peter's & the Vatican, & the greater part of Rome, the new Basilique of St Paul on one side & the place where St Peter was crucified on the other. There was a small chapel here, St[a] Maria d'Aventine, that at one time belonged to the Knights of Malta, when we came away the young lady who shows the place gave us two beautiful bouquets of verbena & roses, and a few leaves & bunches of fruit from the pepper tree which grows here very commonly in the gardens & looks at a little distance something like a weeping willow. Afterwards we just stopped for a few minutes to see the remains of the house of Rienzi[9], the last of the Tribunes & the temples of Vesta & Minerva Median & finished by a visit to the remains of the Tarpeian rock[10], where a little animal of a boy rushed out with a hammer to knock off a piece to sell which of course he did, we were now too tired to do any thing more, so we returned home, Anne & I had had 8 hours of hard sight seeing & that in such weather is no joke.

Sunday July 11 We went to St Peter's at 9 o'clock to hear the mass, we staid an hour & ½ hearing some pretty good music & seeing a great deal of absurd mummery, the Priests fumigating each other & the books seemed to be the principal part of the ceremony which was performed at the back of the High Altar, where nobody ever officiates except the Pope, so

Temple of Vesta at Tivoli, 7th July 1847

they have a small one at the back for common use. There were 3 principal priests who officiated & about 160 in a sort of pew round the Altar, & these were all fumigated once & so thoroughly that they were obliged to turn their faces away to avoid being smothered, the three chief priests chanted a little & then sat down in a row, having a man behind to turn their embroidered robes over the back of the seat while the organ played & the choristers sang, then they got up & bowed a great deal before the altar, & drank something out of a chalice & embraced each other & all the 160 passed round an embrace, and then there was more reading & singing & bowing & then they all walked off into another part of the Church, & we walked round to examine the church itself. The High Altar is under the Dome & under that is the Shrine of St Peter, round which 112 lamps are kept constantly burning, there is a large bronze statue of St Peter, sitting in a chair, near the Altar, the two great toes of which have been nearly kissed away, & are quite bright, we saw several people kiss them & press their foreheads against them & then kiss again. The large mosaic copies of pictures are magnificent & indeed magnificence is the characteristic of the church, but we thought it would have looked better on a Sunday morning if the church had been less showey & there had been more people to make use of it, for the congregation did not amount to above half the number of the priests, & those who were there seemed mostly of the poorest class, & as if they were present from curiosity rather than devotion. There were no seats, so that every body except the Priests either stood or knelt or walked about just as they thought fit. The three chief priests were most superbly robed in crimson & gold & a quantity of point lace, but the underlings who carried the canopies etc were more shabby & mean than I ever saw in any procession at the theatre & so dirty. We took another look at the beautiful monument to Pius 7th & that to the memory of James 3rd of England & his two sons & then returned home very much disappointed at the manner in which the service had been performed in the first Romish Church in the world. In the evening John had a saunter for half an hour & was very much struck by the beauty of the people who were riding up & down the Corso, nobody can help remarking the general beauty of the Roman people, they are handsome & graceful, both old & young & even when they get excessively fat, not an uncommon case, they still have faces that are models of beauty, the old women look like Empresses & even among the carters & commonest people, there are faces that you never see equalled any where else except in antique statues, which they are very like & the upper classes of women look almost as white. It was too hot for Anne & me to try going out again, so with the exception of going down to dinner & catching fleas we were immovable for the rest of the day, there were two most amusing little beggar boys who were always on the door step of a Restaurant[11] just opposite & always wished us good morning when we first appeared at our window, who served greatly to amuse us during our stay in this most stifling climate.

To Florence and Back to the Alps

July 13th to August 6th

BY DILIGENCE TO FLORENCE VIA RADICOFANI AND SIENA · FIVE NIGHTS AT THE HOTEL DE L'EUROPE
BY DILIGENCE TO EMPOLI · BY TRAIN TO LEGHORN · ONE NIGHT AT THE HOTEL THOMSON · BY STEAMER TO GENOA
SEVEN NIGHTS AT THE HOTEL CROCE DI MALTA · BY CARRIAGE TO NOVI · ONE NIGHT AT THE HOTEL L'AIGLE NOIR
BY CARRIAGE TO ASTI VIA ALESSANDRIA · BY CARRIAGE TO TURIN VIA POIRINO AND MONCALIENE
FOUR NIGHTS AT THE HOTEL DE L'EUROPE · BY DILIGENCE TO ARONA AND LAKE MAGGIORE
BY STEAMER TO MAGADINO · BY CARRIAGE TO BELLINZONA, ONE NIGHT AT THE HOTEL L'AIGLE D'OR

To Florence and Back to the Alps
July 13th to August 6th

Tuesday July 13 At ½ past 11, half an hour after time, we left filthy, hot, disagreable Rome, & were so far lucky as to have a coupé to ourselves, the day was burning hot & the dust for miles out of the nasty city almost unbearable, but in a few hours we passed the hills that surround Rome & then we began to breathe, the country between Rome & Florence is bare & desolate & mostly quite uncultivated, & now looked as if it was too dry for even a blade of grass to spring. We passed the Appennines, at least were winding round & round them all day & all night & very slow work it was and very badly managed, for before we had started 3 hours one horse had fallen, and the driver had dropped his whip three times & lost his hat once so that we began to wonder whether even the 48 hours would take us to our journey's end. We stopped to dinner the first evening & dined with the rest of the passengers in the Diligence at a small town the name of which I do not remember, our conductor almost drove us to despair by stopping such an immense time wherever we changed horses. We got through the night as well as fleas & fidgets & mosquitoes would allow & with the assistance of 6 horses & 4 oxen we mounted up to a small town called Radicofani, where we were to breakfast, & when we got out & asked for coffee, there was none, & literally they had nothing but lemonade or sour wine, or what they call in Italy soup, which I believe is nothing but hot water & fat with large lumps of bread swimming in it, this after a hot night's travelling was most refreshing & delightful. We staid here an hour & at 12 o'clock were again en route, & had such a hot ride as it is quite impossible to give any idea of, not a breath of air & the sun shining hot all day like a thousand furnaces, & the dreary country & the slow pace at which we were obliged by the hills to travel altogether made up a sum of human misery almost impossible to calculate. We had to undergo a search at Radicofani & certainly they did search most completely poking into even our little workboxes where I trust they pricked their fingers. Here we

Florence - July 18.1847 -
Naples - July 1847
Naples -
Lazzaroni at Naples -

entered Tuscany & thank goodness got rid of our conductor & got a more business like manager, who did not loiter on his way & we got on much better. We did not dine until we reached Sienna, a large busy & prettily situated town where we arrived about 8 & staid an hour & ½, John & our other passengers, two very well behaved Spaniards had dinner & Anne & I preferred coffee & bread, a hot greasy dinner after such a ride being dreadful to think of. Our chief comfort was the great civility I may almost say kindness of the people at the Hotels, they seem to understand by instinct what you want & if they can are anxious to oblige & serve you with what you wish. We got off again between 9 & 10 & had a dreadful hot restless ride & at 9 o'clock the next morning got to the fair Florence & in good truth it did look fair to us, for it is surrounded by beautiful green hills & valleys & fresh looking trees & clean English looking houses standing in their own grounds scattered over the neighbourhood & moreover almost any place would have looked fair that was to deliver us from our bondage. We had to stop at the entrance of the Town while our fellow passengers luggage was examined, our's had been sealed at the place where it was examined before & a permit given on payment of some trifling sum to prevent our having to go through the ceremony again on our entering Florence. We soon reached the Hotel de l'Europe recommended as the pleasantest in summer & in the course of the day when we had a little recovered from our fatigue, came to the conclusion that it was a very comfortable place. John's feet were so swelled & inflamed by bites he could hardly walk across the room, so he sat with his feet up on the sofa all day and we did not go out either, the people here seem an orderly set, the women wear commonly the large uncut flapping Leghorn hats, & the ladies go out in short sleeves & every thing thats cool that they can imagine, we envied them their clean muslin dresses, such impossible luxuries to travellers.

Friday July 16 John's feet still too much swelled to allow him to move & Anne's rather bad, however she & I went out & sent him home some boots to wear until he could get on his own again, & then to the post office to post a letter to William. We were very much pleased with the appearance of the streets in Florence, they are well paved, not very dirty & with better looking shops than any we had seen since Frankfurt & Brussels, & the people very civil which is more than can be said of the noble Romans. There are a great many English live at Florence & perhaps they have civilised the natives. We went into the Cathedral & listened to a piece of music that was performed, & then just walked round, but there is nothing very striking in the interior, it is very plain, but has some very rich painted windows, the exterior is inlaid with marbles in small pieces more like Tonbridge ware[1] than anything else, & is not so beautiful I think, as plain marble or stone. After dinner Anne & I tried to walk to some public gardens just outside the town, but they were further than we expected & the evening dreadfully hot, when we got near them there was such a pool of filth to wade through, where the street had been watered, that we turned back & went home again, we were most thankful for a storm of thunder & lightening, and a nice shower of rain which we hoped would cool the air. We saw a Turkish lady going to the gardens in an open carriage, she had on a sort of loose white turban superbly ornamented with gems, & seemed decorated with jewels all over.

Saturday July 17 John's feet were still very bad, but he determined to go through the two palaces, where the chief collections of statuary & pictures are kept, so at 9 o'clock we rode to the Imperial palace & saw all the rooms containing the busts of the Medici family, the celebrated Medician Venus, & a very large collection of Statuary & paintings, the most interesting paintings are three rooms of autograph portraits of artists, ancient & modern, there are seven of our English artists only, More, Reynolds, Northcote, Harlow, Hayter, Brockedon & the amateur Prince Hoare, the most striking portrait of them all was Leonardo da Vinci, Albert Durer's is a perfect caricature of a vain youth in an absurd dress, Raphael's very ugly indeed. We could not stay very long, as the galleries were intensely hot & close & it was as much as John could do to limp from one room to the other, however we went on to the Pitti Palace which also belonged to the Medici family & where there is a magnificent collection of paintings, among them that most beautiful one of Raphael's, the Madonna della Seggiola & a very beautiful one of Judith, & 500 other pictures all valuable as they were selected from the best in the churches & purchased by Ferdinand 2nd & afterwards added to by the collection of the Medici Cardinals. When we had walked through the gallery which is itself well worth seeing, built in the 15 century by one of the Italian Princes to outvie another with whom he was at enmity & therefore there was no expense spared in making the building splendid, in one of the rooms is Canova's Venus, we went from there to the Bankers & then John could bear no more so we returned home, where we sat & panted with heat until 4 o'clock when we took a drive to the Cascine, the fashionable drive of Florence but as we are not fashionables we chose to go when nobody else was there, as Italian élite do not turn out until about 6 or 7 in the evening. The Cascine, which is more a park than a dairy, is nicely planted & deliciously shady, with beautiful views of the city, & surrounding country, nice looking country seats round the environs of Florence, situated on the sides of the mountains & the beautiful fresh green looked so new & enlivening after dirty hot Rome that we were delighted with it & enjoyed our ride very much. On our return we drove round the Cathedral which John had not yet seen, & saw the stone in the Square where they say Dante used to sit for hours contemplating the Cathedral. The Campanile, built in 1330 by Giotto who was commanded to build an edifice which in height & richness of decoration should exceed any thing erected by the Greeks or Romans, is of course most superb, it is a square gothic tower inlaid with marbles of different colours & enriched with figures. They say that every square of 3 feet cost a thousand florins and it is considered one of the most beautiful gothic buildings in existence. Our driver, for we had determined to do without the expense & bother of a valet, drove us across the curious old Ponte Vecchio, which is like the Rialto, a street of shops all jewellers & goldsmiths & workers in precious metals. The Arno is a yellow muddy looking stream, though even in this dry weather very rapid & giving evident marks of being a roarer in rainy seasons, it has more than once washed away its bridges & misbehaved itself in numerous ways. The hotel where we staid was just at the foot of the Ponte della Trinita, a very pretty bridge

Costume of Genoa, 1847

ornamented with statues of the four seasons, in marble, the evening & night were dreadfully hot & close.

Sunday July 18 John's feet still very bad but mending & we all determined to have a quiet day. So we sat & read & looked out at window, & wrote, & really it was too hot to do any one of them without great personal exertion. The heat was certainly more oppressive than can be imagined, it seemed perfectly to take away all will or power to employ ourselves, writing, reading, needlework, every thing was a trouble, & there was no relief night or day. We slept with our windows wide open, to the great pleasure & delight of the gnats & mosquitoes, who did not neglect their opportunity as our poor mangled remains testified, having at the writing of this very page 40 bites on my right wrist & hand & others in proportion, & my two poor companions having been crippled since the journey from Rome. However the hope of some day being cool, & leaving venomous animals behind keeps us alive, & thats all. One of the peculiarities of Florence is the trade carried on by the Flower Girls, who are generally very pretty saucy young women, dressed in coloured muslin gowns & gay aprons, & white lace capes and the large Leghorn hat, they carry most lovely baskets of flowers & present them to all the respectable people who pass, who every now & then give them a small sum in payment. The first I saw I thought was mad for it seemed so curious to present every body she met with flowers, & there was a sort of gay flighty manner about her, that I set her down as a Florentine Ophelia, but on better acquaintance with the manners of the place I found there were several Ophelias & they seem to have a very flourishing trade, for one of them we saw go out to fetch a fresh stock of flowers in a carriage, & she had a boy to fill her basket & make up her bouquets, she presented us with some flowers more than once. In the evening we had a curious sight from our window to see the crowds of people returning from the public gardens across the bridge near us, just at 8 o'clock when the gates of the city are closed & a tax imposed on any one who enters after that time. The bridge which is a tolerably wide one was perfectly choked with people for a full ½ hour, & the custom of every one, men & women, ladies & gentlemen, wearing straw hats & bonnets made the crowd look much more gay than an English one, the people generally are flaunting gaudy dresses, but that may be partly attributable to the season, the heat makes every thing thick or sombre oppressive.

Monday July 19 We went to see the interior of the Cathedral & have another look at the beautiful Campanile & to see the curious old Baptistry where all children born in Florence are baptised, a very curious old place, some part of which has been traced back as far as the year 1150, but the exact date of its erection is not known. There are six brazen doors to the Baptistry, most elaborately carved or worked with subjects from Scripture & surrounded with arabesques of fruit & flowers & birds, said to be the finest in the world, the Cathedral is very plain & there are no monuments of interest. We then went to the Church of Santa Croce, the burial place of distinguished Florentines, the pavement is chiefly tombstones. Here we saw the monuments of Dante, Michael Angelo, Galileo, & Machiavelli, we were chiefly interested in going to this church from the remembrance of the beautiful view of it at the Diorama[2] some years ago, it is a curious ruinous old place. We next went for a drive to see the best view of Florence & therefore gave our poor horses the trouble of going up a steep hill called Bellosguardo where we were admitted into a private garden to a terrace & a sight of two most splendid views, one of the city & the other the surrounding country, which is indeed most lovely. The city is a very picturesque one, as the Dome of the Cathedral, the Square Campanile & a very curious tower to the Town Hall & several other spires stand up far above the rest of the buildings, & the fresh green country round on all sides make it a lovely & delicious place in cooler weather I cannot doubt. The garden we went into was like other Italian gardens, rich in beautiful flowering shrubs, but with such a neglected look that it was quite sad. We returned home from here & John & I did not go out again, Anne was taken with a taste for adventure, & went to get a drawing from the Cascine. We made acquaintance today with one of the handsome flower women who positively forced a quantity of roses & pinks & verbena upon us though we told her we had no change to pay for them.

Tuesday July 20 We got up at 5 o'clock and, soon after, we had a tremendous storm of thunder & lightening & very heavy rain, which produced three fine cascades through the ceiling of our bedroom, we were thankful to think it would lay the dust in the roads & cool the air, & as we had just done with the room the cascades didn't signify to us. We breakfasted and at 7 set off in the Diligence for Empoli to meet the railway train for Pisa. Our friend the Flower Woman was ready to say goodbye & present us with some fresh roses at our departure, we had nearly 3 hours terribly hot ride & when we got to Empoli we found we had to wait ¾ of an hour for the train, however there was a tolerably cool decent place to wait in, so we sat watching the carpenters who were working at the quite unfinished station, & unfortunately while so doing remembered that John had left a pretty little cane with an agate handle that he bought at Naples, in the diligence, it was no use making any enquiry, for the lovely conveyance had been gone more than half an hour but it was very mortifying. It took us two hours to go to Pisa & as we were to go on to Leghorn in the evening we proposed leaving our luggage at the Station, but positively they said they had no place where they could put it, & recommended us to take it to an ancient lady who kept a vegetable shop near, so accordingly we left bag & baggage among the cabbages & drove at once to the Cathedral, to do which we had to pass quite through sleepy, dead, deserted looking Pisa. There are

some fine buildings by the side of the river Arno especially one small chapel, ancient Pisa it seems shared the fate of the other large Italian cities & was destroyed by the Goths in the 5th century, who levelled a great many of the temples etc that had been built by the Romans, it was a celebrated & wealthy place again at the time of the crusades, on account of its being then a fine port, which it has now ceased to be owing to the gradual receding of the sea, & Genoa is now what Pisa used to be. The Cathedral was built in 1064 & was 44 years building, it is composed chiefly of the remains of an old Roman Temple, & other remains & the outside is the most singular patchwork of old columns & inscriptions, some the right side up & some the wrong. The interior is one of the most richly adorned in Italy, it is chiefly black & white marble but ornamented by mosaic & painting & magnificent painted windows, the same rich gem like colour as those at Florence, there are some very fine sculptures in marble by Michael Angelo, especially the capitals of two columns at the side of the high altar. In one of the chapels is a shrine for the Host, of chased silver, which cost 170,000 francs but it is kept under a cover so we did not see it. We went to see a very curious old Baptistry close to the Cathedral, very rich in carved marble, the font in the middle is so large that grown people could get into it to be baptised 10 or 12 at a time & there are smaller ones for infants, there is a very curious echo in this place. It is a curious thing that the Cathedral, the Baptistry, the leaning tower & the Campo Santo are all close together on a deserted looking, rather grassy place just outside the city, it is convenient for travellers as they see them all with less time & trouble than if they were further apart. The leaning tower, which is so well known to everybody from the Alabaster models, is much more wonderful & beautiful than the models can give any idea of, we did not go inside it as our time & trouble were both too precious & we did not see any reason why we should. The Campo Santo is a burial place, a sort of cloister, very fine gothic, enclosing a square, or rather oblong piece of ground, as it is 450 ft long & 140 broad, it was built in 1298 for the purpose of enclosing 30 ship loads of earth from the Holy Land by some dignitary of the church, they say that this earth has the property of reducing the bodies to dust in 24 hours but that the space is quite full. The cloisters have been painted in fresco, partly with histories from the Scripture & partly illustrations of Dante, the latter very curious, but sadly spotted by damp & exposure to the weather. There is a collection of sculptured relics, found in different parts of the city & some few modern monuments that are very beautiful, one particularly of a lady said to be inconsolable for the loss of her husband, but with no particular expression of grief about her except that sorrow had made her forget to dress herself. Having seen the chief lions of Pisa we went to the Hotel Victoria to have some luncheon, & while we were there, there was a party of English people came in for the same purpose. I suppose some day it will not be such a rarity to hear an English tongue, but now one almost starts at the sound. In good time we went to claim our valuables at the hands of the fair greengrocer & went to the railway station, where two or three great lounging men wanted to be paid for looking on while our packages were being removed, after about ½ an hour we set off for Leghorn, which is only ¾ of an hours ride & we were quite in hopes that we should be in time to go on board the Columba Steamer that was advertised to sail that evening at 5 for Genoa, so we hurried off to the Steamboat office & there learned that she did not sail until the next day, so we were obliged to make up our minds to stay a night in dirty disagreable Leghorn. We went to the Hotel Nord, but it was quite full, & then we went to the Hotel Thomson, & there were accommodated with the needful for the night & next day.

Wednesday July 21 Anne & John went out for an hour to make some purchases & had no sooner returned than we had another storm of thunder etc & another delicious cool shower came down to wash dirty Leghorn. Of course there is a great sale here for straw hats which are made in the villages between Florence & Leghorn, we saw the women plaiting away with all their might, & the grass that the hats are made of laid to bleach & dry in the sun, the difference in the well to do look of the people in consequence of their occupation is most striking compared with the great part of Italy, there is also a great trade done at Leghorn in coral, also an immense quantity of English cotton goods are sold in the streets, altogether it is a bustling busy place, but so dirty & the people so diseased looking that we were glad to see as little as possible of it. We went on board the New Columba at 4 o'clock & at ¼ past 5 she sailed or rather steamed away to Genoa, there were very few people on board & Anne & I had the single cabin to ourselves. It was a horrid dirty little place but not so hot as one would have expected & the night passed somehow, not agreably certainly though the sea was as smooth as possible, but steamers are vile things, we arrived at Genoa at 5 the next morning.

Thursday July 22 Soon went on shore & got through the search at the custom house very comfortably & went full of hope to the comfortable Hotel de Ville where we were before, but woe's me, it was full & we were obliged to go to the Croce di Malta[3] within a short distance of the other, where we got very nice rooms & breakfast & were soon very glad we had been obliged to take up our quarters there, as it was in a better situation as to view & not quite so near the noisy coppersmiths as the Hotel de Ville.

Friday July 23 Dreadfully hot, the thermometer at 24° of Reaumur[4], we only went out to get some lunch & then sat still & occupied ourselves as well as we could, I wrote to dear old Captn Lowry but really it is quite a task either to work or write when ones fingers are so hot. At dinner at 4 o'clock we met a party of French people, a man, a woman, a child, & such coarse disgusting feeders never were seen, certainly the French

Lighthouse and harbour of Genoa, 27th July 1847

exceed all other people in the satisfaction of being beasts.

Monday July 26 Much cooler, got out for a couple of hours and walked round the bay to the lighthouse. There was a general cessation of business today for a couple of hours for the purpose of seeing 7 or 8 men paraded through the streets who had been condemned to the Galleys, it is one of the few disagreable sights of Genoa to see these poor wretches walking about chained heavily by the legs. We met some English people at dinner but they were sad gubies.

Tuesday July 27 Went directly after breakfast to the top of the hotel to see the curious tower that belonged to the Knights of Malta, we had to go up an all but interminable staircase all of black marble & along endless passages. We had a most exquisite view from the top which is an immense height. Anne staid to take a drawing, & then we went & took a walk on the top of one of the hills where we got a very fine view of the bay & shipping, the Sardinian fleet, by no means a contemptible one, & a beautiful Turkish vessel that had come in the night before & been saluted from the battery. In the evening John & I had another walk & happened to pop upon the small theatre where they have open air performances, so we went in and saw the last act of Don Carlos, one of Alfieri's tragedies, the best places were chairs in a circle in front of the stage, the next were benches outside the circle, there were a great many people there, & really the performance was not bad. As we returned home we went into the Cathedral where they were just performing Vespers and it was as full as it could be, too full to be at all pleasant. The priests were handing round black bags on long poles for Alms, it was a very striking scene, the Altar brilliantly lighted, & the immense number of women in their white veils, but we were glad to get out for it is not pleasant rubbing shoulders with Italian beggars.

Wednesday July 28 John went out for a small promenade but we did not feel inclined to move, at dinner we met the two English people again, the man as disagreable conceited & impertinent an animal as ever lived, the poor wretched wife evidently sighing for her home and children & got snubbed every time she spoke. We pitied her very much & hated him the more, especially as she seemed in wretched health, he wanted John to go to his room to drink wine, but was mistaken in his man. Received a letter from Henry enclosing one from Cousin Susan.

Thursday July 29 At six o'clock with much regret we bade adieu to dear beautiful Genoa & its comfortable hotel, & departed again in our own conveyance at least one that John had hired to take us to Turin, for what the driver had at first the audacity to ask 200 francs, & when John said he would not give more than 100, he consented to take that, there by writing himself down a thorough Italian big thief. We were rather surprised[5] at his stopping before he got out of Genoa to take up a very smart young lady on the box with him, we speculated all the way, whether he was just married & had made up his mind to make this his wedding trip, for they were so very cosy together, but in the course of the day the lady was good enough to explain that she was only going about ½ way to Turin, she was at all sorts of pranks, smoking & taking snuff & occasionally doing a little driving. The road was very beautiful & hilly, the same that we had come on our way from Milan to Genoa, we had to cross the Apennines & a beautiful, rich, lovely ride it is, the mountains so green & every now and then a peep at the sea between them. We stopped to rest the horses & dine at Ronco, a quiet nice little hotel in a lovely situation among the hills, and then proceeded to nasty disagreable Novi to spend the night & found it as noisy & unpleasant as ever, we were at the same hotel where we slept on our way to Genoa the first time & the noise in the market place was just as deafening, & the dreadful tolling of the Church bell just by incessant. We saw the people going in to Vespers, and it was very curious at the termination of the service, I suppose the blessing. All the people in the square, I should say nearly a hundred, went down on their knees & there was a complete hush of voices for about five minutes & then up they got again & the people came out of church & an immense number there were of them, & as soon as the church doors were shut there was a grand performance of a puppet tragedy that collected a very large audience in the square.

Friday July 30 We left that noisiest of places Novi & proceeded over a flat uninteresting country to Alessandria, we passed over the plain where the battle of Marengo was fought, & where there is a museum containing relics of the battle, but we did not care to stay to see them. We had to stop at Alessandria during the heat of the day, 5 hours & very tiresome it was for the place was a nasty place & the hotel a very dirty one & so hot. John asked the waiter if it was always as hot there, & he said 'yes it was, except three years ago when it rained,' so whether it had never rained there since I dont know but the place looked as if it had not & the people all looked asleep from sheer heat, even in the shops. A curious feature of the place was a vessel of water set outside every door for the dogs & they must have been dirty dogs that used some of them, for they looked as if the water had never been changed for months, we set the custom down as the effect of some absurd law unwillingly obeyed. At Alessandria we left our fellow passenger who came to say adieu when we left, and return thanks for having been allowed a seat on our carriage. The country between this & Asti where we put up for the night was mostly very flat & uninteresting, long strait roads with large flat tracts of maize on each side, until within a few miles of Asti it improved & was very hilly & pretty, of course there were plenty of vines on the hills, as this is a celebrated wine country. The day had been so desperately hot that we were all nearly worn out when we reached our destination, & a dirty destiny we seemed to have for the night, but we got some very good coffee & bread & butter & they were wonderful soothers after keeping fast for ten hours.

Saturday July 31 We gladly left dirty Asti & rode a long & a weary way over a flat stupid country until we began to hope that our steeds were transporting us to Turin without stopping to rest, which we were the more surprised at as the poor beasts were so worn out as to require constant whipping. Our hopes proved false, for when we came to a small place called Poirino the horses stopped & we got out & there we staid for about 3 hours amusing ourselves with a collation & our books, &

Old Palace at Turin, 3rd August 1847

then proceeding for another very hot 4 hours. We reached Turin & thankful we were to get there without either dying ourselves or entirely killing our poor horses who were quite unfit for the task imposed on them. The road for some miles before reaching Turin is very beautiful especially from a village called Moncalieri where the King has a summer palace in which he generally lives. Turin seems to stand in a beautiful rich green valley surrounded on two sides by the Alps, it is a handsome looking city as you approach but the nearer you see it the less handsome it is as the houses are of brick & plastered & in some cases not even that & then they have an untidy unfinished look, the streets are very strait & most of them a good width & well paved. We went to the hotel de l'Europe, a very nice looking place & had tea & then went out for an hours walk & were very much pleased with the appearance of Turin, in the evening we had a great deal of lightening.

Monday August 2 We went to see the Royal Palace & very splendid the state rooms are with gilding and velvet & every thing else that Palaces can be made splendid with, but nothing out of the usual way of such places. There were a few good pictures mostly modern, one very fine of the Deluge by a Milanese Artist, & two very interesting miniatures of Marie Antoinette & her poor friend, the Princess Lambelle. Next we went to the Picture gallery, where there are a great many pictures but not a great many first rate ones, then we had a walk in the Palace garden, the view from which was much better than the garden itself, though that was an improvement upon most of those we had seen in Italy and last, we went to see the Armoury. There were several very fine suits of Armour for horse & man, the horses were real skins most beautifully stuffed, some of them had been favourite horses of the Kings, there were suits of Chinese & Japanese Armour, very curious, but there was not much to see & we had soon finished for there was nothing of any historical interest. So we went & did some money spending, which we found easy enough for there are very good shops of all kinds in Turin & the people are excessively civil & charge quite enough to prove their true Italian origin.

Tuesday August 3 At breakfast time we had quite a grand military review at the end of the street, & then about 500 cavalry rode close past the windows in companies 10 abreast and formed a square in front of the Palace close by, & the band played & then we saw them all ride off again & a very fine looking body of men they were. We then went out for a walk and mounted a hill whereon stands a Capuchin Convent & Church & from there we got a most beautiful view of the whole city, with the hills behind & beyond them the range of Alps. Turin is rather a fine looking city from a little distance but wants spires to do away with the flatness, even the Cathedral hardly stands up above the other roofs. We soon made our way down again to the banks of the river Po, and across the iron bridge, and there we seated ourselves under some trees while Anne took a sketch of the curious old Palace & the Convent on the hill. Then we went to a cafe & had some delicious ices, & then we went & bought a new carpet bag, an amber pipe for our dear old friend at Pear Tree Green, & the march that has made such a sensation at Rome, written in honour of the Pope, & a new sketch book for Anne, &

then we returned home for the rest of the day. In the evening we had quite a musical treat in a large orchestrina drawn by a horse that played 4 overtures most beautifully. We were very much amused on requesting to have some tea, by the waiter asking us if it was 'pour boire', we wondered what he supposed we meant to do with it, whether to chew as tobacco or take as snuff. John bought Dicken's Italy[6] today & we were delighted with his very true & amusing sketch of Genoa, most interesting to us who had so lately left it. Curiously enough, in the dining room of the Hotel at Turin we met a gentleman that we had dined with several times at Genoa, nearly two months before, we called him Prince Albert and as he was evidently a traveller like ourselves it was curious that we should meet twice in our wanderings. The costumes at Turin are not at all pretty, a great many of the women wear a straw hat, lined & quite encumbered with blue trimming, some wear a very peculiar castellated sort of cap, one of the most unbecoming & hideous combinations of ribbon & lace that can be imagined & generally worn until it is anything but clean. It is curious a few miles should make such a difference, for the Genoese are so particularly tasteful & elegant looking with their simple white veils, but at Turin you never see such a thing. The King generally lives at Turin, but he has often threatened to take his court to Genoa, as the Turin folk are said to be sad radicals. He was at his country palace 5 leagues off when we were there so that we did not see him, but we saw a full length portrait of him at the palace & he is by no means handsome.

Wednesday August 4 We took a farewell walk round a part of Turin, then packed up & dined, & at 4 o'clock set off in a drenching rain by diligence for Arona & the Lago Maggiore, we had a coupé to ourselves & went as slow as three fat horses could draw us when in the middle of our third stage we came to a mauvais pas, where the road had been completely washed away by a storm & they were repairing it & laying down such heaps of stones, that the horses could not get over, so the men were all obliged to get out & walk for about a mile & ½, which was any thing but a trial to them. There had been a sad blight or storm that had destroyed the indian wheat & the leaves of the trees & all the vegetation for a distance of four miles along the road. Every thing looked as if it had been scorched, it might be the same storm that destroyed the road. Except this tract the crops looked well & we passed some beautiful grassland where they cut 4 crops a year. When we had collected our beaux we went on again at the same very moderate speed until about 10 or 11, when we had a most fearful storm of

Magadino on the Lago Maggiore, 6th August 1847

thunder, lightening & rain, the lightening was incessant & seemed to run along the road in a blue flame just in front of the horses & the rain poured down in such torrents as I never saw above once or twice in my life, the old grey horses luckily jogged on not seeming to care a bit about either lightening or rain, & so we proceeded sometimes better sometimes worse until ½ past three when the concern stopped, & we were invited to get out. I supposed, weak mortals as we were, that we should find a comfortable room & no doubt coffee & other luxuries awaiting our attack, but lo & behold there was nothing but a small office, and we were soon informed that we should have the pleasure of remaining there an hour & ½ & then change our carriage & proceed on our way. Anne was greatly amused on asking the managing clerk what they called the place we were in, meaning the Town, & he said quite seriously that it was a small office (piccolo offizio) which we could have guessed, so there we waited our time & luckily, as the rain was over though the lightening was still incessant. The rest of the passengers, of which there must have been 20 or 30 for there were two carriages traveling together, betook themselves to a cafe or some place of entertainment which I suppose they knew where to find & we had the small office to ourselves & some of us read, & one who shall be nameless in this history had a long nap & at 5 we departed in another diligence & with five horses who went slower than the three, & so it befell that we did not reach Arona until past 10, the last 5 hours being very slow work indeed & very tedious although the road was lovely & the morning really cold after the storm. At 10 we reached Arona on the Lago Maggiore & of course after our ride of 10 hours the first thing we thought of was breakfast, so away we sped to the Hotel d'Italie & breakfasted & then walked to see the gigantic Statue of St Carlo Borromeo & the little ruined chapel standing on the spot where he was born, the figure is indeed immense as they say a man may easily sit inside the nose. It is on a pedestal 106 ft high, the head is very ugly but the figure not so bad, it is of bronze. We just had time to return comfortably before the steamer came up to take us to the other end of the lake, & in we went with a great many other passengers & had a most lovely journey of 5½ hours, called at the pretty villages along the shores to leave or take in passengers or wine or bread as the case might be, the mountains are splendid all the way & the vines just in their very richest foliage & so green & fresh after the last night's rain. We got to Magadino at ½ past six & our fellow passengers hurried off to a diligence to proceed the same evening to Bellinzona but we staid at the small hotel at Magadino, kept by an old Physician & his wife & had sole possession of it & got very clean nice beds & very good coffee & bread & butter & eggs & a bouquet of roses & jasmins the next morning, the view from the hotel across the lake was most lovely, but it is said to be a very unhealthy place & much given to malaria.

Friday August 6 We went out for a dawdle while Anne took a drawing of the mountains & lake & we then proceeded in a horribly dirty little vehicle, through a most lovely valley to Bellinzona, an hour & a half, & took up our quarters at the Aigle d'Or & then went forth to see what we could see. We mounted up to one of the old castles that look down upon the town, of which there are three, that formerly belonged to the

Bellinzona, 6th August 1847

three governors of Uri, Schwyz & Unterwalden. They so completely command the road that Bellinzona was at one time a place of great importance as a pass between Lombardy & Germany, one of these is now used as a prison, but looking in & seeing the gentlemen inside walking about with chains on their legs we did not seek to enter, the other two are empty & I fancy partly in ruins. I quite forgot in our steamboat excursion to note down that there was one of my favourite Capuchin monks on board & in the course of the trip we made many discoveries as to his receptacles for luggage. We remarked that his sleeves seemed very capacious & well stored & found that he kept a library & his stock of linen for travelling inside them, and under a curiously contrived trap door in front that hung down under his chin like a child's bib he kept an immense watch, so that there is no reason to doubt that though his dress looks so simple & plain there are concealed receptacles for immense plunder. Horrid old knaves, it makes one quite angry to see such great strong brawny wretches doing nothing but cheat for their livelihood. We dined at two & then set out in search of the picturesque, which we had not to go very far to look for, Anne composed herself on a low wall by the road side to draw, & we seated ourselves on the same wall to do nothing but look about, first at the beautiful view & then at the disgusting exhibition within a few yards of us, of a party of men heavily chained, at work, guarded by a man with a gun, one of the prisoners was singing Swiss melodies most mellifluously every now and then. Presently a little bit of a boy came and extended himself on the wall close to John, took a book out of his pocket & pretended to read, so John seeing the book was German asked him if he could read it & he said no, & after a great deal of conversation the young gentleman proposed that John should buy his book, but as John had a shrewd suspicion that it was not honestly come by, his offer was politely declined. Unfortunately it soon came on to rain & drove us in, & it continued to rain until 7 o'clock in the evening so no more going out & no more climbing up to the old castles, which was a great disappointment. Anne went out to finish the sketch she had begun but was soon obliged to retreat partly by the cold & partly by the curiosity of the inhabitants of Bellinzona, who expressed themselves very much surprised to see any thing so clean.

Switzerland

August 7th to September 7th

BY CARRIAGE TO AIROLO VIA FAIDO · BY CARRIAGE AND STEAMER TO LUCERNE
VIA THE ST GOTHARD PASS, HOSPENTHAL, ALTORF AND FLUELLEN · EIGHTEEN NIGHTS AT THE PENSION SUISSE ·
BY CARRIAGE TO THUN · FIVE NIGHTS AT THE HOTEL BELLEVUE · BY CARRIAGE AND STEAMER TO GRINDELWALD VIA NEUHAUS,
INTERLACHEN AND LAUTERBRUNNEN · ONE NIGHT AT THE BEAR HOTEL · BY CARRIAGE AND STEAMER TO THUN,
VIA LAKE BRIENZ, INTERLACHEN · THREE NIGHTS AT THE BELLEVUE HOTEL · BY CARRIAGE TO BERNE
TWO NIGHTS AT THE HOTEL FAUCON · BY CARRIAGE TO KRENTZSTRASSE, VIA HINDELBANKE ·
ONE NIGHT AT THE GOLDEN LION · BY CARRIAGE TO ZURICH VIA BADEN

Switzerland

August 7th to September 7th

Saturday August 7 Left beautiful & most picturesque Bellinzona at 7 o'clock & had a delightful ride among mountains & waterfalls & by the side of the Ticino river, the numerous falls of which are amongst the principal beauties of the pass. We changed horses 3 or four times & the carriage once during the day & stopped at a little place called Faido at a nice little clean Inn kept by Germans where we had pleasant indications that we had left nasty Italy behind us in the neatness & cleanliness of the place & people. The Innkeepers on the St Gothard have generally small collections of carved wooden articles for sale, paper knives, nutcrackers etc carved by the poor people of the villages. The chesnut & walnut trees were very plentiful & very fine throughout nearly the whole days journey. After dinner we came to one of the natural passes thro' a narrow ravine where the river rushed down in a series of most beautiful cataracts & the spray dashed up & made rainbows in the sun. We got out of the voiture & walked a little way for the pleasure of looking at the beautiful falls, the road was excellent & in very good repair & a more exquisite ride it is impossible to imagine. We got to our resting-place for the night, Airolo, about 5 o'clock & had time for an hour's walk in the valley by the side of the river & very glad we were to warm ourselves for the ride had been rather chilly for the last hour or two & cold was so new a thing to us that we felt it the more. Anne was fortunate enough to find some fruit in the shape of one wild strawberry, the little Inn at Airolo was to all appearance quite full, as it is the last resting place before beginning the actual ascent of the pass this was not to be wondered at. There were a party of 4 English or, as we suspected, Irish with their two servants, a dirty little village, but tolerably clean hotel.

Sunday August 8 At ½ past 5 we met the Irish people at breakfast & at six we all started for the ascent, unluckily they got off first for it is not permitted to carriages to pass each other on the road & they were a much heavier party than we & constantly fidgetting in & out of their carriage so that they delayed us considerably but we had a beautiful 3 hours ride to the summit of the pass, seeing on our way the source of the Ticino river & numberless lovely waterfalls. The mountains were not nearly so bare as those on the Stelvio but that might be accounted for by the difference in the season of the year. We saw several sorts of flowers growing nearly up to the tops of the mountains, the campanula, dwarf rhododendron, the bright pink dianthus, it was only when we came within a very short distance of the summit that the rocks were bare except for the patches of snow. John walked from Airolo to the top of the pass & was very much pleased with his walk, we lazy people who ride found it bitterly cold so that even wrapped in our cloaks we sat & shivered. In about 3 hours we reached the summit of the St Gothard, where we met John who had ordered coffee etc at an hotel as they call it, but such a filthy place never was seen, dirtier than any English stable I ever saw, however we did not stand much in need of refreshment & therefore resigned the coffee without a sigh. There was a good tempered frenchman there regaling on boiled mutton, we thought his appetite could not be very delicate. We now fortunately got the start of the Irish party & in about an hour were at the bottom of the mountain, trotting merrily down without a thought of drags or any other impediment, the view of the mountains all the way was quite beyond all my powers of description so I shall not attempt any thing of the kind. We changed carriage & horses & all at a little Town called Hospenthal where we saw the Swiss people coming out of church, our new equipage was an open one & we continued our route along a lovely road, still a considerable descent & passing through the tunnel that has been made in the rock for the road to pass through, & over the Devil's bridge[1] or rather over the new one which stands just above the bridge with the respectable name, the little swiss villages perched up among the crags & the cows feeding where you would suppose there was hardly room for a sparrow to stand & the waterfalls & every now & then a sight above our heads of a tall peak covered with snow, but these were rare. There was not so much snow as I expected to see, the sun too shone out quite warm & very glad we were to feel it. We stopped to rest the horses & regale ourselves on bread & butter at one of the prettiest villages that ever was seen, nice clean Swiss houses & the tall mountains all around & a clear rapid river running through the village with a pretty little bridge over it, it was a perfect picture & I should like to have staid there a few days, but fate ordered otherwise & on we went at the end of an hour. We soon came to Altorf, the scene of Tells exploit[2] with his Son & Gessler, it is a small place but interesting from its history & from the inhabitants still treasuring up every remembrance of their favourite hero, there is a fountain where Tell stood to shoot the apple, and another where the pole stood on which the objectionable hat was hung. The greater part of Altorf was destroyed by fire in 1799 & has never been rebuilt, a common fate with Swiss villages on account of their being chiefly composed of wood. A few miles from Altorf we came to Fluellen, the port of the Canton Uri, where we were to wait for the boat to take us to Lucerne, it was amusing to see the boys as we came along this part of the road with their crossbows over their shoulders, & making them an interesting plea for begging. The

Ascent of St Gothard from Airolo, 8th August 1847

costumes too were some of them new to us, the women many of them wore the funniest little black caps or a large silver arrow put through their hair at the back of their heads & others had the long plaited Swiss tails that always make a part of the stage costume. We had some dinner at Fluellen & by that time the steamer was come up & in an hour we steamed away down the beautiful lake, & passed Tell's Chapel on the spot where he escaped from Gessler, & after a three hours sail through the most lovely scenery we arrived at ¼ past 8 at Lucerne. The day had been most beautiful, the sun as bright as an Italian sun, but climate in the evening & morning was not at all Italian but very cold & we were very glad to find on landing from the steamer that there were still rooms enough left for us at the immense new Hotel Pension Suisse on Schweitzer Hof, though for some little time we feared there was a doubt of their being able to accommodate us, for it was very full. We had some tea & went to the most comfortable beds we had had for some time, and a clean sweet room looking over the little town & a nice garden.

Monday August 9 We had to search for a dressmaker to help us to refit as travelling makes people sad shabby objects & we had collected a great deal of dust on our journeyings, we waited at home for an interview with a nice little cheerful woman recommended by the hostess, & then it began to rain, & rained incessantly for the rest of the day so we did not go out at all, John went to the Post office but that was all. At the Table d'hote the people were mostly English & rather stiff. We were almost driven wild by the crying of a poor little croupy child in the next room to us & the cruel scolding nurse, they were a party of three Belgian children with an English nurse & French bonne, who were left in charge while the father & mother made a tour among the mountains & the way in which first one cried & then another was so distressing that we were obliged to beg for another room which we were promised for the next day.

Tuesday August 10 We made a sorti directly after breakfast and went first to the post office & then had a very pleasant walk in & about the curious little town & by the side of the river & we were soon quite enchanted with Lucerne. It was so sweet & clean & fresh & the people have such nice good-natured open countenances & curious costumes all with their long plaited tails & black velvet boddices, they are a civil well behaved people too, & have the same kindly habit of bidding one good day when one meets them in the lanes & fields that Saxons have, & are not such impertinent starers as the French & Italians who sometimes seem to stare for the mere purpose of annoying one. We walked through the market, where they were selling live poultry & eggs & vegetables in no great variety, & no fruit except little hard dry stony pears which abound in this part of the world. The shops in Lucerne are not such as to tempt much money out of one's pocket, they are mostly tobacco & soap shops or repositories for the sale of the wood carvings with one or two shoemakers, one or two tailors, & a stationer or two, & thats about all. The streets are narrow but sweet & clean & the place altogether so quaint & old fashioned with its pointed spires & curious old wall & watch towers that we were quite charmed with it. In the middle of the day we were fortunate enough to make our escape from the young Belgians & moved into new

Lucerne, 10th August 1847

rooms at the other end of the house, John had been obliged to get up & scold the nurse in the night for her unkindness to the poor children & to threaten to write to her master, the noise must have been awful before he would have gone such lengths, we were very glad to get away from the poor little animal's painful cry. When I keep an hotel[3] I wont take in any children for my own sake as well as that of my other customers, three parties in the day had complained of the noise of our tormentors. At dinner the party were mostly novelties, a very nice party of 4 youths taking a trip during their holidays & very merry & happy they were. I was very much annoyed at an old wretch of an Irishwoman who was bragging & giving herself airs all dinner time & after dinner was mean enough to pocket some of the fruit & cakes, nasty sneaking old thing, I do hate such shabbiness, & she thought she did it so well & looked so respectable & so unconscious all the time, that I was determined she should see I was watching her, & I shall again, for I dislike such people very much.

Wednesday August 11 We went soon after breakfast to see the monument[4] carved in memory of the Swiss Guard who were killed while defending the royal family of France at the revolution in 1792, it is a gigantic lion wounded by a spear but defending the shield with the fleur de lis to the last, the countenance of the poor beast is admirably expressive of pain & the whole design exceedingly beautiful. It was by Thorwaldsen but executed by a sculptor from Constance, the names of the officers who fell are engraved under the lion, it is carved on the solid rock in the grounds of an old General who permits visitors to see it, & there is an old man who has the care of it who professes to have been in the Guard at the time of the revolution, but fortunately for him he was not at Paris, or he would not have been at Lucerne to tell the tale in 1847. There is a small chapel close by the monument where they make a great fuss with an altar cloth worked by the Duchesse d'Angoulême, but when it was uncovered for our admiration it was only a very coarse piece of worsted work. We had a pleasant hours strole through the fields & the curious old cloisters of the church & then returned home for the rest of the day. We had quite got now into the tide of English tourists and heard more of our own language than any other, this difference in language is, to me, one of the most striking things in travelling, to think that on one side of a mountain you have nothing but Italian, or at most a very few words of French, & on the other, the distance of a days journey, you come to a place where Italian is unknown & German or English the only tongue you hear, except among the waiters & they generally understand French all over the Continent. The trades people at Lucerne understand nothing but German & much pleasanter they are in their dealings & manners than their neighbours on the Italian side of the pass.

Thursday August 12 We took a long walk up towards Mount Pilatus & were still more & more enchanted with Lucerne, the walks in every direction are most lovely, it was rather too hot, but we managed to walk for about three hours & then went into a small inn and got some very good bread & butter & honey & beer for luncheon & returned home again for the day. Met three very pleasant talkative people at dinner who had been great travellers, one of the gentlemen we thought was a retired military for he had been in India, America, & every where else apparently, told marvellous stories about his friend's combats with tigers etc.

Friday August 13 Anne & John went out for a walk, but 'little pig staid at home' having rather overdone it the day before.

Saturday August 14 Sallied forth again on our adventures directly after breakfast, & after walking for about an hour & a half we found we had succeeded in losing ourselves, & asked a man whom we saw at the window of one of the houses to direct us. We proceeded as he directed us when we were stopped by a boy who told us we were trespassing in a field that we were crossing, we quietly turned back & soon met our friend from the window who was the owner of the field & had kindly come out to put us in the right way, not only that but he asked us to return to his house for rest and refreshment. We declined doing so & then he said if it would not be disagreable he would walk part of the way with us, & so he did & he & John had a great deal of conversation about things in general & among others the quarrel among the Cantons at the present time about the expulsion of the Jesuits, which he said must lead to a riot & that we had better send over the Duke of Wellington to put them to rights. He was a very clever intelligent old man, a perfect specimen of an upright simple Swiss, & we were very much pleased at meeting with such an instance of civility. He put us beyond the possibility of mistaking our route & then said he would go further if we wished but thought we could now find our way, & that when he came to England he had no doubt we would do the same for him & we took our leave. We walked on & on & were very hot & tired & very thankfully turned in to one of the little road side inns, just such as one reads of in books, so clean & neat & in such perfect Swiss shape, the old landlady & her daughter as neat as two pins, in Swiss costumes, long tails & white sleeves & all, the windows filled with flowers, hydrangeas & roses & geraniums, the floor cleaner than Italian tables & the delicious bread & butter & honey & beer & clean wooden benches to sit on, made us think it a small wooden paradise & all this luxury did we get for the small sum of one franc. It was well worth that to see the picturesque place & the kind old lady with her long grey plaited tails. We sat for a while much to the edification of two of the peasantry who we felt sure came in for the purpose of seeing the strange beings eat, & therefore never took their eyes off us but still there is nothing impertinent in the way in which they watch over here & one felt amused & not annoyed by the interest they took in our manner of eating bread & butter. We then started off again along a dusty road every winding of which we hoped would bring us in sight of Lucerne, & at last, but not until we were sorely tired, we saw the two pointed spires of the Church, & were not a little glad to find ourselves at home again, for even beautiful walks tire one in 4 hours & especially in very hot dusty weather & after being unaccustomed to much exercise for some weeks.

Sunday August 15 A dreadful hot day. Anne & I went to the English service performed in the German Protestant chapel, very tolerably read but a very stupid sermon from the

Lucerne, 23rd August 1847

minister who I suspect is very poorly paid, the prayers & sermon all performed strait on without stopping except to put on his gown, for there is no accommodation for music & therefore they very wisely dispense with it. There were a great many people & we were surprised to find them ridiculously overdressed which in such a place as Lucerne is very much thrown away, such flounces & fine bonnets & footmen to carry the books, & to go to such a poor little shabby poverty stricken place seemed rather a contradiction, but we'll hope they were all very rich & put a great deal into the plate for the poor parson, the day was too hot for walking so we read & looked out at window at the good people in their holiday trim, their straw hats trimmed with flowers & gay ribbons. In the evening we saw the Pope's Nuncio[5] who lives at Lucerne come out for a crawl, a great fat bloated looking creature dressed like a Priest, with purple stockings and a gold chain & cross round his neck & three servants, two in livery, walking behind him, & the people some of them went down on their knees as he passed & all bowed. Just as he got opposite to the hotel it seemed to occur to him that it looked like a storm so off he walked again & the storm soon began & very beautiful it was as we watched it gradually pass across from the Righi to Pilatus & then down came the rain & monstrous glad we were to see it, for it had been so desperately hot all the afternoon that we had quite wished for a storm but we rather pitied the poor people who were coming home from Fluellen in the steamers & there are generally a good many go from the hotel & return at night. It must be a wearysome life to keep an hotel like this, where there is accommodation for 200 people, & where they seem to change them almost all every day & while we were there I believe it was full every night. The poor chambermaid said she had 48 beds to make every day & she only had the care of one floor, & the waiter said he did not go to bed until near 12 & was up every morning at 3, so they do not have a very easy life of it during the season which lasts four months, & then they are dismissed until next year.

Monday August 16 John had a lame foot again, so Anne & I went to the post office & got some letters & papers & then to the bankers & got some money, & having deposited all the valuables with John, we went out again in search of the picturesque for the sketchbook & one has no need to search far at Lucerne. The morning was very fine but hot, & the steam rising from the wet ground made the air feel like a vapour bath & to my great horror my parasol chose this indiscreet time for going to immortal smash, or rather split, & there was I in a desert place as regarded shops & shipwrecked for a parasol. However, go on with such a tattered concern I could not, so I determined to go to all the *first rate* shops & seek for the important article, bewailing on my way the perverseness of parasols & other things of like disposition that they will not wear out at places like Turin, where there are thousands more, but desert one where we cannot replace them. However seeing a parasol in a shop window we went in & were surprised to find a choice of at least a dozen, dreadful rubbish they were too, but better than nothing, and as the lady merchant told us that parasols without fringe were much used in Paris we deemed ourselves fortunate in meeting with one minus that ornament & wending our way home again rejoicing in having become fashionable of necessity. At dinner we met our pleasant friends again who had made an unsuccessful attempt to get on to the Brunig pass – but found such difficulty with their luggage, & such exorbitant demands on their purses, that they came back again intending to go by some other route, a useful lesson to us who had had some notion of going by that road too. After dinner Anne & I went out again while she sketched Mount Pilatus & were rather annoyed by one of the poor idiots that are so numerous in Switzerland, he came quite close and made faces at us, the poor creatures are very unpleasant to meet in a lonely place. It is curious to hear the watchmen round Lucerne in the evening blowing their horns & answering each other from the different stations & then every quarter of an hour singing a sort of short chant, the words of which we were never near enough to discover.

Tuesday August 17 Had a beautiful walk among the hills & woods on the further side of the lake & walked through the curious old roofed bridge decorated with paintings of the Dance of Death, very old & curious they are too as well as the bridge itself. The day was intensely hot, nevertheless we enjoyed our walk very much, the winding walks through the woods are so lovely, & the shade was not the least agreable part, we went to get some lunch at one of the small confectioners who complained very much that there were so few visitors this year, which he attributed to a fear of the reported war, but most of the foreigners say that the English cannot afford to travel this year because they have spent all their money on the Irish. There must be a great many on the move, too, when the hotel is full every day & we hardly can meet the same people twice at dinner.

Wednesday August 18 Again had a long walk to a village in the neighbourhood, but not so pleasant a one as yesterday, for we kept along the road & it was dreadfully hot & dusty. Today the little tormenting children that had been such a nuisance to us when we first came, went away with their father, a Belgian Count & their french mother, no wonder the children are badly managed, a French mother is reason sufficient. Their place in our affections is filled by two English girls in the room underneath us, who tease a poor unfortunate piano all day long from 9 in the morning until ½ past 10 at night, & such playing as would surely kill any old woman's cow that came within hearing. Sometimes of an evening there is a party of men come past the Hotel who sing what we suppose to be a national hymn most beautifully, one night there was a universal clap from the windows of the hotel, but they did not repeat the performance, so I suppose they are a party of amateurs, who sing for their own amusement and not for ours.

Thursday August 19 The weather so intensely hot that we agreed it was pleasanter to sit still & therefore did so. A party of 30 came in by the steamer at 11 o'clock & dined at the ½ past 12 table d'hote for there are two dinners here each day, & upwards of 30 went away at 2 o'clock which looks like getting in the harvest though they complain of so few travellers coming this year. The heat was most oppressive & we could not help laughing at the Chamber maid when she came into John's room in the evening saying in German 'Well are you hot enough,' she is quite an oddity & seems very much puzzled at John's writing so much, she has said to him once or twice 'You are always busy.'

An entirely new party except my favourite fruit-stealing old woman today at dinner, nearly all foreigners, the people who have been up the Righi do not encourage one much, yesterday a party here told us they had spent the night before at the small hotel on the summit in company with 61 people, the house so overfull & noisy that sleeping was hopeless even if the sheets had not been so damp as to be quite unsafe, they saw the sunrise but the sunset was cloudy. Most people that we have seen have failed in seeing either, I think it wont do for us.

Saturday August 21 John went off by the steamer at 5 o'clock to Weggis to go up the Righi which he accomplished in three hours, but in coming down again was drenched with rain, & had three tumbles from the slippery state of the road. He got home sorely tired and stiff at 5 o'clock. Anne & I had a very pretty walk in the morning by the side of the river & along the road to Berne, & saw more old fashioned flowers in the cottage gardens than we had seen for months, most lovely major convolvulus & nasturtiums & many of our old friends that we were glad to see again. The cottages are all pictures of neatness & all, if they have not a garden, have pots of nice flowers in all the windows, the Swiss are thorough lovers of flowers, thats quite plain. We saw also, hanging outside some of the cottages, picturesque garlands of onions, they always have plenty of them in their gardens. Today we had a Sir George Rose[6] & his lady & toady at dinner, they sat next the dear old lady that prigs the fruit & whom in the course of conversation we found was a Mrs Tighe an Irishwoman & we 'thanked our stars to be rid of a knave'. I'm glad she's not English, she Sir George'd away all dinner time in the most approved tuft hunting[7] fashion, pity she has not any proper pride to prevent her committing petty larceny.

Sunday August 22 Went to the small chapel which was quite full, when we came out it rained & the congregation had to scramble home as it best could, the rain was not heavy & they had not far to go, for Lucerne is a small place. At dinner old Mrs Tighe had a countryman next her & actually had the impudence to say 'She could not deny that the English had been liberal to her countrymen, but she did not think they had the *head* to govern them,' whereupon old Sir George gave her a good rap, for he said, it was a pity they could not govern *themselves*. An old scamp, I like her to be snubbed but it is not easy for she has all the impudence of her race. The Table d'Hôtes are very amusing but one meets with very few pleasant people.

Thursday August 26 Had a long days journeying again from six in the morning to 9 at night which brought us safely to Thun, a cloudy & rather wet day but a beautiful ride nonetheless through green valleys & by the side of roaring rivers & over numbers of the curious old covered bridges for in Switzerland the bridges are almost all roofed. We stopped 3 or 4 times to rest or water the horses who were fed with brown bread & water with flour stirred in it, & we were fed with coffee & bread & butter & cold ham etc etc & as we got towards the end of our journey we had a little adventure that amused us very much. We had had another party following us some way on the road & at last when we stopped to dinner they took the unhandsome advantage to gain over our driver to let them go first in order that they might have the best chance of rooms at the hotel which at that season was generally full, so we let them go first & kept quietly behind until their man, who did not know the road, took the wrong turning & was driving off to Berne & then we thought we might as well have our own again, not that it signified so much to us as our rooms had been ordered two days before, but we did not like their meanness in tampering with our driver instead of speaking to us. They were rightly served, for when they got to the Hotel it was quite full & they were obliged to seek for quarters elsewhere.

Sunday August 29 Went in the morning to the Chapel built by the owner of the Hotel for his English inmates, a very nice plain little building in a beautiful situation in his own grounds. We had a sermon & collection for the relief of the Protestant Clergy in Ireland, and a very good collection it seemed to be. We then went for a walk & a beautiful one we found by the side of the roaring river & through lanes of cherry & walnut trees, the houses real Swiss Chalets of wood many of them beautifully carved & with moral inscriptions carved on the beams between the windows. The costumes here are somewhat different to those at Lucerne especially the headdresses which are like large black butterflies with clear lace wings set upon the women's heads, the men most of them wear clothes made of the wool of brown or black sheep undyed & very respectable everlasting looking clothes they are. They keep Sunday very strictly here, everything being very quiet and the people sitting chatting outside their pretty houses, evidently spending their Sundays in a serious & respectable manner.

Monday August 30 Anne went out by herself to sketch & when she returned we all went out for a walk & went to one of our favourite little Inns for some bread & butter & honey & then Anne & I went up to the Church yard which stands quite above the town & where she got a very good view of it, & I had a conversation with an old Sexton whom I nearly frightened to death by appearing unexpectedly at the door of the church while he was sweeping it. He told me the owner of a beautiful Schloss[8] that they are building by the side of the river is a banker from Paris, certes he has one of the loveliest gardens that one can imagine, large beds of dahlias, hollyhocks, scarlet geranium, hydrangea & I do not know what else in full bloom but from the steamer in passing along the river it looks like a perfect blaze of bright colours. The afternoon was wet, we had two good natured Germans at dinner who spoke very good English.

Tuesday August 31 A cloudy morning, nevertheless being strongly moved in the spirit to go and see the glacier of Grindelwald, away we went by the steamboat at ½ past 8 & had a tolerably pleasant trip down the Aare though the mountains were so hidden by clouds that we could only now & then distinguish their forms. The Captain of the boat had the most magnificent Newfoundland dog I ever saw, he was like a gigantic black bear but very good tempered & amiable to the passengers. We got to Neuhaus at the other end of the Lake in an hour & a ¼ & as good luck would have it our voiturier who brought us from Lucerne was on board, and introduced us to a very nice carriage & a respectable driver & worthy horses to take us on to Grindelwald, so we went strait from the boat to the carriage not

Thun, 30th August 1847

a hundred yards, & drove through Interlachen, a beautiful valley full of Hotels & Pensions & a wonderfully favourite place with the migratory English who live there in the said Pensions or boarding houses at the charge sometimes of 3 francs a day. It is a lovely place & looked as we passed through quite swarming with visitors. On we went until we came to the village of Lauterbrunnen, where we were told we must stay, & walk up to see the fall of the Staubbach, so being obedient out we got & being provided each with a huge cotton umbrella for it rained fast, we trudged off ¾ of a mile along a slippery wet path, where we came to the best view of the fall, which is certainly very fine. It dashes down over the face of the rock 995 feet & becomes little else besides spray before it reaches the bottom, in fine weather when the sun shines it must be splendid. We were beset by the little beggars who made pretence to help us when we wanted no help, & by the elder persons who put themselves in your path & began one of their unearthly Swiss howls to persuade a little money out of your pocket, but there is one good thing about them, they are satisfied with a mere trifle. When we got back to the hotel we consoled ourselves with some very good bread & butter & coffee, & then proceeded on our way, the rain continued to fall and the mists to hang most provokingly round the mountains, but with all that there was sufficient left to wonder at & admire, for such a wild scene I never saw before, immense mountains covered with fir trees & strewed with huge blocks of stone, the remains of the ravages caused by avalanches in the winter. Here now & then we drove through a complete trench of rough stones & earth that had been washed down the sides of the mountains, then through a stream that ran across the road & then over one of the unsafe looking bridges that they put up where the torrent has washed away the road entirely. Now & then we passed a wooden chalet & a few poor looking wooden huts, some of them made only of rough logs, the people we saw looked poor & diseased & the sickly looking children came in numbers to sell their little stocks of plums or pears or more frequently to beg. We saw an immense herd of goats feeding on the mountain & their attendant herd treated us as we passed to a few notes from his long horn, decidedly more melancholy than musical. We were entertained very much at being stopped by a voiturier whom we met, & who told our driver that 'the Eagle was full, so he must take us to the Bear'. It seemed as if we had been brought into a savage wild to be made a meal of, either by birds or beasts. At last, after mounting & mounting until we wondered whether our good steeds were going to take us quite up into the clouds, we came in sight of the two Glaciers & the sight quite repaid us for our long rough journey, they are indeed very singular & wonderful things quite unlike anything else & no description can give any idea of them, further than that they are like an enormous river or sea down the side of a mountain, completely frozen and in the clefts & cracks of a bright deep blue, the rest white, except where the earth & stones have fallen on the surface, the largest of the two at Grindelwald is said to be 115 square miles in extent. We were prevented going upon them for they are an hours walk from the hotel & the rain fell so fast that we did not feel inclined to go out in such a cold climate for a two hours walk, so we contented ourselves with the very good view we had of them from the windows of the 'Bear' & at 5 o'clock sat down with the other visitors to dinner, these consisted of six Americans & five

Glacier of Grindelwald, 31st August 1847

English. We soon got to be very sociable with the Yankees who were very intelligent nice people though rather rough until we got used to them. After dinner the three American ladies retired but we did not like to leave a nice snug wood fire, so there we sat all the evening talking to an old American who did not belong to the other party, a very agreable old man & very free from the prejudices that are considered a part of the American character & really, to say truly, we have, since we left home, met with more pleasant Americans than English, the latter have been very much the reverse.

Wednesday September 1 We had a great deal of fun with the Yankees about the wooden carvings that are for sale in the hotels through Switzerland, one of the ladies said she could not have enough of them but her husband seemed to look on them as rather an inconvenient addition to the luggage, having already sent off a large case of them to meet him at Paris on his return homewards. We saw them all mount their horses to take the overland track to Lucerne & then we got into our less adventurous vehicle & returned by the same road we had come as far as Interlachen, at a short distance from which we came to the Brienz Lake where we were to meet the Steamer which was to take us to see the fall of the Giesbach, we had to wait an hour & a half so Anne & John mounted up the side of a hill to a small pavilion from which there was a good view & I waited for them on the old covered bridge. At 11 we started in a small & remarkably slow steamer down the Lake of Brienz which is about 8 miles long & in some places is as much as 2100 feet deep, the range of mountains on each side most magnificent & fortunately quite cloudless. We were an hour performing the voyage & landed at the foot of the fall, & mounted in company with a large party up a very steep winding path to a small hotel built where the best view of the entire fall is to be obtained, we walked to several points of view which was sometimes rather a slippery business as the rain of the previous day had made the narrow pathways anything but agreable, but we were amply repaid by the beauty of the scene. We had some bread & butter & some of the celebrated fish caught in the lake, called Lotte, a kind of eel, & by the time we had withstood several vigorous attempts to induce us to buy a parcel of wood carvings, it was time to start on our downwards journey in order to avoid going down in a string with all the other visiters, so we made our descent and sat on a bench on the small ricketty sort of pier from which the passengers go on board the steamer & passed our few minutes in trying to get a little information out of a juvenile cake & pear selling peasant, but she was rather obtuse & we did not learn much beyond where she lived & other things of like interest. An hour took us back to Interlachen where our voiture was waiting to convey us back to the lake & the other steamer, & we accomplished our voyage back to Thun in comfortable time, the day very cold but not wet so we thought ourselves very fortunate.

Saturday September 4 Cold wet morning, left Hotel Bellevue & Thun at 11 & had a rainy ride to Berne of 3½ hours, the country pretty & nicely cultivated all the way but as this was just the manuring season there was nothing to be seen but beautiful green pastures covered with small black heaps, which rather spoiled their beauty & became very monotonous after we had seen several miles alike. The rain & mist quite obscured the tops of the mountains but we passed some nice clean looking houses & beautiful bright gardens full of major convolvulus & dahlias. We arrived at the Hotel Faucon at Berne somewhere about 3 & had dinner & then went out for a walk which is quite practicable even in wet weather as the chief streets in Berne are built with stone arcades in front of the shops, the said shops being dark dull looking little holes, but apparently well stocked with the necessaries & a good many of the luxuries of this world. We sauntered about for a couple of hours looking at the curious old fountains in the middle of the streets with the quaint looking stone figures, & the numerous repetitions of the Bear, the Emblem of the city, which you see in every size & material from a Gentlemans shirt pin to the Colossal stone figures at the sides of one of the gates.

Sunday September 5 We went out directly after breakfast to pay our respects to the bears that are maintained by the City & after wandering in search of them for about an hour arrived at the pit, where we saw one of the poor bears wandering about apparently in very low spirits, next we walked round the Cathedral & saw a handsome bronze figure[9] that was in the process of erection in honour of somebody, but there was no name on the pedestal. The Cathedral is rather a fine old Gothic building & has a curious doorway carved with figures representing the wise & foolish virgins in the parable, with the Last Judgement in the centre. There is a pleasant terrace walk at the back of the Minster from which in fine weather there is a good view of the chain of Bernese Alps, but today it was thick & misty with perpetual showers. Next we went to see the old Rathaus & then sauntered about so as to be in time to see the curious mechanism of a very old clock in one of the gate towers, just before the clock strikes a cock flaps his wings & crows, then a figure turns an hour glass & several others perform divers other little interesting tricks but it is a childish affair, we then went home as the drizzling rain did not make the idea of a walk agreable. The party spirit between the Protestants & Papists seems carried to a sad length at present between the respective Cantons. Berne is Protestant & therefore all the print shops have caricatures of the Jesuits & other hits at the Priesthood, & the bedrooms at the Hotel were all furnished with a french edition of the Testament which one might be inclined to admire if one did not feel that it was done rather in the spirit of opposition than for peacemaking, for where there is a mixed population each side thinks it necessary to be more bigotted & violent than where they are more distinct & that is quite the case evidently in Berne, however it is a curious & interesting old town so I wont abuse it. The houses are all built of good substantial stone, & it is an improving place too, for they have just finished a very handsome bridge at one end of the town & are now building one at the other end to make the approaches to the town more easy as the old road was a very steep ascent and the bridges will level it considerably. We were a large party at dinner mostly English and very common place but at the bottom of the table was Lord Ranelagh[10] who is by no means common looking at any rate.

Monday September 6 Left Berne a little after 7, a wet cold uncomfortable morning, we stopped at Hindelbanke, a small village two hours from Berne to see a very curious monument[11] to the memory of the wife and child of one of the pastors of the village. It is intended as a representation of the spirits of the lady & her infant bursting from the tomb on the last day, a beautiful idea & very finely executed, the stone lies on the floor of the small church and is apparently just burst into 4 or five rough pieces as a stone would break, & you see the forms of the mother & her little naked infant in the grave, the face of the lady is very beautiful but some mischievous wretch had chipped off the nose which had been replaced, but left an unsightly mark where it was joined. We continued our route for a couple of hours again & then stopped to rest the horses & dine, & then on again through beautiful grass pastures & such orchards & miles on miles of apple & pear trees, loaded with beautiful ripe red fruit & through some few fir forests, the rain continuing to drizzle & making the roads very stiff & trying for the poor horses & the views of the distant mountains very indistinct for us, however we got very comfortably to our journey's end about six to Kreutzstrasse. Just before we got there we met a gentleman walking along the road & Anne said 'that looks like Mr Dodsworth'[12] & so we proposed that he was taking a pedestrian tour through Switzerland with no creature comforts but his umbrella, as we knew him to be a self denying old pet, however on we went & secured rooms & tea at the Golden Lion. While we were at tea in the Salon there was tea prepared for two other travellers at the same table, & we began to wonder whether it could possibly be Mr & Mrs Dodsworth, thinking it almost impossible to meet anybody we had ever seen before in such an out of the way place as Kreutzstrasse, when presently in walked the said Simon Pure but not with Mrs Pure, but Archdeacon Manning, a bird of similar hue, two holy crows, funny enough we had seen two crows sitting chatting together in the morning & wondered what good luck it portended. The old fox did not seem to recognise his lambs again so we did not hold any communication, he was going to Lucerne to hunt among the Jesuits, I suppose.

Tuesday September 7 We were up and on our way before our two clerical friends were stirring & had a great mind to write their names in the travellers book as an indication that Daddy ought to have known us, but we didn't. The morning was cold & wet & the afternoon not very fine, we stopped to rest the horses at Baden, a nasty little town celebrated as its name implies for baths, the people at the hotel proposed our dining at the table d'hote which was just ready, so we did & a very curious party we met, some very decent people, some quite the reverse, as the old individual that sat next me was certainly the most disgusting animal I ever saw, out of a sty. I expect it was market day & they were a collection of the genus clodhopper. We got to Zurich about 5 o'clock & went to the Hotel Baur, a very large but comfortable place to which we had been strongly recommended by some people we met at Lucerne. The evening was wretchedly cold, so we had the stove lighted & soon made our room warm enough. The days journey would have been a beautiful one in more favourable weather, the hills were lovely & the plentiful crops of fruit, especially the bright rosy apples that abound in Switzerland are very pleasant to look at, but in such damp dull cold weather one does not feel able to enjoy them as one ought.

Zurich and the Journey Home

September 8th to October 9th

ZURICH · TWENTY NIGHTS AT THE HOTEL BAUR · BROTHER HENRY AND HIS BRIDE ARRIVE
BY CARRIAGE TO RHEINFALLS, BY BOAT ACROSS THE RHINE · TWO NIGHTS AT THE WEBER HOTEL
BY CARRIAGE TO FREIBERG VIA THE BLACK FOREST · ONE NIGHT AT THE ZAHRINGER HOTEL · BY TRAIN TO HEIDELBERG
FOUR NIGHTS AT THE PRINZ CARL HOTEL · BY TRAIN TO MANNHEIM · BY RHINE STEAMER TO COLOGNE · ONE NIGHT AT THE HOTEL D'HOLLANDE
BY TRAIN TO LIÈGE · ONE NIGHT AT THE HOTEL CHEMIN DE FER · BY TRAIN TO OSTEND · ONE NIGHT AT THE HOTEL D'ALLEMAGNE
BY STEAMER TO DOVER, BY TRAIN TO CROYDON, BY CARRIAGE TO MITCHAM · ONE NIGHT AT WILLIAM'S HOME
BY CARRIAGE TO WIMBLEDON, BY TRAIN TO SOUTHAMPTON AND HOME

Zurich and the Journey Home
September 8th to October 9th

Wednesday September 8 Directly after breakfast went out to see Zurich, & very much pleased we were with it, it seems a nice flourishing clean place, well supplied with everything, & the people look prosperous & thriving. It is a great manufacturing place for steam machinery, for silk, woollen & cotton goods, there are two very rapid rivers run through the town turning several mills & meeting just outside Zurich, & the numerous ins & outs & crannies & curious old bridges make it a very amusing place to walk about in. We went up to a promenade on what used to be the fortifications and got a pretty good view of part of the line of snowy Alps. When we had had walking enough Anne & I returned into the streets to hunt for thick boots, & went to one of the shops where they sold the fine embroidery that the Swiss are celebrated for, & some very beautiful work we saw and a very stupid old woman to show it, & then we returned home. The evening most bitterly cold again but we cheered ourselves with a bottle of champagne to drink the health of Henry & his bride whom we had been wishing all day might share the bright sunshine that we had been enjoying at Zurich.

Thursday September 9 Rather a cloudy day but we walked off to one of the sights recommended to the visiters of Zurich, viz: a hill called the Weid about three miles from the town where there is a very fine view of Zurich & the environs & when clear, of the mountains beyond, but the day we were there it was not clear, so the mountains were in a great measure left to the imagination. We had some very good bread & butter & some very strong ham & cheese at the little hotel on the hill, & then returned by the village of Kussnacht home, the neighbourhood of Zurich is very pretty but not to be compared with Lucerne. Received a nice long letter today from Gilbert, the party at the Table d'Hote a small one & all English, in the evening were driven into having the stove lighted, by bad colds.

Friday September 10 We went to see the Botanical Gardens, from which there is a beautiful view of the Alps of Glarus with their snowy tops, the gardens are very poor, very full of indifferent flowers, & not in very nice order, we found the weather quite changed warm again, a very agreable find.

Copy of a printed description of the Town of Zurich hung in all the rooms of the Baur Hotel, Zurich: '*Capital of the Canton the oldest & most important manufacturing town of Switzerland, distingtified above all others for prosperous industry and natural situation, may by reason be called the most agreable stay. Nowhere we find a more healthsome state of atmosphere than here and scarcely travellers will find in no place of Switzerland more diversion. Without trouble inconveniencey or danger they enjoy on every points the most delightful view upon the lake and the chain of the Alps. So the most pleasing features in the proximity of the town are the following, Botanical garden etc etc etc more distant, The Weid, The Hochlei, etc, etc. On all this points travellers find every possible comfort. But also the internal part of the town offers many interesting things. The old arsenal, containing a great number of ancient armours and coats of mail, The town library close to the stone bridge formerly a church contains an addition to 62,000 vols several logical & historical works of celebrety. The museum club contains a capital reading room where more than hundred of the best continental journals & litterary gazettes are taken in, it is open from 9 in the morning to tea in the evening & finaly a quantity of industrial, medical & instructive stablishments, The new builded hospital, the building for blinds & deafs & dumbs are very beautiful & deserve to be seen. The Steam boat goes twice the day in Summer time from Zurich to Rapperschwyl & to the other end of the lake. Both sides of the shores offer very good new roads, and excursions in a carriage or a boat to Kussnacht or Thalwyl 3 English miles from Zurich are most pleasing. On account of the tickets of admission for the different stablishments as well as for carriages, travellers may adress themselves to the bureau of the hotel. Travellers having no time to see the already named points of views will indenitify themselves for this loss by visiting the Belvedere of the hotel, which likes a walk (containing 300 ft in the length by 16 in the broad) nothing can be more delightful than this view, particularly at sunset, from this point extending over the smiling & populous shores of the lake of the distant peaks & glaciers of the Alps of Glarus, Uri, & Schwitz, tinged with the most delicate pink by the sinking rays. On this Belvedere of the hotel travellers find every comfort for refreshments, Dejeuners, tea in the evening every thing is wound up by means of a mecanism.*' This description was too amusing to be lost so I copied it verbatim.

Saturday September 11 We went out with the intention of finding our way to the top of what they call the little Righi, a hill about an hour & half walk from the hotel, we had a very pretty walk & thoroughly tired ourselves, but missed the path & could not find our way to the top of the hill. The quantities of Apple & pear trees are beyond belief & several times we tried some of those that had fallen off into the road but they are the nastiest rough sour little wretches, quite impossible to eat, more like a crude tasted sawdust than anything else I can imagine, I believe the common wine here is made from them & therefore is more easily imagined than described. We saw a curious procession pass the hotel today, one of the professors of the college at Zurich was leaving home for a short tour & the students were paying him the compliment of accompanying him some distance, a few of them in open carriages and others on horseback in black velvet dresses & scarlet & white scarfs, they looked very gay. There is nothing much to notice in the Zurich costume, we saw a few women with a short black petticoat over a long scarlet or blue one but no costume equal to that at Lucerne.

Sunday September 12 Went to the Morning & Afternoon services at the English Chapel & heard two most clever & impressive sermons from the old Chaplain, a Swiss, but who speaks English very well, as it was only from two or three peculiar expressions that he used that we discovered he was not an Englishman. The Chapel is very plain but clean & comfortable, a collection was of course made at the doors for its maintenance, in the churchyard adjoining is the grave of Lavater[1] with only a plain stone slab to his memory, his monument is in one of the large churches in Zurich.

Monday September 13 We had a very long and beautiful walk to the top of a hill called Höckli where there is a splendid view of the lake & town of Zurich. It was rather hard work to get up the steep steps to the place where we were to see the view, but we were fully repaid by its beauty and the fine sight we got of the range of Alps. We went into the small hotel half way down the hill & had some bread & butter & Gruyere & wine & John found a book there, extracts from German Authors, that pleased him so much that he went straightway & bought it on our return to the Town. The day was bright & so hot, & the people all busy gathering their apples & pears, they say that they distill a great deal of brandy from them, there was an enormous crop & they were shaking them off the trees & carrying them away in sacks. We saw a great many poor people pass through the town on their pilgrimage to the Shrine of Our Lady of Einsiedeln[2] taking their provisions in wallets on their backs.

Tuesday September 14 John went by the Steamer at 8 o'clock to Rapperschwyl at the other end of the lake intending to walk to Einseideln to see the pilgrims & ceremonies there which only take place once in three years but the day proved wet & he thought it more prudent to come back. Anne & I went out to get some presents to take home & then tried to get a walk but the rain drove us home too, John came home at ½ past five very much delighted with the beauty of his trip despite the bad weather.

Wednesday September 15 Had a nice long letter from Gilbert with account of Henry's wedding. John wrote to Wm & then we went out to watch for the arrival of the Steamboat as we expected it would bring back a great many of the pilgrims & as they came an immense distance from all parts of Switzerland the costumes were well worth seeing, but we had made some mistake as to the time of its arrival & did not see it. After sauntering about for an hour & walking round the Cathedral & curious old cloisters, & looking in at all the shop windows which are not very inviting, we went to the bankers to get some money, & there found that they shut up shop every day from 12 to 2 so we had to do another hours sauntering & then returned & found the goodnatured old banker & a great sack of quinces, from which we inferred that he had been spending his time in agreable society. We then returned home & saw a great many of the pilgrims pass in parties looking sadly tired & footsore, poor creatures.

Thursday September 16 As soon as breakfast was over we summoned our resolution & set forth to find our way to the top of the Hütliberg, a hill from which there is a fine view of the Bernese Alps on one side & the Alps of Glarus on the other & the whole length of the Lake of Zurich. We had a beautiful walk, a winding path ascending to the top of the hill with trees on each side. We just reached the top in time to get a look at the view, though the mountains were somewhat indistinct, when it began to rain, a pleasant prospect for us as there was no way but Shank's naggy of getting home again, we waited & had some lunch, & then as there seemed no probability of the rain ceasing & the more it rained the more slippery & dangerous would be the path, away we went & a most adventurous walk we had, we turned our gowns over our heads and made up our minds to plunge through thick & thin, but the paths were clay & so excessively wet & slippery, that it was with the greatest difficulty & only by means of setting our feet firmly down in the softest mud we could find that we could keep upright at all, & some of the steep corners we had to get round were especially awkward, luckily however by clinging every now & then to anything within reach, John being pioneer & helping us round dangerous corners, we kept on our feet & trudged back to Zurich, about 4 miles, & precious dirty & wet we were when we got there. I would willingly have sneaked into the hotel any back way that I could, but woes me, there is no way into the Baur but up the broad stone staircase, where we left the track of our wet feet at every step behind us. Of course we had to change our garments & by that precaution & a nice hot fire we escaped all evil from our adventure & had the amusement of drying our valuable wardrobe the rest of the day, the rain never ceased & the wind blew a perfect hurricane & banged the outside shutters all night.

Friday September 17 Had a letter from Henry at Brussels promising to be with us by Sunday & at one o'clock went to get some lunch at a quiet little pastry cook's & then Anne went to take a sketch & John & I went wandering about & came upon the preparations for a fair held under a long avenue of trees outside the town. The booths were full of all sorts of merchandise, pipes & tobaccos to put in them, worsted slippers, gloves, toys, millinery, looking glasses, & everything else one can imagine, the gloves seemed mostly sold by Tyrolese people with their high crowned hats adorned with gold bulbous tassels, some of the merchants professed to come from Milan & Vienna. There was a theatre at which the grand sea fight at Trafalgar was to be performed accompanied by a barrel organ, also a shew of a family born with wood instead of hair on their heads & other curiosities usual at fairs, we did not walk far as we had not quite recovered the fatigue of our yesterday's trip.

Saturday September 18 We went out to lunch & then to see how the fair was going on but found almost all the best booths closed on account of their owners being Jews, we fancied. The wind was very high & blew the dust in our eyes terribly, so John soon got tired & went home. Anne & I walked about a mile

Lake of Zurich from the Höchli, 24th September 1847

along the shores of the lake & then went home too. The afternoon & evening were very cold & wet.

Sunday September 19 Went to the two services at the chapel & had no sooner got home than the Clergyman Mr Myers was announced to our great surprise, he called very kindly to say he would be happy to be of use to us in any way that he could if we were going to make any stay in Zurich. He sat & talked nearly an hour about Mr Dodsworth & other clergymen & Zurich & things in general & wound up by asking us to go to tea at his house which we declined as we were expecting Henry & his wife, but we were very much pleased at the little man's kindness, & we found he was a Norfolk man & not a foreigner & had only been a few months in Zurich.

Monday September 20 Mr Myers called at 10 o'clock to take John to the reading room & we sat & worked until his return & then had an hour's strole to the fair & along the side of the lake, the day cloudy & disagreable. At night made up our minds that of course Henry & his wife would come & had the stove lighted & everything prepared to welcome them, but in came the Basle diligence & no Henry & wife, so we began to wonder if they would ever come or if they had got to some place where nobody could understand what they wanted. Very cold frosty night.

Tuesday September 21 John went to the post office & to buy himself some stockings, but we did not go out all day as it was cold & wet. In the evening came Mr & Mrs Henry Wilson & very glad we were to see them, they were very tired of their long journey, we sat & talked until near eleven & seemed as if we never could get through all we had to say.

Thursday September 23 Up before six to get breakfast ready for the lady & gentleman to set off at 8 to Lucerne, but the poor lady had such a cold that she could not in prudence get up, so John & Henry went off by Steamer to see the lake of Zurich, & we three staid at home to nurse & try to drive away the enemy. We spent a quiet day with books & conversation & Anne & I went to call on Mr Myers, but he was at dinner so we did not go in. John & Henry came home very much pleased with their trip & found the invalide convalescent.

Friday September 24 In the morning some of the party had to write letters & then as it was a beautiful day, we all set off to mount the Höchli, luckily we missed the way we went before & found a beautiful winding path that was new to us & a very lovely walk was had. We wanted to persuade the invalide that it was too far for her to go, but she was so anxious to find herself at the top of a real mountain that our remonstrances were useless & so we all went up except Anne who is no climber, we left her to sketch away half way up & away we went up the steep steps. Unfortunately the mountains were very cloudy when we got to the top, but we had the view of the beautiful lake & the shores on each side, with the innumerable white houses & pretty steeples standing up here & there, we sat & rested for a few minutes & then home. The fields through which we walked were strewed with apples & pears that had fallen from the trees, the

Lake of Zurich, 26th September 1847

trees themselves were some of them perfect models, the apples were such a brilliant crimson & in such quantities, but very bad to eat. Mr Myers told us that people were considered welcome to help themselves to any that lay on the ground, but there is no temptation for they are nasty crude little affairs. The fields we passed through were very gay looking with the lilac flowers of the Colchicum or autumn crocus. At dinner we met the Honorable & Reverend Baptist Noel[3] & his wife & daughter, he is a pleasant looking man.

Saturday September 25 Henry & Anne went out in the morning, one to draw & another to fish. They returned at 12, the one having caught some sketches & the other lost his line & float & then we all set out together to the Weid, & had a hot walk to it, the day being very close & cloudy. We stopped to lunch there & then home again. Mr Mayer came to dinner at six & very much pleased we were with him, he is a pleasant intelligent little man, he has the living of Langham Episcopi in Norfolk, but has leave of absence for two years, he was very anxious we should go to tea at his house to meet Mr Noel & some of the Zurich people, but setting aside all other disabilities we had no visiting costume at hand.

Sunday September 26 Went to Chapel to hear Mr Noel preach & did not like him at all, he being as we thought little else than a methodist. The morning was drizzly but cleared up afterwards & John and Henry went for a walk to Kussnacht & Anne went again to Chapel, & Charlotte & I sat & read & talked. Mr Mayers waylaid Anne & wanted her to promise that we should go to a party at his house on Tuesday, but as our arrangements were made for leaving before that time, we did not come in for a sight of the Zurich grandees, but his kindness & hospitality to us as strangers was the same.

Monday September 27 Busy by 7 o'clock packing up again & after breakfast I went to take back a little basket that the kind little clergyman had sent us some grapes in & when I got to the house the maid insisted on my going upstairs, so up I went & saw Mr Mayers & his daughters. I took an affectionate leave of him, & then he said he must go & take leave of the rest of our party, & so as soon as we had finished our packing he came in & sat with us for half an hour & begged we would recommend any of our friends who visited Zurich to him & then away he went, & soon after away went we in a very capacious carriage where we all had plenty of room. The day was very gloomy & cold until about one when it cleared up a little, but was still very cold. We stopped for half an hour's rest & bread & butter at Winterthur & then proceeded to Weber's hotel at the Rheinfalls near Schaffhausen which we reached about 5 o'clock & had some dinner, & then as we had no sitting room & the Salon was very cold we went early to bed.

Tuesday September 28 Directly after breakfast we went to see the falls from all the different points of view that travellers are recommended, though we could not have had a finer one than we had from the windows of our rooms which were just opposite & a most wonderful & magnificent sight it is to see a whole river like the Rhine precipitate itself down 70 feet

Rheinfalls near Schaffhausen, 28th September 1847

over the rocks, there are two picturesque blocks of rock that stand up in the middle of the scene & break the fall & much increase the beauty of it. We crossed in a boat just below the falls to the Castle of Lauffen inhabited by a person, half hotel keeper & half artist, who shewed us the views from various little galleries & summer houses in one of which John got a considerable wetting from the spray, & then introduced us to a picture gallery & small warehouse for the sale of prints etc which were so kindly & warmly pressed upon us both by Master & Mistress, that John was driven into buying some prints & then was called upon to pay a charge of a franc apiece for the privilege of going over the house. After we had seen the falls from above & on a level with the water, we walked along a beautiful winding path by the side of the river where we were agreeably amused & interested by searching for walnuts that had fallen from the trees we passed, then we came to some vineyards, the grapes looked hard & sour & some who tasted them said it was safe in some cases to judge from appearances. We were greatly amused by a very savage & terrific harangue that a young swiss peasant treated us to, as he was wheeling his barrow through the same vineyards where we were walking. The best of the joke was that we did not understand what it was all about except that he was threatening to take us before somebody when we got into the town, but having quietly continued our walk through the town & not been taken up before anybody we still remain in ignorance of our offence & the intended punishment. We had a beautiful walk & then a very nice luncheon & made our first & last acquaintance with the favourite Swiss cheese called Schabzieger[4] which is in appearance & taste the most unpleasant thing imaginable, being green to look at & tasting like a pigstye. We crossed the river again by a bridge and walked through the curious old town of Schaffhausen, where the outsides of the houses are many of them painted in fresco & have nice little bow windows looking out into the street, this is about an hours walk from the Hotel, & we were rather glad to get back again as we had been walking several hours. Anne & John went first for the purpose of sketching the falls & we took it easily & fell into the rear, we dined at the so called table d'Hote at 5 at which there was nobody present except ourselves & in the evening amused ourselves by reading & writing journals etc & the shattering of the windows served for a musical entertainment, for the wind was rather high & shook all the windows & doors most delightfully.

Wednesday September 29 Up before sunrise, that is at ½ past 4 & saw the sun rise over the falls & a beautiful sight it was, the immense cloud of foam rising from the water, which gradually cleared away as the sun rose. We had a beautiful view of the snowy peaks of the Alps before we left the Hotel Weber at 6, the morning was dismally cold & cloudy. We had not got more than a hundred yards from the Hotel when we came to a new piece of road that was unfinished & wherein a waggon heavily loaded had stuck fast & all the strength of six horses & two oxen & the attendant drivers failed to move it. The road was very narrow & we had to wait some time while they removed what they could out of our way, & then we all got out while the man manoeuvred the carriage past the unfortunate waggon & then we all got in again & had a beautiful up & down days ride. The two beaux had several long up hill walks to relieve the horses who had nevertheless a tremendous days work, 50 miles, from six in the morning until nearly 8 at night when we reached Freiberg. We stopped to dine & rest the steeds at a small hotel at Lenzkirch, a place where they make a great many of what in London are called Dutch clocks, we had a curious collection of them in the room where we dined. The road from there for several hours was one succession of very steep hills on each side clothed with trees of such brilliant colours as I never saw before, the mountain ash of a bright scarlet, the beech something between red & yellow & others of the brightest yellow or green, a great part of the way there was a small but rapid river running by the side of the road & altogether it was as beautiful a ride as ever was seen. Some part of the days journey was through the Black Forest & another part was called the 'Valley of Hell' but much more beautiful than one can imagine the infernal regions to be. We got rather tired & cramped after it became dark so that the last hour or two were somewhat wearisome & we were right glad to find ourselves in one of the most comfortable hotels we had been in since we left England, the Hotel Zahringer at Freiberg. Mr Mayer at Zurich had written a recommendatory letter to the landlord & he & his people were so civil & everything so good & comfortable that we were almost sorry we could not stay more than one night. Poor Charlotte was so tired that she went off direct to bed but we sat up to have some tea etc & then followed her example. The crops along our days route consisted principally of hemp & flax which were lying in rows on the ground to rot, but there was wheat coming up and Indian corn still unripe & a very untidy ugly crop it is, when nearly ripe they gather all the leaves & only leave the two or three cobs of corn on the plant. We saw nothing peculiar in costume, most of the women wearing a red handkerchief on their heads & the rest of their dress like poor English women.

Thursday September 30 John woke us early to say that we must go and see the Minster before 9 o'clock if we wished to see it at all, so up we got & at 8 o'clock went to the Cathedral, where the service was going on. It is a beautiful Gothic church with one of the most lovely open carved spires I ever saw, that, & the fine painted windows are the chief beauty. There were several curious old monuments & a very singular piece of sculpture of the last supper, with figures the size of life, just opposite the Minster is the curious old exchange ornamented with statues of four Emperors & other architectural trimmings. We returned to the Hotel to breakfast & at 11 o'clock departed by the railway to Heidelberg, the road was very pretty all the way & we had tolerably agreable companions considering that they were Germans. We got to Heidelberg at ½ past five and made our entrance to the Prinz Carl Hotel in a heavy shower of rain & there found that they had only one decent bedroom left & so John & Anne & I were obliged to adjourn to a couple of wretched cold little attics. We descended to the salon to dinner & tea & then did all the sleep we could in our lofty roosting place.

Friday October 1 A damp uncomfortable morning so we staid indoors until after the table d'hote dinner at one, & then went out to see the Castle, & a very splendid ruin it is, standing on the side of a hill surrounded by fine trees, but overtopping them all. The colour of the ruin is most picturesque, as it is built

Heidelberg, 1st October 1847

of red sandstone & has become darkened by time & the effect of fire, by which it was destroyed the last time when the fire lasted 8 days & nights, it was set on fire by lightening in 1764. It had been twice destroyed by fire before, during a war, & rebuilt & one of the huge towers was blown up by the French, & the side that was blown out instead of falling to pieces fell into the moat in one mass where it still lies & gives a very good idea of the strength & solidity of the building, the walls in some places are 24 feet thick. The most perfect part of the ruin is that called the Knight's Hall where the finely carved doorways & chimney pieces still remain. It was built in 1559 & is richly decorated outside with statues etc, the chapel is still tolerably perfect but all the other buildings are roofless. We went down of course to see the celebrated tun which is said to hold 800 hogsheads, in the same cellar where the tun is kept is a wooden painted figure of a jester who belonged to one of the Electors, & by his side what looks like a large wooden clock, & the girl who shows it says it was the jester's clock & desires you to pull a string at the bottom when out flies a fool's tail in your face & a bell rings at the same time, & your surprise gives infinite pleasure to your guide, as I suppose it was wont to do to the Jester himself. One of our conductors over the ruin was a girl of about 15 who talked very good English which she said she had picked up from the visiters in the course of 15 weeks, & she certainly had picked it up very well & was most amusing. Heidelberg is not a nice place though full of good shops, especially print shops which abound here, it has been a such unhappy place in its time, having been 5 times bombarded, twice laid in ashes, three times taken by assault & given up to pillage. During the thirty years war it was given up to the soldiers to be sacked for three days, there is a university & the town is consequently overrun with students & riotous & disagreable looking people they are & celebrated for the number of duels they fight. The grounds round the castle did not look to advantage when we were there for the day was gloomy & damp & every place smelt mouldy, there is one garden pointed out as having been planted for an English Princess, Elizabeth, daughter of James 1st, who married one of the Electors & lived here, & they shew a triumphal arch to one of the gardens which he had built in one night as a surprise to his bride, 'Very gallant in a husband' our young conductress said & seemed very proud of the English expression she had learned. I think, taken for all in all, Heidelberg is one of the most interesting places we have seen but there is something very melancholy in seeing such magnificence in ruins, & if I was the Duke of Baden I should feel strongly tempted to try restoring some part of it at any rate; some of the towers that have been blown up are quite hopeless, but he might restore some of the inside buildings that are more perfect, if he has plenty of money.

Saturday October 2 A lovely bright morning so Anne walked up again to the old Castle to spend a long day in sketching, & at 11 o'clock the rest of us set off for a walk by the side of the river Neckar to a village six miles distant called Neckargemünd, a most pleasant & beautiful but rather too long a walk, a row of walnut trees almost the whole way served to beguile the tediousness to some of our party who kept up an unceasing attack on the defenceless fruit all the way, besides buying a kreutzers worth consisting of as many as they chose to

Blown-up tower at Heidelberg, 2nd October 1847

take, that being the bargain the merchant made, they grow them here in immense quantities for the sake of the oil. We had a most lovely walk as the river ran close to us all the way, we went between two richly wooded hills & stone quarries in the red sand stone rocks. We stopped to rest & lunch at the beforementioned village & then toiled home again the same way, & sorely tired we were before we reached the Prinz Carl, but we did reach it at last & found Anne just returned from her drawing expedition. We made ourselves as snug as we could with the lighted stove in the evening & went early to bed to rest our jaded frames after our 12 miles walk.

Sunday October 3 The party were three of them rather late in getting up so directly after breakfast we went to Chapel & heard the service very respectably performed & a good short sermon, the Chapel was quite full which we were rather surprised to see but I fancy there are a good many English residents at Heidelberg. After chapel we had lunch & then a long walk to the Wolf's Brunnen, so called from a spring that rises there and a tradition that an Enchantress[5] was once devoured by a wolf on that spot, it was in the same direction as we had walked the day before, but up on the hill instead of by the river's side. There is a small Inn where the people go to eat trout & drink beer, we saw the trout in quantities in the small stream, where they are preserved by means of boards fixed on the top of the water for the fish to get under. We dined by ourselves at five, for we did not find the Table d'Hote at all to our minds, and had a fire again in our rooms for we found the evenings very cheerless & cold as soon as the sun went down.

Monday October 4 We left Heidelberg by the 11 o'clock train & had a pleasant ride to Mannheim, only an hour. We went to the Hotel & ordered rooms & luncheon & then went to see the wonders of the place which we found neither numerous nor splendid. There happened to be a fair in operation which served to pass away the time, also we went in like babies to see a wild beast show that had a splendid picture outside of Elephants etc, when we got in we found it consisted of one poor miserable rhinoceros, which we staid and looked at during a long oration made by his happy possessor & then took our leave. Henry & his wife returned home, & we went for a walk along the bank of the 'beautiful Rhine' & beautiful indeed it was for the weather was like spring, so sunny & fine. We had a pleasant walk through the public gardens & then home to dinner, & in the evening Charlotte & I amused ourselves with the intellectual game of dominoes, while John & Henry went to see an exhibition of rope dancing and feats of strength in a booth at the fair.

Tuesday October 5 At 6 o'clock, only just daylight & a nasty wet morning, we were on board the steamer to enjoy the beauties of the Rhine, we first thought of breakfast and by the time that was done & we had got to the pretty part of the scenery the rain came down in such good earnest that we found decking was ducking too & so down we all came into the cabin. We were rather a large party when all assembled, some few English but mostly foreigners, nasty frenchwomen & equally nasty frenchmen, some we fancied from their manners & appearance were gamblers from Baden[6], however there we were, and tried for some time every now & then to get up stairs for a peep, but the deck was so wet & the scenery so misty & wretched that we were obliged to give it up in despair & get on as well as we could by means of watching our fellow travellers. We had dinner at one which passed over an hour & after that the afternoon seemed terribly long & tedious as we did not reach Cologne until nearly nine, pitch dark & though not actually raining when we arrived it was damp & wretched & Cologne did not smell any sweeter than usual. When we arrived there John & Charlotte & I rushed off to the Hotel d'Hollande where we were before, to secure rooms, while Anne & Henry looked after the luggage. We received a very kind welcome from young Mr Illig who is an active clever young man, & soon got all the rooms ready & tea, & we were heartily glad to exchange the close hot cabin for a room by ourselves & were thankful to have performed a long tedious days journey without greater fatigue.

Wednesday October 6 After breakfast I went with John & Henry to the Bankers & such abominably dirty streets I certainly never saw elsewhere, they being considerably muddier than usual in consequence of a nights rain & perpetual heavy showers. Charlotte wanted to go out to seek for some presents for her nieces, but it was quite impossible, for John went out & nearly got up to his knees in mud. We dined at the Table d'Hote at one, a very large party, two or three of whom we remembered meeting at dinner when at Cologne before. As soon as dinner was over we went by railway to Liege where we were to spend the night in order to divide the long journey to Ostend. We got to Liege between 8 and 9 and as the railway guard had kindly recommended our going to the railway hotel & it was of course close to the station we preferred taking his advice to getting into an omnibus & having to take all our luggage into the city which is some little distance from the station. So we walked off to the Hotel Chemin de Fer, & were received by a remarkably loud tongued Frenchwoman, the hostess thereof, who summoned her myrmidons & seized our luggage & took us upstairs to our rooms before we had time to think what a very dirty entrance she had to her most desirable hotel, luckily the bedrooms were very clean & nice & what we had to eat & drink very tolerable & we managed very well for one night, but did not wish to prolong our stay on account of the excessive comfort of our quarters.

Thursday October 7 Before breakfast went out for a walk through the city of Liege and was much struck by seeing a very beautiful gothic church with a notice on the door that it was for sale. Several churches in Liege are used as Iron works, which seems at first a terrible thing, but on second thoughts, as they were only Romish churches they perhaps do less harm as they are. We left Liege at 8 and had a very pleasant ride to Malines, where we had to change carriages as the road branches off here to Brussels, we waited ¾ of an hour & were then put into a carriage with a couple of nasty french people who chose to keep the window up all the way, which as the sun was burning hot & the carriage quite full nearly stifled us, they luckily only went as far as Ghent & we were still alive & able to open the window, which speedily revived us & the rest of the way we did very well. We got to Ostend about 4 & went quite by chance to the Hotel d'Allemagne close to the station & very much pleased we were to find it the most comfortable we had been in since we left Home,

Terrace at Heidelberg Castle, 2nd October 1847

for the Ostend hotels have always been celebrated for dirt & discomfort, but luckily this was a new one and on a new plan, & most comfortable we were, & only sorry to leave it so soon. The night was a complete storm of wind & rain & lightening, a pleasant prospect for bad sailors on the morrow.

Friday October 8 Up before daylight, breakfast & on board at 7 & there have the pleasure of finding that the steamer is fast on the mud & refuses to move so there we stay, & there stays poor John, whom we here parted with as he was going into Holland, looking down on us from the quai. The steamer puffs and blows to no purpose for not a bit did we move, neither did we for an hour & a ½, which if we had but known we need not have hurried from our snug beds, however at last the tide rose & then we gave a last nod at John which he returned & away we go, and away I go downstairs, there to stay for 7½ dreadful hours, the vessel rolling awfully in consequence of the wind in the night, & almost all the women on board ill. All things come to an end at last & so did our voyage, and before we landed Henry who was on deck recognised William who had come down to see us land, we were sure of a kind welcome from him and went off to the Ship Hotel where he had made preparations for us, and where we learned with much regret that we must alter our plans & hurry home if we wished to reach it in time to take leave of our dear old friend Captn Lowry. William had kindly made all the arrangements for us to go that night to his house at Mitcham & return to Southampton the next day, so as soon as we had got our luggage from the Custom house we left Dover by the 4 o'clock train[7] as far as Reigate where we took leave of Henry & Charlotte who were going to Ewell, & we went on to Croydon & there met a fly that William had ordered to be there & got to Mitcham about 7, dreadfully tired but very glad to have got over so much of our journey in so short a time, thanks to railways & kind brothers. We had half an hour of dear Arthur's company before he went to bed & then sat & talked for an hour or two with William & Emily & went to bed too.

Saturday October 9 At 10 o'clock we leave Mitcham in a fly with Nurse & Arthur as far as the station at Wimbledon & there take leave of the dear little child & away by the train. The day was drizzly & unpleasant but we got comfortably to our journey's end & leaving our luggage to be sent on to Shirley, we went straight over to Pear Tree Green[8], where we had the grief of finding we were too late to receive a last kind word from our dear old friend. We spent the rest of the day with Miss Lowry & returned to our own home in the evening, where we were kindly welcomed after our long absence and were very glad to find ourselves once more safe at home & with so many pleasant remembrances of our journey to talk about during the winter that was approaching.

Reference Notes

INTRODUCTION

1 · William Gilbert, 1725-1797, of The Gables, Little Carlton, South Muskham, Nottinghamshire.
2 · Jasper Capper, Gracechurch Street, Linen Drapers, by Appointment to Her Majesty. Anne Wilson wrote: 'I have often heard my father speak, with interest and pleasure, of having talked with many of the great men, and most important women, of that period. Rather a change for the poor farmer's son!' 'Her Majesty' was Queen Charlotte, wife of George III.
3 · The widow was Martha Jones who, after the death of her husband, ran her small pottery in Vauxhall Walk, where John Doulton found employment in 1812. In 1815 Martha Jones formed a partnership with her foreman John Watts and the young hardworking thrower John Doulton. In 1820 she sold her share and retired to Hertfordshire, whilst the small pottery developed into the well-known Royal Doulton. No wonder the Wilsons had a keen interest in ceramics and wanted to see over the Meissen factory.
4 · At the Victoria and Albert Museum the painting by John Constable, 'Trees at Hampstead, the path to the Church, Sept. 1821', was probably painted at Greenhill.
5 · Sydenham Teast Edwards, 1768-1819. The son of a Welsh schoolmaster, he was a protégé of William Curtis, who published one of the first complete English botanical works, *Flora Londinensis*, between 1775-1787.
6 · The Wilsons did not own their homes. Family houses of quality, for sale, were in short supply until later in the century when large estates were broken up and developed. However, the Mitcham Grove estate, with the Mansion, 620 acres of land and farms, dwellings and mills, was sold by auction in twelve lots in 1828. Wandle Grove, Lot No. 12, with gardens, meadows, farm buildings, cottages and two water-powered corn mills, two snuff mills and a paper mill, was sold for £2440. The Wilsons could have afforded this sum but were not house-hunting until the following year. It was more convenient to have a lease from the new owner for a house they liked than go on searching for a house to buy.
7 · The linen shop closed down in 1901, at the time when the West End department stores were becoming well established and popular. Economic problems were not the reason for the closure; by this time the Wilsons were into the upper regions of the middle class and it was unacceptable to be working in the trade.
8 · Edward Wilson, 1813-1878. His biography in the *Australian Dictionary of Biography* and a sketch in *The Golden Age* by Geoffrey Serle do not give a full picture of Anne and Mary Wilson's brother, who battled for what he believed in until his death. His remains were buried in Melbourne and he wrote instructions for this arrangement in 1876, ending: 'people are best laid to rest in the vicinity of those places in which their best work has been done. And perhaps when the struggles of life are at last at an end even such enemies as I have made may acknowledge that I have been tolerably staunch in my devotion to my public duties and in my appreciation of the public interests.' His portrait, a statue by his friend Thomas Woolner (a founder of the Pre-Raphaelite movement), is in the State Library of Victoria in Australia but is not on view.

STAGE I
FROM ENGLAND TO SAXONY

1 · One of the world's first railway hotels, near London Bridge Station where trains left London for Dover. Trains from Southampton arrived at Nine Elms Station in Vauxhall (Waterloo Station opened in 1848). The Wilsons may have taken a boat between the two stations; there was a regular service and the River Thames was a major highway for travellers.
2 · Here Mary Wilson is forgetful or confused. Until 1806 large parts of Europe were in the Holy Roman or German Empire, including the Netherlands. Belgium was part of the Netherlands until 1830 when, after a revolt against the Dutch, it was declared a separate nation.
3 · The first Royal Exchange, the traditional meeting place for merchants in the City of London, was built in 1570 and modelled on the Antwerp *Bourse*. It was burned down in the Great Fire of London in 1666. A new Exchange was built in 1669 – the building Mary Wilson would have known when growing up in London. It was in turn destroyed by fire in 1838 and replaced by a third Royal Exchange, opened by Queen Victoria in 1844, after the Wilsons had moved to Hampshire.
4 · Nicholas Wanostrocht, schoolmaster, musician and author. He played county cricket for Kent, using a pseudonym to avoid upsetting the parents of his pupils. Early cricket was a disreputable game and Felix made an effort to end the bribery and gambling. He was a popular player, making jokes with the spectators and wearing an unconventional cap. His testimonial match at Lords in 1846 was attended by Prince Albert.
5 · Mother of Constantine, 274-337 AD, the first Christian Roman Emperor. Helena went on a pilgrimage to the Holy Land and found the Cross and Christ's Sepulchre. She also brought back the marble staircase from the Roman Proetorium at Jerusalem. It is preserved in Rome near the Lateran Church.
6 · The legend of Saint Ursula tells of the beautiful

and pious daughter of an English King on a pilgrimage to Rome before her marriage. On the way home she and her eleven companions (it was only discovered in modern times that there had been a mistake over the number) were slaughtered by barbarian Huns at Cologne. Some years after the Wilsons visited the church, an English anatomist declared that most of the bones were not human remains.

7 · Thomas Waghorn, 1800-1850, served in the Navy from the age of twelve. He became well-known for his plan to build a new and more economical route between Alexandria and Suez. The plan and its construction was the great work of his life and when complete in 1842 he returned to the Royal Navy as a lieutenant. The Suez Canal was constructed in 1869, making the journey to India and back even more economical and convenient.

8 · Marie-Joseph Sue, 1804-1857, a popular French author. The son of a doctor in Paris, he became a ship's surgeon but gave it up to write seafaring novels. Later he wrote sensational novels of Parisian low-life.

9 · Here Mary Wilson is remembering their first visit to the Rhine in the summer of 1834.

10 · Johann Dannecker, 1758-1841, a German sculptor. The statue, with the figure reclining on a leopard, was placed in a museum in the garden of Mr Moritz von Bethmann's villa. Later it was presented to the town of Frankfurt.

11 · The play – in German – of the extraordinary life and gruesome death of Count Johann Struensee, 1737-1772, a first minister of Denmark, was a formidable challenge for the English visitors.

12 · The 'Battle of Nations' in 1813, when Napoleon was defeated.

13 · Where the two great German poets died, after a close friendship.

14 · Possibly bogus names for the hotel register in order to get better service.

15 · Joseph Anton Poniatowski, 1762-1813, was born in Poland, the grandson of Stanislaus, a Prince and Marshal of France. He had a distinguished army career and Napoleon made him a Marshal just before the Battle of Leipzig. Being pressed by the enemy on the banks of the swollen Elster, he spurred his horse into the river. His body was found several days later and taken to Cracow for burial in the sepulchre of the Polish Kings.

STAGE 2
SOJOURN IN DRESDEN

1 · Joseph Tichatschek, 1807-1886, a great Bohemian tenor. His friendship with Madame Schroeder helped his career and he was appointed to the Dresden Royal Opera in 1838. He performed in *The Magic Flute* at Drury Lane in 1841.

2 · Wilhelmina Schroeder-Devrient, 1804-1860. A brilliant soprano who retired at the end of this Dresden season. She toured England several times in the 1830s and sang at Covent Garden.

3 · John Woodhouse Audubon, 1813-1862, the younger son of the naturalist John James Audubon, 1780-1851. He was working with his father on drawings for the engravers preparing the first volume of *The Viviparus Quadrupeds of North America*. In 1845 he made a long trek with a scout to Texas, looking for specimens, and the following year visited Europe with his wife and family who stayed in England. He toured the Continent engaged in 'making figures of those arctic animals, of which accessible specimens exist only in the museums of that quarter,' wrote his father. He left Europe in May 1847.

4 · Karl Christian Vogel, 1788-1868, a painter and professor at the Academy of Dresden, where he had studied. He painted portraits and some decorative works including frescos in the King's new summer palace at Pillnitz.

5 · In Bellini's opera *I Capuletti ed i Montecchi*.

6 · The Queen Maria, second wife of Frederick August II and a daughter of Maximilian Joseph, King of Bavaria.

7 · Friedrick Flotow's opera tells the story of Alessandro Stradella, 1645-1678, a composer and accomplished musician who was murdered in Genoa after a long and complicated love affair.

8 · The Palace of Albrechtsberg, built in 1481, had been the residence of the Margraves of Meissen, Princes of the Holy Roman Empire. It was set up as a porcelain factory by an alchemist named Böttcher in 1710 and became the Royal Porcelain factory, with 650 workers. It closed down in 1863 when a new factory was built outside the town.

9 · Jean Victor Moreau, 1763-1813, had a long and distinguished career in the French army. His success turned sour when Napoleon began to consider him as a rival and then as part of a royalist conspiracy. He was banished and retired to America. In 1813 he accepted an invitation from the Russian Emperor to assist the allied armies against France. He took part in the Battle of Dresden and was mortally wounded, dying soon after the amputation of both legs.

10 · Wilhelm Richard Wagner, 1813-1883, was conductor at the Dresden Royal Opera from 1843 until 1848 when he went into exile for political reasons.

11 · Mozart's *Don Giovanni*.

12 · Probably a merchant and John's business associate. Zittau was the centre for one of the oldest Saxon industries – the manufacture of linen damasks. The weavers lived and worked in the surrounding villages. From the catalogue of the Great Exhibition 1851, page 1107, No.51:

> 'Beyer's Widow & Co, Zittau.
> (Agents John Wilson & Sons, 159, New Bond Street.)
> Manufacturers. Linen damask table cloths; with napkins and doyleys – raw, white and bleached.'

13 · Once the home of Albrecht von Waldstein, 1583-1634, Duke of Mecklenburg, Friedland and Sagan. A statesman and general who found fame in the Thirty Years War.

14 · To slive: to creep about in a stealthy way, or to idle or lounge about, in Nottinghamshire dialect.

STAGE 3
BERLIN AND THE JOURNEY SOUTH TO THE TYROL

1 · Pauline Viardot, one of the daughters of Manuel Garcia, 1775-1832, a Spanish tenor, composer and teacher. His two wives and several sons and daughters were all international singers. Pauline became a famous mezzo-soprano, making her debut in 1837 and singing in Rossini's *Otello* in London in 1839.

2 · This opera by Meyerbeer had its première in Paris in 1836 and was performed at Covent Garden in 1841.

3 · Also by Meyerbeer, the opera had its première in Paris in 1831 and was performed at Covent Garden in 1832. In 1847 it was performed in London again with Jenny Lind making her English debut.

4 · *The Sleepwalker*, by Vincenzo Bellini. The opera was performed in English at Drury Lane in 1833 with Mademoiselle Garcia's sister Maria Malibran.

5 · A light and lively Polish dance.

6 · Bertel Thorwaldsen, 1770-1844, considered by many in the nineteenth century to be the greatest modern sculptor. The son of a poor woodcarver in Iceland, he was born and died in Copenhagen, but studied and produced most of his work in Italy.

7 · The village of Alexandrowka was built in the great park at Potsdam in 1826, the year after Nicholas 1st became Emperor of Russia. According to a modern guidebook, it was founded for Russian choir singers.

8 · Peter Vischer, 1450-1530. The monument to St Sebald, the sculptor's most famous work, was made between 1506 and 1519, with the help of his wife and five daughters-in-law as well as his five sons.

9 · Adam Kraft, 1460-1508.

10 · Eugène Beauharnais, 1780-1824, stepson of Napoleon. After a distinguished career under the Emperor, he retired with his family to Munich to live at his father-in-law's court, with the title Prince of Leuchtenberg.

11 · The British Museum in Bloomsbury. Originally Montague House, it became too small to hold all the collections donated and sold to the Nation, and the main part of the new museum was completed in April 1847. A permit had to be obtained to visit the galleries until 1879.

12 · Antonio Canova, 1757-1822.

13 · Philip Melanchthon, 1497-1560, eminent German scholar and reformer. In 1518 he was appointed professor at the new University of Wittenberg and became Luther's colleague. They were close friends and after Luther's death, Melanchthon continued with work for the Reformation.

14 · Lola Montez (Marie Gilbert) 1818-1861, was born in Ireland and, after an eventful childhood, eloped to avoid an arranged marriage. Left by her husband, she took Spanish dancing lessons and started performing at theatres in European capitals. In 1847 she appeared in Munich and captivated the elderly King who took her into his Court, giving her Bavarian nationality, a title and big income.

Under her influence the government was dismissed and the university closed down. In 1848 there was an insurrection, Lola was banished and the King was forced to abdicate. Her astonishing career, with two more marriages and tours of America and Australia, ended in New York where she cared for women outcasts.

15 · Carriages used by Queen Victoria and her family when staying at their seaside home on the Isle of Wight.

16 · Products of the Royal Painted Glass Manufactory. The designs, like transparent mosaic, were very expensive due to the complicated method of production which involved heating the glass seven times.

17 · In memory of Benjamin Thompson, 1752-1814, an American schoolmaster with scientific interests. During the War of Independence, he led a regiment loyal to the English and returned to England in 1784 where he was knighted. While travelling, he met the Bavarian Royal Family and was appointed to high office in Munich. He introduced military reforms, helped with social problems and was made a Count. Back in England, he was elected a Fellow of the Royal Society and continued to write on scientific and philosophical subjects.

18 · In 1755, with 30,000 deaths.

19 · Andreas Hofer, 1767-1810, a Tyrolese patriot. In 1809 he headed an insurrection against the Bavarians and French who occupied the country, but he was betrayed and shot at Mantua by order of Napoleon. In 1823 his remains were removed to Innsbruck and buried with full honour.

STAGE 4
OVER THE ALPS AND ACROSS LOMBARDY TO GENOA

1 · A Coachman, especially one that drives at a rattling pace. From the Bible, 2 Kings 1.2. The son of Nimshi.

2 · 1827-1883, a young aristocrat who liked fast horses. Later in life he became a leading racehorse owner and master of foxhounds.

3 · 'The German voiturier does not engage to provide you with meals as the Italian, but he expects to be allowed to stop at inns of his own choosing – a condition to which travellers are not compelled to agree, though they rarely object': from *Murray's Handbook* (1840). It is not surprising that the voiturier found these English travellers exasperating if he usually had his customers inside the carriage and not walking ahead.

4 · The Wilsons' astonishment was a little naïve. They had just entered the world's leading Roman Catholic country, and the Santa Maria hospice was on an important route between Britain and Rome. Whilst they were in Berlin on May 5th, Daniel O'Connell (1775-1847), the distinguished Irish politician and the first Catholic Member of Parliament at Westminster, died in Genoa, during a devotional trip to Rome. The hospicekeeper's wife may well have known about this before the Wilsons.

5 · The Villa Serbelloni, built in about 1800 by G. Albertolli on the site where the younger Pliny had a villa in the first century AD.

6 · Giudetta Negri, 1798-1865, a famous Italian singer. She studied at the Conservatorio in Naples before marrying the tenor Pasta, and sang in England several times between 1816 and 1850. She died at her villa on Lake Como.

7 · Maria Taglioni, 1804-1884, the greatest dancer of the golden age of romantic ballet and a pupil of her father, the choreographer Filippo Taglioni.

8 · Queen Caroline, 1768-1821, wife of George IV, lived here from 1814 after being acquitted of all guilt in the wake of serious accusations by her husband – and much publicity. She returned to England in 1820 to claim her rights as Queen when her husband succeeded to the throne, but was not allowed into Westminster Abbey for the Coronation. She died soon after this snub.

9 · The Arch of Peace, started in 1807 to celebrate the marriage of Viceroy Beauharnais with Princess Amalia of Bavaria, with funds from Napoleon. Work stopped in 1814, was resumed in 1816 and the arch was finished in 1838.

10 · A mechanical instrument designed by Abbé Vogler in 1789 that imitates an entire orchestra.

11 · St Carlo Borromeo, 1538-1584, was made a cardinal and archbishop of Milan by his uncle Pope Pius IV.

12 · Published in London in 1812, this Holy Bible had maps and numerous engravings, together with philological and explanatory notes by John Hewlett well known in the literary world.

13 · A district in Milan where a large hospital and community housing were founded and built between 1488 and 1506. Originally for lepers, it was the scene of Carlo Borromeo's saintly work.

14 · Richard Cobden, 1804-1865, an English statesman. Mary Wilson's deep dislike may have had both political and personal reasons. With John Bright, Cobden helped to form the 'Anti-Corn-Law League' in Manchester and in 1841 was elected a member of Parliament. His work helped to bring about the repeal of the Corn Laws in 1846 with the result that English farmers were no longer protected from foreign competition. Cobden and Bright and other radical politicians in Manchester influenced Mary Wilson's brother Edward in the years before his business failure and subsequent departure to Australia.

15 · The gun-brandishing coachman and ex-convict in *The Mysteries of Paris*, written in 1842, and the first French novel to be printed in serial form in an English newspaper. The book was translated and published in London in 1844.

STAGE 5
STEAMER TO NAPLES, BY DILIGENCE TO ROME

1 · *Galeotti* in Italian, the name given to criminals condemned to hard labour, who were at one time employed as rowers on board the galley boats.

2 · Luigi Lablache, 1794-1858, an Italian bass, the most famous of his generation. He was born in Naples, the son of a French merchant, and made his English debut in 1830. He became Princess Victoria's singing teacher.

3 · It was near the Grotto of Posillipo – 950 metres long and now closed to traffic – that the two-year-old W.S. Gilbert (of Gilbert and Sullivan fame) was kidnapped by brigands and ransomed in 1839. This may have been the reason for Mary Wilson's nervousness.

4 · The Cappella di Santa Maria della Pietà del Sangro, later converted into a museum. The statues are 'Modesty' by Corradini, 'Disillusion' (a man struggling in the net of vice) by Queiroli and 'The Dead Christ' by Sammartino. The Wilsons' guide gave them inaccurate information.

5 · Tommaso Aniello, a young Neapolitan fisherman. He led the poor market people into revolt when a new tax was put on fruit and vegetables in Naples in the seventeenth century.

6 · The large Paris cemetery which the Wilsons visited in 1838.

7 · A street entertainer, usually playing a shawm – a medieval form of oboe.

8 · This is situated in the volcanic region between Naples and Cumae, known as the Phlegrean Fields, with many craters and hot springs.

9 · Lucullus, 115-56 BC, a rich Roman soldier noted for his magnificence and self-indulgence, served under the Roman dictator Sulla. He introduced the cherry tree into Europe and spent vast sums on his estate at Naples.

10 · The Wilsons travelled round part of Ireland in 1835.

11 · Fra Diavolo (Friar Devil) was Michele Pezzo, 1771-1806. With Cardinal Ruffo he formed an army of resistance against the French invaders in 1799. He fought for the Italian royalty and the Catholic faith and was made a Colonel by King Ferdinand of Naples. In 1806 he stopped the advance of Massena and defended Craeta, near Terracina, but was later defeated and hanged by the French. An opera *Fra Diavolo* was written in 1830 by the French composer Daniel Auber, 1782-1871, and the Wilsons may have seen a performance before their visit to Italy. In it, Pezzo is portrayed as a brigand and villain – the French view; he was also an Italian resistance fighter and hero.

12 · Here Mary Wilson was seeing a continental method of threshing. The wheat was placed in the roadway so that horses and vehicles would pass over it to dislodge the grain.

STAGE 6
ROME

1 · 'Home' was the Hotel d'Allemagne in Via Condotti, listed in a guidebook as 'less expensive than the best' in Rome. It was a rambling old building next door to the famous Cafe Greco and was demolished in 1911.

2 · The Fontana della Barcaccia by Pietro Bernini in the Piazza di Spagna. The Via Condotti enters the Piazza opposite the fountain and the Spanish Steps.

The fountain commemorates the great flood in 1598 when a boat on the River Tiber was washed up to this point.
3 · Guido Reni, 1575-1642, Italian painter.
4 · The large equestrian statue, a relic of Ancient Rome, survived the Middle Ages when most bronze statues were melted down.
5 · This was most probably the Fontana di Trevi, situated between the Colosseum and the hotel.
6 · Pius IX reigned longer than any other Pope, from 1846-1878, outliving Mary Wilson by five years.
7 · An ancient and mutilated statue of Menelaos, excavated in 1501 and placed at the corner of the Palazzo Braschi. A popular legend tells of a witty and prosperous tailor who lived opposite the Palace and worked for the papal court. When he died, his name, Pasquino, was given to the statue and it became the mouthpiece for the people of Rome, who attached critical writings to the pedestal. Pasquino had a partner, another statue standing at the foot of the Capitol Hill, called Marforio. Together they had dialogues which upset the Popes and Marforio was enclosed inside the Capitol museum. This did not end the notorious dialogues and the number of 'talking' statues grew.
8 · The Basilica was built by Pope Sixtus III, 432-440, in an attempt to convert the many Roman women who still frequented the pagan temple of the Mother Goddess Juno Lucino. The snow legend refers to an earlier church built by Pope Liberius, 352-366, on the Esquiline Hill of which nothing remains.
9 · Cola di Rienzi, 1313-1354, incited the people of Rome into revolt against the Government in an effort to restore the political system of the Ancient Republic.
10 · Where traitors were hurled to their death until the fifteenth century. The name derives from Tarpeia, the daughter of a custodian of the Roman fortress, who opened the city gates to the Sabines for their golden bracelets. She was crushed to death for treason.
11 · The Trattoria del Lepre (*lepre* = hare) was on the other side of the Via Condotti, in the courtyard of the Villa Lepre. It is no longer a restaurant, but the sign of the hare can still be seen affixed to the building.

STAGE 7
TO FLORENCE AND BACK TO THE ALPS

1 · A form of parquetry work perfected during the early nineteenth century at Tonbridge in Kent for decorating furniture. Geometric patterns were created by cutting strips of veneers from different natural woods.
2 · A scenic exhibition, invented by a Frenchman, Daguerre. A painting was viewed through an aperture and use was made of lighting from above and behind the picture, which was painted with a combination of transparent, semi-transparent and opaque colours. The degrees of light from different angles gave a magical effect, from twilight to daylight. In London, the Diorama was housed in a building designed by John Nash in 1823, near Regents Park (close to Chester Terrace where the Wilsons lived from 1838-43). In 1840 two pictures were exhibited – the Coronation of Queen Victoria and the interior of the Church of Santa Croce in Florence.
3 · The hotel was run by a Mr Masso who received a medal at the Great Exhibition of 1851 for his display of filigree work. One of the principal shops where this exquisite work could be obtained was inside the hotel.
4 · 30° Centigrade.
5 · According to *Murray's Handbook* the *vetturini* were accustomed to having a full complement of passengers – four in the carriage and one on the box. Single travellers and couples shared with strangers unless they were willing to pay more. Therefore, when the Wilsons managed to halve the fare for their journey, they lost their privacy.
6 · Charles Dickens, 1812-1870, toured Italy with his family in 1844. Part of his account of the journey was printed in the columns of the *Daily News* which he edited. It was published in collected form as *Italian Notes* in 1846 and later, after corrections by the author, as *Pictures From Italy*.

STAGE 8
SWITZERLAND

1 · Over a deep gorge and the River Reuss, the new bridge was finished in 1830. It was a major feat of engineering, built to replace the old bridge begun in 1118 by Abbot Gerald of Einsiedeln. The scene of many terrible battles, the old bridge was frightening to cross since it had no parapet above the 70-foot drop.
2 · The William Tell legend tells the story of the folk hero who shot the apple off his son's head whilst his own life was being threatened by Gessler, a bailiff under Albert I of Austria, the oppressive ruler of Switzerland and Germany in the fourteenth century.
3 · This European journey would have been a good preparation for this ambition but available records do not suggest Mary Wilson achieved it. The tradition in the family was that women worked – her mother in the shop, one grandmother at the pottery and her other grandmother ran the farm after her husband's death.
4 · The lion monument in General Pfyffer's garden, 28 feet long and 18 feet high, was executed by Ahorn in 1821 from a model by Thorwaldsen. 786 soldiers of the Swiss Guard fell in the defence of the Tuileries on August 10th 1792.
5 · Envoy in residence. Lucerne was the capital of a canton and mainly Roman Catholic.
6 · Sir George Rose, 1771-1855, an English diplomat and statesman. After retiring from Parliament in 1844, he became active in missionary and evangelical work.
7 · Tuft hunting: seeking the society of titled people.
8 · The castle of Schadau, built in Gothic style and finished in 1850 for M. Rougemont of Paris.
9 · The monument to Berchtold of Zähringen, the founder of Berne, being replaced after restoration. It had originally been erected by the town in 1600.
10 · Thomas Heron, Viscount Ranelagh, 1820-1885. With an army career, the Viscount was a member of London's high society in the early 1840s. He met and desired the ex-wife of Captain James who, as Lola Montez, was preparing for her debut on the London stage. On the evening of June 3rd 1843 at Her Majesty's Theatre, on to the stage danced the beautiful Donna Lola Montez from Seville and from a box a voice was heard to call, 'Why, it's Betty James!' Soon the enthusiastic applause turned to hissing – Lord Ranelagh had exposed the woman who had rebuffed him and it was the end of her career in England. He died unmarried and the Viscountcy became extinct.
11 · Housed in a chapel, the monument by the sculptor Nahl of Madame Langhous, who died in childbirth.
12 · The Rev. W. Dodsworth, MA, first vicar of Christ Church, Regents Park, where the Wilsons worshipped when living at Chester Terrace.

STAGE 9
ZURICH AND THE JOURNEY HOME

1 · Johann Kaspar Lavater, 1741-1801. The son of a physician in Zurich, he was ordained into the church, became a poet, philosopher and Protestant theologian, and was well-known as a physiognomist. He was murdered in the troubled times after the French Revolution.
2 · The Benedictine church and monastery at Einsiedeln were founded in 934 AD. The great festival of the Miraculous Dedication is still celebrated on September 14th. The most frequented place of pilgrimage in Switzerland.
3 · The Honourable and Reverend Baptist Noel, 1798-1873, Minister of St John's Chapel, Bedford Row, London. In 1841 he was gazetted one of the Queen's chaplains and in 1848 joined the Baptists. He was one of the most popular preachers of his day.
4 · Schabzieger cheese was peculiar to the canton of Glarus. Made with the herb *Melilotus Caerulea*, from the plant blue melilot which was cultivated in gardens throughout the canton.
5 · Jetta. After her unfortunate end the Emperor moved his Court to Mannheim.
6 · Baden was one of the most fashionable watering-places in Europe with more than twenty mineral spas and hot springs. Bath houses, hotels and gambling saloons were developed in the nineteenth century when the population trebled during the Season - from May to October. The notorious gambling saloons were closed down in 1872.
7 · This railway line was opened in 1844. A railway network for south-east England was developing, based on a plan which started in 1839 with a line from London Bridge Station to Croydon, with three branches – to Dover, Brighton and Southampton.
8 · A village about one mile east of Southampton.

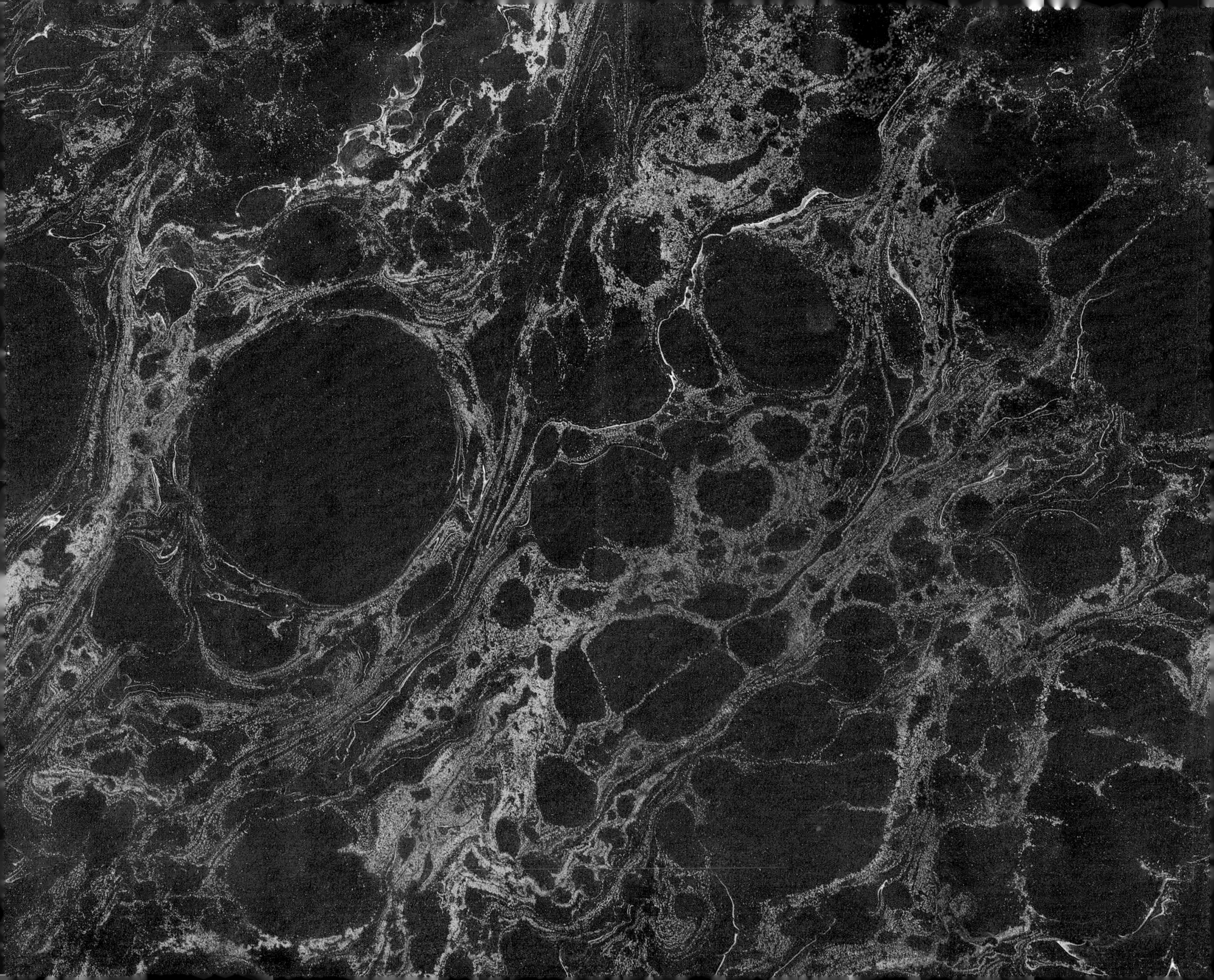